James Benning's Environments

Politics, Ecology, Duration

Edited by Nikolaj Lübecker and Daniele Rugo

EDINBURGH
University Press

Edinburgh University Press is one of the leading university presses in the UK. We publish academic books and journals in our selected subject areas across the humanities and social sciences, combining cutting-edge scholarship with high editorial and production values to produce academic works of lasting importance. For more information visit our website: edinburghuniversitypress.com

© editorial matter and organization Nikolaj Lübecker and Daniele Rugo, 2018
© the chapters their several authors, 2018

Edinburgh University Press Ltd
The Tun—HolyroodR oad
12 (2f) Jackson's Entry
Edinburgh EH8 8PJ

Typeset in Garamond MT Pro by
Servis Filmsetting Ltd, Stockport, Cheshire

A CIP record for this book is available from the British Library

ISBN 978 1 4744 1794 5 (hardback)
ISBN 978 1 4744 1795 2 (webready PDF)
ISBN 978 1 4744 1796 9 (epub)

The right of the contributors to be identified as authors of this work has been asserted in accordance with the Copyright, Designs and Patents Act 1988 and the Copyright and Related Rights Regulations 2003 (SI No. 2498).

Contents

List of Figures	v
Notes on the Contributors	vi
Acknowledgments	viii

Introduction   1
Nikolaj Lübecker and Daniele Rugo

Intellectual Environments

Surveying James Benning   15
Scott MacDonald

Utah and the *Times*: Governing Temporality in *Deseret*   39
John Beck

Violence and Landscape in the Films of James Benning   55
Nikolaj Lübecker

Material Environments

Constructing the Transversal Time-image: Ecosophy, Immanence, and Corporate "Land" in James Benning's *Four Corners* and California Trilogy   75
Colin Gardner

Men in Huts in Woods: Independence, Transcendentalism, and Technology in James Benning's Thoreau and Kaczynski Documentaries and Exhibition   94
Silke Panse

The Earth as Material Film: Benning's Light Glance Making a Material-Image 114
Felicity Colman

Perceptual Environments

A Lake-Event 129
Tom Conley

Defacing the Close-Up 143
Kriss Ravetto-Biagioli

The Adventure of Patience 160
Daniele Rugo

Filmography 177
Index 180

Figures

1 From *Stemple Pass*, 2012 — 4
2 From *Easy Rider*, 2012 — 11
3 From *American Dreams*, 1984 — 18
4 From *small roads*, 2011 — 28
5 From *Deseret*, 1995 (I) — 44
6 From *Deseret*, 1995 (II) — 50
7 From *Landscape Suicide*, 1986 (I) — 58
8 From *Landscape Suicide*, 1986 (II) — 68
9 From *Four Corners*, 1997 — 83
10 From *El Valley Centro*, 1999 — 84
11 From *Concord Woods*, 2014 — 95
12 From Architectural Rendering (*Two Cabins*), 2015 — 102
13 From *casting a glance*, 2007 (I) — 118
14 From *casting a glance*, 2007 (II) — 118
15 From *13 Lakes*, 2004 — 130
16 From *Faces 1973*, 2010 — 150
17 From *Faces*, 1968 — 155
18 From *Ruhr*, 2009 (I) — 161
19 From *Ruhr*, 2009 (II) — 170

Notes on the Contributors

John Beck is Professor of Modern Literature and Director of the Institute for Modern and Contemporary Culture at the University of Westminster. He is the author of *Dirty Wars: Landscape, Power and Waste in Western American Literature* (2009) and co-editor, with Ryan Bishop, of *Cold War Legacies: Systems, Theory, Aesthetics* (Edinburgh University Press, 2016).

Felicity Colman is Professor of Film and Media Arts and Director of Research at Kingston University, United Kingdom. She is the author of *Film Theory: Creating a Cinematic Grammar* (2014), *Deleuze and Cinema* (2011), and editor of *Film, Theory and Philosophy: The Key Thinkers* (2009). Her current book projects are on "Digital Feminicity" and "Materialist Film."

Tom Conley is the author of *Cartographic Cinema* (2007) and co-editor of the Wiley-Blackwell *Companion to Jean-Luc Godard* (2014). More recently, with Clara Rowland, he is co-editor of *Falso movimento* (2016), a book of essays on writing and cinema. Tom Conley teaches in the Departments of Visual & Environmental Studies and Romance Languages at Harvard University.

Colin Gardner is Professor of Critical Theory and Integrative Studies at the University of California, Santa Barbara, where he teaches in the departments of Art, Film & Media Studies, Comparative Literature, and the History of Art and Architecture. Gardner has published two books in Manchester University Press' "British Film Makers" series: *Joseph Losey* (2004) and *Karel Reisz* (2006) as well as *Beckett, Deleuze and the Televisual Event: Peephole Art*, a critical analysis of Samuel Beckett's experimental work for film and television (2012). His most recent books are *Deleuze and the Animal* (Edinburgh University Press, 2017) and *Ecosophical Aesthetics* (2018), both co-edited with Patricia MacCormack.

Nikolaj Lübecker is Professor of French and Film Studies at St John's College, University of Oxford. His publications focus on contemporary American and European cinema, French literature, and critical theory. His most recent book, *The Feel-Bad Film* (Edinburgh University Press, 2015), investigates logics of unpleasure in films by directors such as Claire Denis, Lars von Trier, Gus Van Sant, Bruno Dumont and Harmony Korine. His current research projects concern the so-called "nonhuman turn" in the humanities.

Scott MacDonald is author of the series, *A Critical Cinema: Interviews with Independent Filmmakers*, in five volumes from University of California Press, and twelve other books, most recently, *American Ethnographic Film and Personal Documentary: The Cambridge Turn* (2013), *Avant-Doc: Intersections of Documentary and Avant-Garde Cinema* (2014), and *Binghamton Babylon: Voices from the Cinema Department (a nonfiction novel)* (2015). He was an Anthology Film Archives Film Preservation Honoree in 1999 and was named an Academy Scholar by the Academy of Motion Picture Arts and Sciences in 2012. He teaches film history at Hamilton College.

Silke Panse is Reader in Film, Art and Philosophy at the University for the Creative Arts. She has written about James Benning's films in "The Work of the Documentary Protagonist: The Material Labor of Aesthetics" for *A Companion to Contemporary Documentary Film* (2015) and in "*Ten Skies, 13 Lakes,* 15 Pools" and "Land as Protagonist: An Interview with James Benning" for *Screening Nature: Cinema Beyond the Human* (2013). She was the co-investigator of the AHRC-funded *Screening Nature Network* (2013–14), co-edited *A Critique of Judgment in Film and Television* (2014) and is currently working on a monograph about documentary between realism and materialism.

Kriss Ravetto-Biagioli is the author of *The Unmaking of Fascist Aesthetics* (2001), *Mythopoetic Cinema: On the Ruins of European Identity* (2017), and is currently working on "Digital Uncanny." She teaches at UC Davis in the departments of Cinema and Digital Media and Science and Technology Studies.

Daniele Rugo is Senior Lecturer in the Department of Arts and Humanities at Brunel University London. He is the author of two books, *Philosophy and the Patience of Film* (2016) and *Jean-Luc Nancy and the Thinking of Otherness* (2013), and his articles have appeared in various journals including *Angelaki, Third Text, Cultural Politics,* and *Film-Philosophy*. He is the recipient of an Arts and Humanities Research Council Innovation Grant for the project "Following the Wires," which uses film to examine post-conflict scenarios in Lebanon.

Acknowledgments

The editors would like to thank Gillian Leslie and her very supportive team at Edinburgh University Press; and Maia Gianakos and Dylan Lustrin at Gallery neugerriemschneider Berlin for their hospitality, help, and support. Special thanks to James Benning.

All figures are courtesy of James Benning and Gallery neugerriemschneider, Berlin and New York.

NIKOLAJ LÜBECKER AND DANIELE RUGO

Introduction

Since at least the early 1970s, James Benning has committed himself to a systematic investigation of the relations between man, environment, and the filmic medium. The heterogeneity of Benning's work notwithstanding, a sustained attention devoted to the human marks on the world defines much of Benning's filmmaking achievements. These investigations often (but not always) result in medium- or feature-length films that embrace both the experimental tradition (particularly in the form of structural filmmaking) and the documentary form (at least in their reliance on real-life locations and ambient sound). Benning's films, installations and related activities test, challenge, and prod many of the oppositions and distinctions we have come to take for granted when discussing "landscape" and the "environment," showing their fragility. While Benning demonstrates awareness of the tradition of landscape painting (the Hudson River painters for example), his focus on the environment is not a device for an elegiac consecration of nature. This point can be easily seen in Benning's choice of subjects. Rather than focusing on the immediacy and innocence of nature, Benning turns to land use and multiple social natures. A glance at Benning's films shows a number of recurring subjects: agro-industrial processes and large-scale farming, along with the machinery and labor relations they involve; the traces of water infrastructure in the landscape (aqueducts, spillways, pipelines), their "civilizing" effect (the birth and expansion of Los Angeles) and the intense desertification they cause; steelmaking and its communities (in Milwaukee and in the Ruhr); the topographies of second natures such as cities, roads and railway networks; man-made lakes and man-made clouds; invisible boundaries and very visible ones created by the built environment. An even more prominent example of Benning's attempt to complicate nature is his interest in two crucial figures in American history, provocatively brought together as epitomizing nature as the source of dissent and violence. The reference here is to Henry David Thoreau and Ted

Kaczynski, better known as the Unabomber. In the films and artifacts (such as the replica cabins) that Benning has dedicated to these two, nature is presented as the locus of a social antagonism that takes the form of civil disobedience and solitary political violence or individual terrorism. Rather than being conciliatory and aesthetically appeasing, what we could (once) call the "natural environment" in Benning is a complex, ambiguous, politically charged field, which is both always entangled with man and technology and capable of resisting and reversing man's designs.

Benning has adopted this approach since the 1970s, when he moved from mathematics to filmmaking under the influence of the structural filmmakers,[1] and has applied it to various locales such as the Midwest, Utah, California, and Germany. In other words, Benning stands today as an important precursor to the non-pastoral attitude to ecological and environmental thought required by the Anthropocene, the acknowledgment of man as a dominant geological and climatic force. Environmental concerns, the relevance of which was once limited to natural sciences and literary romanticism, have now acquired capital importance and occupy center stage in public debates. Within academia, the arts and humanities have in the past fifteen to twenty years embraced the responsibility bestowed on them and reoriented their priorities in order to address with more urgency the demands of climate change and the meaning of human existence in the Anthropocene. The explosion of environmental humanities and ecocriticism is evidence that environmental concerns can no longer be separated (if they ever could be) from ethical, aesthetic, cultural, economic, and political issues. Questions around unequal access to primary resources, energy scarcity, and the impacts of climate change on farming are now discussed by environmental scientists as much as by scholars in political science and development studies. The adverse effects of climate change are also acknowledged as one of the main sources of conflict and social unrest, and demand the concerted efforts of scientists and policy makers. The humanities as a whole are being reinvented under the pressure of these developments and are questioning their own human-focused approach, turning to varying degrees to a renewed sensitivity to matter, nonhumanism and post-humanism, objects and things, relational processes, assemblages and networks. These new conceptual constellations all sanction different, more or less diffuse, more or less flat agencies. To use Timothy Morton's words, "ecological thought" has infected all "other areas of thinking" (2010: 2); James Benning has paid attention to these issues since the beginning of his career and has therefore for many years been a key filmmaker of the contemporary situation.

A political reorientation is also taking place, inasmuch as older forms of environmental activism, predicated on discrete categories and limits, conservationism, and ahistorical images of nature are showing themselves to be less and less capable of coping with the intricate ambiguity of technonatural flows. Environmental issues are becoming more and more ubiquitous, at times invisibly embedded in various and diverse practices, sometimes requiring a far subtler political imagination than most Green ecologies are equipped to mobilize.

Benning's ecological practice is clearly one that anticipates and gives sensuous form to many of these currents. It is rooted in the importance of being "in situ," of an experience of place, while understanding the interconnectedness of different (at times very distant) sites. Benning's work on landscape is never just an homage or an appropriation of the picturesque tradition, it is rather a rejection of that in view of a more politically aware, charged confrontation of and intervention in various environments. Even when a sense of the picturesque is deployed—his films often have a classical beauty about them—Benning uses it to trigger confusion rather than abandoned satisfaction. Benning acknowledges that coexistence precedes him, and shows through formal explorations often dominated by duration the political side of this coexistence. As briefly indicated in relation to Thoreau and Kaczynski, for Benning the political does not merely take the form of advocacy for more balanced relations with the natural environment and its resources and mechanisms, but strikes a specific note in relation to the history and geography of America. Benning is a thoroughly American filmmaker, in the sense that his work is embedded in the American territory and in its nation-building processes. In many films, Benning uses the land and the environment more generally to criticize hegemonic narratives of America, the mythologies of its "discovery" and faith in unending progress. Often Benning invokes singular moments in the history of the United States in order to recuperate to official chronicles those forgotten instances of radicalism, social utopias or minor histories. Benning contributes with his work on landscape to create a parallel narrative for America or to highlight the dissensus at the heart of the American dream, whether by addressing racial conflicts, minoritarian identities or social pathologies.

There is then a third element that makes Benning's work important today. Even if his production is heterogeneous, it is fair to say that most of his major works insist on the time it takes for images to begin revealing their significance. When Benning insists on landscape, he does so through the use of fixed-camera durational shots. While this formal strategy has been in development since the very beginning, it became more prominent with *Landscape Suicide* (1987) and reached its peak after Benning moved from 16 mm to digital video, eventually producing one-shot films such as *Nightfall* (2012, 98 minutes) and *BNSF* (2013, 193 minutes). In the last of these films an arid landscape is cut almost in half by a railway. The movement is negligible until a train travels across the screen. *Nightfall* is a study of light in a forest near Benning's residence in the Sierra Nevada. Considering the minimal happenings in the films, it is clear how

Figure 1 From Stemple Pass, 2012. Courtesy of the artist and neugerriemschneider, Berlin

duration plays a very important role, at times even replacing narrative, character development, and dramatic tension. This type of filmmaking, predicated on the adventure of patience, rewarding only once one has readjusted one's own perceptual expectations, is again anticipatory of many durational works that have become prominent in recent years, prompting a series of more or less illuminating criticisms as to their significance. This aesthetic baggage, the combination of landscape and duration, is one that is now more familiar to audiences worldwide, but it is fair to say that Benning has made of this a peculiar feature well ahead of the time. For these and many reasons that fall beyond the scope of the present volume James Benning can be considered among those filmmakers whose work broadens our temporal, scalar, and conceptual bandwidth.

This volume offers a number of interpretative frameworks drawing on film theory, environmental humanities, visual culture, and philosophy to respond to Benning's work. The chapters in this collection highlight the thematic and formal coherence of Benning's practice while providing readers with a context to understand his experimental film work. Rooted in the structural cinema movement of the 1960s and 1970s, Benning's career offers an unrivaled exploration of the many ways in which politics and economics mark the landscape (in particular those of his native North America) while engaging in an original reflection on the relations between image, text, and sound. The structure of the book emerges from the ambition to contextualize Benning's work in relation to the most important artistic and sociohistorical influences on his work; analyse Benning as an eco-filmmaker with perspectives from environmental studies and eco-cinema; and explore Benning's films in view of their aesthetic, political, and epistemological import. Taken together, the three parts of the present volume aim to provide a framework to reflect on the richness and significance of Benning's career also in light of his contribution to contemporary critical discourses.

The first part of the book offers an introduction to some of the *intellectual environments* that shaped Benning's filmmaking. This part establishes a historical and formal context to the director's work, reconstructing the major influences on Benning's work and defining his relation to American experimental filmmaking of the 1960s and 1970s. In addition this part investigates his relation to American culture, politics, and mythologies, emphasizing how Benning confronts many of the political events of his time, deliberately misrepresenting official histories (as Colin Gardner puts it), while also maintaining a strong connection with American counter-culture.

The second part—*Material Environments*—is dedicated to readings of Benning's work that focus on environmental concerns. As mentioned, Benning's films are often structured around land use activities (from forestry and agriculture to mining and the establishment of a national rail network), providing ambiguous narratives of the changing human relationship with nature. Landscape is seen not as ordered and immutable, but as open to entropy, the coexistence of construction and destruction. In addition, landscape is not seen in terms of scenery, but often as a field of negotiation, at times hospitable and at others inhabitable. Benning's films can be said to provide vistas for an inclusive understanding of the lived environment by shaping our thinking about energy, ecology, sustainability, and challenging our cultural assumptions about "nature."

The third part is concerned with the analysis of Benning's films as *perceptual environments* by focusing on the perceptual experience produced in and by these films and their epistemological value. Benning's explorations of the close-up, the question of duration, and the investigations of place as a function of time dominate these analyses. The ideas expressed here revolve around Benning's demand on himself and the audience. This demand can be described as the achievement of a different kind of vigilance, a non-instrumental and non-cumulative attention to the singularity of the events on the screen, however minimal they might seem at first (the quasi-immobility of a lake, the light reflecting on a passing cloud, the movement of a woman's lips).

The volume develops these topics in detail, intertwining and overlapping them, so that the three environments are never discussed independently of each other. While in each chapter one environment might be privileged, the influence of the others is always felt. In the first contribution of the volume Scott MacDonald discusses James Benning's various crossings of America, both in terms of the films' cultural, geographical, and historical references and in the physical journeys they imply. Emphasizing Benning's autodidacticism, MacDonald's chapter focuses on those artists and artist–filmmakers whose work has been important to Benning. They include Henry David Thoreau, Edward Hopper, Robert Smithson, Yvonne Rainer, Hollis Frampton, Michael Snow, Andy Warhol, John Knecht, Sharon Lockhart, and a variety of outsider artists. Particular writers, artists, and filmmakers have been important during particular moments in Benning's filmmaking career. American landscape/cityscape painting was important in his breakthrough films *8½ × 11* (1974), *11 × 14* (1977), and *One Way Boogie Woogie* (1977), and landscape/cityscape has remained a passion. The text-image work of Frampton, Rainer, Snow, and George Landow is celebrated in Benning's *Grand Opera* (1978), and inspired a series of feature films employing text in imaginative ways: *American Dreams* (1984), *North on Evers* (1991), *Deseret* (1995), and *Four Corners* (1997). Andy Warhol's "slow cinema" has always been important for Benning and has been celebrated in several recent digital works, including *After Warhol* (2011) and *Twenty Cigarettes* (2011). This chapter shows how Benning has built on these varied crossings of the American's intellectual and physical landscape and, in the process, has created an entirely unique body of work.

John Beck's chapter focuses on *Deseret*, Benning's idiosyncratic chronicle of the state of Utah over 150 years. The chapter excavates the counter histories embedded in the film, demonstrating how Benning's engagement with this reputedly conservative state manages to draw out what Beck describes as a "revolutionary impulse . . . in Utah." This impulse partly originates in Utah's ability to be "out of step with the times." In formulations that resonate across Benning's work more widely, Beck's chapter details how *Deseret* gives form to an alternative management—and politics—of time. This does not mean that Benning instrumentalizes Utah in an attempt to "get at" the East Coast establishment (represented by the *New York Times*). Instead, the chapter aptly concludes that it is "Utah's strangeness—its resilience, awkwardness, and its socialistic, utopian willingness to imagine the world otherwise—that makes it essential for Benning."

Continuing the exploration of Benning's alternative histories, Nikolaj Lübecker's chapter considers a series of projects about *how* and *why* violence may erupt in a particular individual: the 16-year-old Bernadette Protti's murder of her classmate Kirstin Costas; the famous Ed Gein case that also inspired Alfred Hitchcock's *Psycho*, Tobe Hooper's *Texas Chainsaw Massacre*, and Jonathan Demme's *Silence of the Lambs* (in *Landscape Suicide* [1986]); and the terrorist activities of Ted Kaczynski (in *Two Cabins* [2010] and *Stemple Pass* [2012], for instance). Drawing on the work of Félix Guattari and Isabelle Stengers, the chapter examines how Benning places individual histories in a socio-political context, while at the same time raising the question of what part the natural environment plays in the formation of pathological subjectivities. With this focus on landscape, violence, and the processes of subjectification, the chapter aims to bring out a provocative dimension that sometimes remains occluded in humanist and/or environmentalist readings of Benning's work.

The section *Material Environments* is opened by Colin Gardner's analyses of Benning's time-images. Applying Guattari's idea of "vectors of subjectification" to *Four Corners* (1997) and the California Trilogy—*El Valley Centro* (1999), *LOS* (2000), *and SOGOBI* (2001)—the chapter explores the ecosophical ramifications of Deleuze's time-image. Gardner focuses on the duration of Benning's shots as a transversal link between landscape (the perceptual view of the land) and the corporate ownership of "land" (with its concomitant exploitation of indigenous people as well as cheap immigrant labor). Describing Benning's methodology as exercising a "subjectivity without a subject," Gardner explains how *Four Corners* explodes the artificial intersection of four state lines. This allows Benning to open out the four horizons beyond the "confines" of Utah, Colorado, New Mexico, and Arizona, to a potentially infinite series of deterritorialized subjectifications. Next, Gardner's analysis of the California Trilogy details how Benning discloses an ecosophical relation between the corporate wealth of Los Angeles and the irreversible despoliation of Owens Valley, the historical source of its water supply. In this way, water—where it comes from, where it goes to, and who owns it—becomes the virtual vector that ties the films together as an ecosophical project, constructing a pure immanence that is also, as Deleuze puts it, "a life."

Silke Panse's chapter turns to Benning's renegotiations of the transcendentalism of Henry David Thoreau in *Concord Woods* (2014), *Stemple Pass* (2012), and the *Two Cabins* installation that formed part of the exhibition *Decoding Fear* (2015). Considering the ways in which the videos and the installation map the relations between humans, objects, and their environment, Panse establishes a critical dialog between Benning and arguments on independence advocated by the transcendentalists. Panse moreover discusses similarities and differences between Kaczynski's and Heidegger's approach to technology and freedom, and considers Kaczynski's suggestion, read by Benning in *Stemple Pass*, that looking and listening is more than mere sense perception. Panse concludes by underlining that these works ask uncomfortable questions about independence and ethics.

In the final contribution to the part of the book dealing with *material environments*, Felicity Colman analyses how nature continuously comes to be in the films of James Benning. Focusing on *casting a glance* (2007), she shows that for Benning "landscape" is a verb, an activity, at least as much as it is a noun (Colman writes about "landscaping at work"). These processes of materialization include spectator, technology, and matter, allowing for an understanding of the image as "an actualisation of the experience of matter." In this sense, Benning's materialist filmmaking style (*13 Lakes* [2004]; *casting a glance* [2007]; *RR* [2008]) is in direct and indirect conversation with that of Robert Smithson (*Spiral Jetty* [1970]), Robert Smithson and Nancy Holt (*Swamp* [1969]; *Mono Lake* [1968–2004]), in terms of their respective filmic emphases on the duration of seeing the matter of the Earth, and its organization, as its own materialist film site. Colman's chapter unfolds these activities for the reader, paying particular attention to the diffractive work of light and explaining how in Benning's film "the event is the light."

The third part of the book, *Perceptual Environments*, opens with Tom Conley's discussion of *13 Lakes*. Drawing largely on Deleuze's *The Fold* and on the French philosopher's reading of Whitehead, Conley approaches Benning's film, composed of fixed shots of thirteen lakes across the United States, as producing what he calls (in terms that complement Colman's analysis) a "lake-event." Conley argues that over time the gazes of both the film and the spectator converge, producing a scale of intensities. By way of a sense of layering of surfaces set over each other according to "degree" or latitude, what emerges is world changing according to the relation that its "zones" (frigid, temperate, torrid) hold with each other. The lake becomes the world on which, here and there, drifting or ever-changing islands float. The lake-event would be intensities of molar and molecular differences that when pictured could take the form of a globe in which masses of water and land gain "intensity" through their iteration or repetition and difference. Where the various lakes suggest different degrees of atmosphere they are continually "beginning" and "becoming."

Kriss Ravetto-Biagioli focuses instead on the close-up, analyzing the encounter between the camera and the human face in Benning's *Twenty Cigarettes* (2011), *Faces* (2010), and *Faces 1973* (2010). After making forty films over the span of four decades (using a 16 mm Bolex camera), Benning switched in 2009 to high-definition digital video. It is during this period and with the use of the digital format that Benning begins to explore the close-up and, with it, the human face. This exploration of the human face marks a major shift in Benning's œuvre, previously characterized by largely de-peopled landscapes. *Faces 1973* stretches two three-second close-up shots of a face (one woman and one man) into a twenty-minute installation piece. These portraits have been digitally scanned from footage that Benning shot on 16 mm in 1973. The scanning process makes these seemingly still portraits change in color and brightness, animating and blurring the features of the faces as it unsettles the distinction between movement and time. *Twenty Cigarettes* captures twenty people smoking one cigarette (a whole pack in total). Each shot lasts as long as it takes the subject to smoke the cigarette, and each sequence is clearly demarcated by a fade to black—it is a formal exercise in duration. *Faces* is both a partial and a literal copy of John Cassavetes' film: Benning copied the original film with his digital camera, but only captured a selection of the individual faces shot in close-up, calculating how much air time was given to each character. Ravetto-Biagioli argues that these works point to the shifting architecture of the close-up, its untimely duration, and the ungrounding of the pose itself. While Benning's work has often been described as observational and structural cinema—and therefore rigorously formal—the chapter shows how Benning's work also makes us aware of a complex set of relations—between posing, acting, setting up a shot, shot-consciousness, casting a glance, recording, scanning and reflecting back.

Daniele Rugo concludes the collection with a chapter that focuses on "the adventure of patience." While duration was an important component of James Benning's work from the very beginning, with the California Trilogy (*El Valley Centro* [1999], *LOS* [2000], *SOGOBI* [2001]) the length of individual shots has progressively increased—thanks also to the move to digital cameras—from 2½ minutes to the hour-long take of a coke-processing tower in *Ruhr* (2009). These extreme durations deliberately test the audience's perceptual faculties and ability to withstand the passing of time. Benning has explained this evolution of his style as the attempt to show "landscape as a function of time," an assumption that imposes on both filmmaker and audience an investment into the most minute changes. In addition, Benning pairs this radical duration with the complete reduction of contextual information. While his earlier works included interviews, voice-overs and on-screen text that in different ways guided the reception of the image, films such as *El Valley Centro*, *13 Lakes* (2004), *Ten Skies* (2004), *RR* (2007), and *Ruhr* (2009) offer almost no complementary or expository element. The audience has to work harder, but this means at the same time being able to surrender to the uneventfulness of the image. With specific reference to the work of Alfred North Whitehead and analyses of the tradition of contemplation in landscape painting, Rugo discusses how these films simultaneously demand, from both director and audience, responsiveness and relinquishment, blurring the lines between activity and passivity, and thus producing an environment dominated by patience, understood at once as endurance and urgency.

The decision to divide the collection into three environments recalls Félix Guattari's *Three Ecologies* (1989) and more recent eco-cinecritic variations on this volume, such as Adrian Ivakhiv's *Ecologies of the Moving Image* (2013). Guattari's text introduces a distinction between a socio-political ecology, a mental ecology, and an environmental ecology that includes both landscapes and built environments. This systematization allows for a fine-grained analysis of the many complex ways in which these various ecologies connect and interact.² Throughout these analyses he keeps the question of human subjectification at the heart of matters: the ambition is to understand how the subject is woven into—and out of—the fabric of the social and the environmental, and how this weaving must be done in order for the subject to escape the many pathological crystallizations that so easily take hold.

As demonstrated by a number of contributors, some of Benning's projects very obviously lend themselves to a Guattari-inspired approach insofar as they investigate the movements between mental pathologies, landscapes, and socio-political structures. But more generally, Guattari's idea of overlapping ecologies leads to a focus on how the dynamics between the various ecologies are articulated, how they can be modified, and what the consequences of such modifications could be. To address these questions Guattari introduces the notions of "practice" and "micro-politics." He is interested in how our daily practices can be conceived as interventions that modify the existing ecologies. Such ideas have relevance for the practice of Benning, too, insofar as they can inspire an analysis of his filmic interventions. When Benning proposes (in an interview with Silke Panse, cited by several contributors) that "duration is what helps bring the political back into the shot," he can be understood to operate at the micro-political level. By extending a shot, Benning modifies the relation between spectator, image and the subject matter appearing in the image; this durational politics furthermore marks out the films in the wider cinematic landscape, pulling Benning's works away from more conventional, narrative forms of filmmaking. Such (seemingly minor) adjustments in the distribution of the sensible (Rancière) therefore have wide implications: they allow spectators to see (their own place in) the world differently, they work to challenge and expand our understandings of what film art can be. From this new viewpoint, the detailed reworking of a close-up (Ravetto-Biagioli) or the construction of a cabin (Panse) is inextricably tied up with the modification of larger ecological and political structures; furthermore, the distance between a lake-event (Conley) or earth-matter (Colman) and films about American history (Beck) begins to shrink. Indeed, from this perspective all Benning's projects form part of practice that remaps existing ecologies, thereby inviting us to think differently about our imbrication in the world.

The present volume is unable to give anything like an exhaustive overview of Benning's large—and rapidly expanding—filmic corpus. We have chosen to prioritize the aspects that most obviously speak to contemporary debates about perceptual and environmental ecologies, about American national identities. As mentioned, these dimensions have been present in Benning's work for decades, and Benning has therefore been one of the key filmmakers of our time,

Figure 2 *From* Easy Rider, *2012. Courtesy of the artist and neugerriemschneider, Berlin*

long before our time realized it. At the same time Benning's diverse productions outstrips contemporary critical debates, and will undoubtedly be taken up in many other ways in the future (as it has been in the past).[3] Indeed Benning himself is already engaged in this work. The compilation film *52 Films* (2015), for example, contains a sequence sometimes referred to as "13 Other Lakes."[4] The footage for this film has been appropriated entirely from Youtube videos. In a series of brief sequences, "13 Other Lakes" works its way through the *13 Lakes* that Benning filmed for his feature film. Because of the brevity of these "other lakes" (a total running time of 8 minutes 26 seconds, compared to the original's 135 minutes), and because of the much larger role played by human beings (swimming, fishing, diving, and gliding through the image on a paddling board), these "other lakes" take us by surprise. One may speculate that Benning felt the need to step out of the world created by the previous film (and perhaps by the reception of this film?), or at least to expand this world by introducing a humorous dimension that was less evident in *13 Lakes*. But the reworking also points to the substantial self-reflexive and media-archeological dimension that can be found in many other of Benning's films. As suggested, Benning engages carefully and playfully with existing visual cultures, reworking films by other directors (Warhol, Cassavetes, Hopper) and by himself (*One Way Boogie Woogie, Faces 1973, casting a glance, 13 Lakes* . . .) and gleaning images from the internet and other sources. This practice inscribes itself in a long history of twentieth-century *avant-garde* art, and it also energetically signals to viewers that no work is definitive: ecologies are there to be reworked and retuned, and such activities can be joyful undertakings.

Notes

1. Benning often recounts the anecdote of how he discovered "art." While a mathematics undergraduate at the University of Wisconsin, Benning found himself attending a talk by an artist reading an abridged version of Joyce's *Finnegans Wake*. Benning was later to discover that the unknown artist was in fact John Cage.
2. As regards ecologies, Guattari does not restrict himself to systematizing in *threes*. In other texts he writes about scientific ecologies, machinic ecologies and media ecologies (see for instance Félix Guattari (2013): 65).
3. This is the place to pay tribute to the work of the Austrian Filmmuseum, publishers of the first edited volume on James Benning (Barbara Pichler and Claudia Slanar's *James Benning* [2007]), and, not least, of the DVD editions of Benning's *American Dreams (Lost and Found)*, *Landscape Suicide*, *Four Corners*, *Deseret*, California Trilogy (*El Valley Centro*, *Los*, and *SOGOBI*), *casting a glance*, *RR*, *Natural History*, and *Ruhr*.
4. In fact Benning uses the same title twice—*13 Lakes*—thereby emphasizing that the lakes are identical, and also complicating any attempt to distinguish between "serious art cinema," and amateur home videos.

Works Cited

Guattari, Félix (1989), *Les trois écologies*, Paris: Gallilée
Guattari, Félix (2013), *Qu'est-ce que l'écosophie?* Paris: Lignes/IMEC.
Ivakhiv, Adrian (2013), *Ecologies of the Moving Image: Cinema, Affect, Nature*, Waterloo, ON: Wilfrid Laurier University Press.
Morton, Timothy (2010), *The Ecological Thought*, Cambridge, MA: Harvard University Press.
Pichler, Barbara and Slanar, Claudia (eds.) (2007), *James Benning*, Vienna: Österreichisches Filmmuseum/SYNEMA Gesellschaft für Film und Medien.

Intellectual Environments

SCOTT MACDONALD

Surveying James Benning
(For Peter Hutton)

No filmmaker has referenced a broader spectrum of American geography and history than James Benning; traversing America is as fundamental to Benning's work as it was to Jackson Pollock's. In fact, though Benning has traveled reasonably widely over the years, he had made more than thirty films before he shot and used footage shot outside the continental United States.[1] And he decided to make *Ruhr* (2009), his first film about a non-American subject (and his first digital film), because "Duisburg reminded me of Milwaukee, so I felt like I could do something important there." The borders of the United States seem to have been Benning's way of limiting a territory so that he could both move and concentrate. Indeed, his personal movement across America, as a filmmaker/teacher, predicts the movement in so many of his films.

When I teach Benning's films to students finding their way into independent cinema, I often tell them that, at first, Benning's significance seemed to be a function of his Midwestern background: he was the first noteworthy independent film artist to have been nurtured in what some have called "the fly-over zone." During the 1960s and 1970s independent cinema was identified primarily with the East Coast (particularly New York) and the West Coast (San Francisco); the huge territory between the coasts was seen as the (non-cinematic) zone one flew over to get to those places where innovative independent work was being produced. Not only had Benning been raised in the Midwest, in Milwaukee, but most of his early films (*8½ × 11*, 1974; *I-94*, 1974 [co-made with Bette Gordon]; *9-1-75*, 1975; *Chicago Loop*, 1976; *11 × 14*, 1976; and *One Way Boogie Woogie*, 1977) celebrated Midwestern spaces: Milwaukee's industrial valley, Chicago, and the landscape of the upper Midwest from Wisconsin to Rapid City, South Dakota. At first, Benning seemed proudly, even defiantly, a Midwesterner—something new under the American cinematic sun. Then in August 1980, after teaching briefly at the

University of Oklahoma and at the University of California—San Diego, he moved to New York City.[2]

If the move to New York seemed, at least at first, a capitulation to the Art Gods and a betrayal of Benning's roots (in retrospect, a bit like LeBron James leaving the Cleveland Cavaliers to play basketball in Miami), those of us who lived in the Northeast were glad to have Benning one of us: his New York films (*Him and Me*, 1982; *American Dreams*, 1984) were different from the earlier Midwestern films, but very interesting in their own right—and we could understand why a film artist might want to move to New York, since, after all, New York was, we thought, the Center of the Art World—and so much interesting filmmaking had been, and was, going on there.

Then in 1988 Benning moved to California—and not to San Francisco, where independent cinema was thriving, but to Valencia, just north of LA.[3] At the time, this seemed—at least to us New Yorkers—a second capitulation: how could a serious filmmaker move to the center of film commerce; was Benning going *Hollywood*? The fact that he had found a home at California Institute of the Arts—the art school developed by Walt Disney!—seemed to confirm this capitulation to something other than serious filmmaking.

In retrospect, Benning's moves from the Midwest to New York to LA no longer read as failures of artistic integrity, but as evidence of his hunger to use filmmaking as a means of exploring American geography and history—and himself. Of course, Benning's early years also included *The United States of America* (1975, co-made with Bette Gordon) and *Grand Opera* (1978), both of which involve cross-country excursions: in *The United States of America*, from the Brooklyn Bridge to the Pacific Ocean; in *Grand Opera*, from New York to California (one section of the film recapitulates *The United States of America* in 99 seconds) and from the upper Midwest to Texas. During the past half-century, Benning's relentless exploration of the United States has allowed him to engage national, environmental, artistic, and personal history in a considerable range of ways.

STRUCTURAL FILM

At first, Benning's films seemed a slightly late addition to what P. Adams Sitney had defined as "structural film." Like other structural filmmakers, Sitney listed as part of this movement (Michael Snow, Hollis Frampton, Ernie Gehr . . .), Benning frequently used the extended shot that Warhol had pioneered, and relied on serial structures that fit Sitney's definition of a "cinema of structure in which the shape of the whole film is predetermined and simplified, and it is that shape which is the primal impression of the film" (1974: 407). Every shot in *The United States of America* is recorded from a camera mounted in the rear of the car that Benning and Gordon drive, so that the front windshield of the car becomes a movie screen through which we see a series of shots (of varied lengths) of American landscape and cityscape, from east to west; in *I-94* (1974) Benning and Gordon are visible in alternating frames so that Gordon's movement away from the camera and Benning's movement toward it are experienced simultaneously; and *One Way Boogie Woogie* is a series of sixty one-minute shots of Milwaukee's industrial valley.

Benning, like the other structural filmmakers, saw himself in rebellion against conventional, commercial, narrative-bound, illusionary cinema; and like them, he was fascinated with the idea of using filmmaking as a means of exploring the cinematic apparatus itself (*One Way Boogie Woogie* playfully explores cinematic framing in the way Snow playfully explores camera movement in *Back and Forth* [1969]). In interviews and in his films, Benning has frequently paid homage to Snow's *Wavelength* (1967), perhaps the quintessential structural film (the recent *52 Films* meta-film, completed in 2015, includes a digital remake of *Wavelength*), as well as to Frampton: Benning's computer piece, *Pascal's Lemma* (1984), is a conscious nod to *Zorns Lemma* (1970).[4] And *Grand Opera* (1978) includes portraits of Snow and Frampton (and George Landow/Owen Land, who was also identified by Sitney as a structural filmmaker).

Time has helped us to recognize that Benning was also, like Yvonne Rainer (the fourth portrait in *Grand Opera*), in rebellion against what had come to seem the (male-centered) establishment of *avant-garde* cinema and those critics and critic/filmmakers—Sitney, Jonas Mekas, and Peter Kubelka—who were chronicling its history and establishing its canon at the then-new Anthology Film Archives. For Benning (and for a good many other filmmakers) it seemed preposterous that the repertory at Anthology, the first American museum dedicated specifically to serious cinema of all kinds, would be made up solely of what the Anthology Selection Committee (Ken Kelman, James Broughton, Sitney, Mekas, and Kubelka) had decided were the essential films for serious cineastes—and this became increasingly frustrating as it became clear that no changes would be made in the repertory.

Grand Opera can be read as Benning's final major statement on the history of *avant-garde* cinema as of the early 1970s and on the emergence of structural film. The title of *Grand Opera* comes from a comment by Brakhage, who is heard on the soundtrack early in the film, to the effect that whatever sound does offer in other areas of the arts, it continues to retard the art of cinema; Brakhage: "I'm not against sound though I rather think of it as grand opera" (MacDonald 1992: 222).[5] The central incident of *Grand Opera*, described in an early rolling text, involves a building, a *structure*, that explodes. A young boy, fascinated with the mathematical concept of π (as Benning himself has always been), witnesses the explosion and destruction of the structure, though he remains more fully focused on a book in which he has written the endless digits of π.

The idea of structural film, films in which "the shape of the whole film is predetermined and simplified," would remain a crucial element of Benning's filmmaking, but he would reject the world that had grown up around structural film and the other forms of cinema identified as *avant-garde*, a world that seemed generally oblivious to immediate socio-political realities and the ways in which these realities were being expressed within modern popular culture. What distinguishes Benning from all the structural filmmakers Sitney discusses and some of the *avant-garde* filmmakers who preceded them (Maya Deren and Stan Brakhage, for example) is what may be a fundamental paradox of his career: the fact that Benning's consistent, lifelong rebellion against commercial cinema and television and American capitalism in general has *not* involved a dismissal of year-to-year political events or the ongoing evolution of popular culture. After *Grand Opera*, Benning became, and has remained, quite open about this.

American Dreams is Benning's most detailed review of the influences on his childhood and youth. It uses a "predetermined and simplified" structure to present a collection of Hank Aaron memorabilia and the handwritten text

Figure 3 *From* American Dreams, *1984. Courtesy of the artist and neugerriemschneider, Berlin*

of Arthur Bremer's diary scrolling across the bottom of the frame (as Bremer pursues his quest to assassinate a political figure), accompanied by dozens of quotations from public comments by political figures, activists, entertainment celebrities, and from the popular music of the time. The combination of these elements is Benning's means of exploring, during the heyday of second-wave feminism, the problematics of American masculinity and the issue of race, as embodied in Hank Aaron's quest to challenge Babe Ruth's homerun record; in Arthur Bremer's obsession with trying to assassinate Richard Nixon and later, segregationist George Wallace; in Benning's elaborate, even obsessive, presentation of his comprehensive collection of Aaron memorabilia—*and* in his determination to make a challenging but politically engaged structural film.[6]

POLITICAL AND AESTHETIC CONTEXTS

Benning came to adulthood and to artistic maturity during the 1950s, 1960s, and early 1970s; and his early influences are, in large measure, characteristic of our generation (both Benning and I were born in 1942): Benning was 15 in 1957, 26 in 1968. While the members of every generation probably feel that life in their time is in a state of dramatic evolution, the changes that took place in American culture from the 1950s to the 1980s continue to seem especially dramatic; and most anyone who grew up during these decades will have felt the power of particular personalities and moments. The various major events of that era—the Korean War; the Cold War; the construction of the American Interstate Highway System; the revolution in Cuba; the arms race; the election of John F. Kennedy; the Cuban missile crisis; the civil rights struggle; the moon landing; the assassinations of JFK, Robert Kennedy, Malcolm X, Dr. Martin Luther King, and Medgar Evers; women's liberation; the Vietnam War and resistance to the war; Black Power; Nixon's election and impeachment—were reflected by major transformations in popular culture: the proliferation of television and the expansion of television broadcasting, the arrival of folk music, country music, and rock music and a new generation of popular musicians, as well as by new developments in the art world: in the Fifties, Abstract Expressionism and assemblage art; and in the Sixties, Pop Art, Happenings and Performance Art, minimal and conceptual art—and the expanding availability of a range of new kinds of cinema from abroad and from within "the Underground."

Of course, *influence* is a problematic concept: we are influenced by virtually everything we experience and are fully as capable, as the years go by, of forgetting important inputs into our lives and work, as we are of remembering them—and of distorting those we do remember. What can be traced, however, is those influences that seem evident in particular films, whether the filmmaker was/is aware of these influences or not, My listing of some of the events of the era when Benning was growing up references figures and events that show up again and again in his films. For example, many of the public figures quoted in *American Dreams* have continued to reappear in later films. President Eisenhower's announcement of the desegregation of the public schools in Little Rock, Arkansas, is excerpted in *American Dreams*; and Eisenhower's warning about the military-industrial complex in his "Farewell Address" is heard in *RR* (2007) and in "Ike," a section of *52 Films*. An announcement of the assassination of President Kennedy in Dallas, Texas, in 1963 is included in *American Dreams*, but Benning had already filmed the location of the assassination for *The United States of America* and would revisit it in *North on Evers* (1991)—the Zapruder footage is included in the "two moments" section of *52 Films*.

In the era before an expansive, multi-leveled film culture was available to most Americans, thoughtful young people coming to maturity were likely to spend a good bit of time listening to the continual transformations in pop music and to regularly find their way to movie theaters. No canonical independent filmmaker (with the possible exceptions of Bruce Conner and Kenneth Anger) has been as tuned in to popular music as Benning. During *The United States of America* we hear a wide range of music apparently coming from the car radio: excerpts from recordings by Elton John, Johnny Cash, John Lennon, the Everly Brothers, Bob Dylan. *11 × 14* includes the entirety of Bob Dylan's "Black Diamond Bay" (7½ minutes) twice—once to accompany an extended single shot during which two lovers relax in a motel bed; and again, to accompany an extended single shot of a smokestack spewing white smoke. *American Dreams* begins with excerpts from recordings by Johnny Ray, Eddie Fisher, Etta James, the Del Vikings, Peggy Lee, Richie Valens, and Frank Sinatra; and one of the first speeches excerpted in the film is from an interview with Elvis Presley (Benning would visit Graceland in *North on Evers*).

If the American adult population in the 1950s and 1960s was turning to television for audio-visual entertainment, thoughtful youths of Benning's generation remained moviegoers, attracted to horror films, romances, and comedies, and to films by the two most visible auteur directors of that era: Alfred Hitchcock and John Ford. Benning's early films, and to some extent his later films as well, resonate with evidence of his experiences with Hitchcock and Ford. That characters in *11 × 14* make a road trip to Mount Rushmore seems an obvious echo of *North by Northwest* (the crop-dusting shot in *SOGOBI* (2001) and shot 7 of *small roads* (2011) also allude to the Hitchcock film);[7] and Benning's interest in the Wisconsin murderer Ed Gein in *Landscape Suicide* (1986) is not only a function of his always considerable interest in his own native region, but also an echo of Hitchcock's *Psycho* (1960), for which the story of Gein, via Robert Bloch's novel, *Psycho* (1959), was an inspiration—no moviegoer in 1960 could have failed to be affected by the Hitchcock film.

For Benning's generation, John Ford's use of Monument Valley as a central emblem of the American West transformed what in earlier decades had been a relatively unknown area into a pilgrimage site; and Benning makes his pilgrimage in *North on Evers*, first, visually, as he travels through the southwest early in the film and, near the end (in the film's only flashback), as he textually remembers the details of his visit to Monument Valley, when he gave a Navajo woman a ride to her home there. Of course, Benning's fascination with Western landscape (and the residue of the actual history that commercial Westerns mythify) is obvious throughout his work, and is a central subject of *Deseret* (1995), *Four Corners* (1997), *UTOPIA* (1998), and the California Trilogy (*El Valley Centro*, 1999; *Los*, 2000; and *SOGOBI*, 2001).

Benning has always seen himself as a film *artist*, though he has tended to resist the commercialization of the art world. His fascination with art seems to have developed along with his passion for filmmaking (he earned an MFA in filmmaking at the University of Wisconsin in Madison in 1975). His most obvious art-world influence has been and remains Robert Smithson, and in particular, Smithson's *Spiral Jetty* (1970). The Spiral Jetty first appears in *North on Evers*, where it is a crucial location; and it has continued to fascinate Benning who has returned to the site many times to film it: for a sequence of *Deseret* (1995); then as the sole subject of the feature *casting a glance* (2007), for which Benning made many trips to the Jetty to demonstrate "how it changes over time"; and most recently, for *measuring change* (2016), an hour-long, two-shot meditation on the Jetty. Benning's commitment to *The Spiral Jetty* as a primary pilgrimage site remains something of an anomaly: it is the one canonical work of non-cinematic art, and the one instance of what is now called "destination art," that has so captivated him.[8]

Benning did not study cinema history or art history during his undergraduate college days; he studied mathematics, earning a BA in mathematics at the University of Wisconsin in Milwaukee in 1966 (he sometimes teaches math at CalArts). However, as he found his way into filmmaking and the independent film scene, he learned art history by going to museums—though an unusual range of artists' work has found its way into his films. The title "One Way Boogie Woogie" refers to Piet Mondrian's *Broadway Boogie-Woogie* (1943) and *Victory Boogie-Woogie* (1944); a Mondrian painting is carried through the forty-seventh shot of *One Way Boogie Woogie*—and the film's sixty shots are composed in ways that graphically evoke Mondrian and refer to the painter's commitment to red, yellow, and blue. The titles of *13 Lakes* (2004) and *Ten Skies* (2004) seem a nod to LA photographer/painter Ed Rusha's titles *Twentysix Gasoline Stations* (1962), *Thirtyfour Parking Lots* (1967), and *Nine Swimming Pools and a Broken Glass* (1968). Claude Monet's *Poppy Field in a Hollow near Giverny* (1885) is the first of four paintings seen in *Four Corners*; the others attest to the particular breadth of Benning's artistic taste: the second painting is *George Washington* (1989) by Alabama outsider artist Mose Tolliver; the third, a pictograph that Benning calls "Holy Ghost" that he imagines was painted by a Native American named Yukuwa, circa AD 100; the fourth, Jasper Johns' *Flag* (1955).

The inclusion of Mose Tolliver evidences Benning's long-time interest in outsider or "vernacular" artists and art. On his way east in *North on Evers* Benning tries to find Tolliver—"Mose T"—and recalls visiting him some years earlier, when he bought a Tolliver painting for his daughter Sadie); and in that same film, he also visits a man in Texas "who made things out of cement, but they looked like they were made from trees," and the Reverend Howard Finster, a Georgia preacher/folk artist who paints religious signs. Benning's interest in vernacular artists seems part and parcel of an empathy with the struggles of American minorities (particularly Native Americans, African Americans, and Chicanos) that was fundamental to his maturation and has been fundamental to his filmmaking at least since *American Dreams*. Indeed, Benning has come to understand himself as something of an outsider—an artist who works outside the confines of institutions and collaborators and beyond the expectations of critics. It is also true that, at least in New York City during some of his most productive years, Benning was under-appreciated: it was not until the sixteenth annual "Views from the Avant-Garde" that a Benning film—*small roads*—was screened as part of the annual review of *avant-garde* cinema at the New York Film Festival.

Visual Text and Cinematic Space

Though he works alone, Benning has stayed in tune with particular cinematic issues raised by his independent filmmaker colleagues. His adoption of the principles of structural film in many of his early films has been mentioned—and remains equally evident in recent decades. During the 1970s and 1980s, a more specific focus of many filmmakers was the use of visual text as image. There are premonitions of this issue from the earliest decades of filmmaking: Edwin Porter's *College Chums* (1907) is a particularly early instance, and several formative landmarks of *avant-garde* film—Charles Sheeler and Paul Strand's *Manhatta* (1921), Marcel Duchamp's *Anemic Cinema* (1926) and Luis Buñuel and Salvador Dali's *Un Chien Andalou* (1929)—employ visual text in inventive ways. And of course, the issue of whether visual text (particularly in the form of intertitles) was/is "cinematic" was debated by feature film directors during the 1920s.[9]

The 1960s saw a renewal of interest in visual text, to some extent as part of independent cinema's challenge to Hollywood movies, which rarely used visual text except in conventional ways—but also as part of a widespread consideration of the limitations and possibilities of written language.[10] Bruce Conner's *A Movie* (1958) and *Cosmic Ray* (1963), Robert Nelson's *Oh Dem Watermelons* (1965), George Landow's *Film in Which There Appear Sprocket Holes, Edge Lettering, Dirt Particles, Etc.* (1966), Bruce Baillie's *Tung* (1966), Paul Sharits' *Word Movie/Fluxfilm* (1967), Joyce Wieland's *Sailboat* and *1933* (both 1967), Taka Iimura's *White Calligraphy* (1967) and Hollis Frampton's *Surface Tension* (1968) are among the many premonitions of an explosion of cine-visual-text in the 1970s—in such films as Jonas Mekas' *Walden* (1969), *Reminiscences of a Journey to Lithuania* (1972) and *Lost Lost Lost* (1976); Frampton's *Zorns Lemma* (1970) and *Poetic Justice* (1971); Yvonne Rainer's *Film about a Woman Who . . .* (1974) and *Journeys from Berlin/1971* (1979); Morgan Fisher's *Projection Instructions* (1976), Anthony McCall and Andrew Tyndall's *Argument* (1979)—and in the early 1980s: Su Friedrich's *Gently Down the Stream* (1981) and *The Ties That Bind* (1984), Michael Snow's *So Is This* (1982), Peter Rose's *Secondary Currents* (1983), and Benning's *American Dreams*. Of course, some of Benning's 1970s films—*11 × 14*, *One Way Boogie Woogie* and *Grand Opera*—make considerable use of visual text as an element of the landscapes and cityscapes depicted in these films, and in *Grand Opera* Benning includes a range of experiments with words and numbers.

The computer piece, *Pascal's Lemma*—a premonition of Benning's later embracing of the digital—uses a various kinds of visual text as part of a riff on the mathematical wizardry of Blaise Pascal and its implications for modern calculation (a computer programming language is named after him) and art-making. Originally exhibited by the Kitchen in 1984, the piece was revived and shown as *Pascal's Lemma (After Warhol)* in 2014 (in its recent iteration, the installation includes a Warhol silkscreen of an electric chair). In either version, the piece evidences a variety of textual approaches—texts that scroll across the middle of the frame, mathematical notations in letters and numbers, paragraphs of text that explain various dimensions of Pascal's discoveries; titles, dedications. These texts (along with various graphs of mathematical curves and illustrations of paintings by Piet Mondrian, Frank Stella, and Josef Albers that exemplify mathematical concepts) evoke many of Benning's typical interests: the history of π and of mathematics in general; the furor surrounding Hank Aaron's approach to Babe Ruth's homerun record, the environmental dangers of weapons testing in Utah . . .

North on Evers, Benning's meditation on turning fifty, uses the handwritten scrolling text he developed for *American Dreams* in a more complex way. Beginning early in the film, the text that rolls across the bottom of the screen explains that though he enjoys living in the small town of Val Verde, Benning has "decided to leave for the summer. I had been feeling anxious and thought travel might help." In time it becomes clear that *North on Evers* documents *two* trips: the first recorded in the rolling text; the second, documented by the visual imagery and sound, which was recorded a year later when Benning revisited the same sites and people. In *North on Evers*, the scrolling text is superimposed over other forms of imagery so that some words are obscured: a periodic frustration that functions as a way of visualizing the ephemeral quality of memory. Of course, Benning's trip across the country to New York and back to Val Verde also includes many instances of environmental text, including Maya Lin's Vietnam Veterans Memorial where Benning finds the name of a friend who died in 1970—the first moment in *North on Evers* when the textual description of Benning's first trip and his recording of image and sound a year later are in sync.

Benning continued to work with text, and often visual text, in a variety of ways for the better part of ten years: most obviously, in *Four Corners* and *Deseret*. *Deseret*, Benning's first film entirely about the West, does include environmental visual text, though the film's primary textual experiment involves syncing his exploration of the geography of Utah (originally called "Deseret" by the Mormons) with Fred Gardner's reading of edited versions of ninety-three *New York Times* stories about Utah dating from 1852, when the *Times* was founded, until 1992. Each shot in the film lasts as long as a sentence in the *Times* story (each *Times* story is separated from the next by a shot without narration).

Four Corners is a rigorously, even mathematically, organized feature about the area of the Southwest where Arizona, New Mexico, Colorado, and Utah meet—a synecdoche for the Cartesian grid system for the American West, designed by Thomas Jefferson and instituted by the Continental Congress in the Land Ordinance of 1785. The film divides into four structurally identical sections. Each section includes four distinct elements, beginning with a scrolling text providing a brief history of the artist who produced the particular artwork that is revealed immediately after the scrolling text. Each artwork is accompanied by a spoken narrative about a particular element of the history of the American West—each narrative is read by the differently accented voices of Hartmut Bitomski, Benning himself, Yeasup Song, and Billy Woodberry. Each section concludes with a thirteen-shot sequence, arranged seasonally; these sequences depict the pueblos in Chaco Canyon (New Mexico), the Milwaukee neighborhood where Benning grew up, various scenes at Mesa Verde (Colorado), and the city of Farmington, New Mexico.

In general, *Four Corners* traces the history of Native-American/European-American relations (the Milwaukee narrative includes the Black Hawk War of 1832 that displaced the Menomonee and Potawatomi tribes and opened the way for the settlement of Milwaukee by Euro-Americans) and surveys how that history remains evident in the Four Corners area and in American culture in general. That the rigorous structure of *Four Corners* is precise not only in a general sense, but in its specifics—each rolling text includes the same number of typographic characters (1,214) and each narrative, the same number of words (1,186)—implicitly places *Four Corners* within the era of personal computers, and can now be read as another premonition of Benning's subsequent embrace of the digital. Benning's fascination with text would reemerge, in a more traditional way, after 2006 as he developed his Two Cabins project.

SPACE EXTENDED THROUGH TIME

While his work with visual text in *American Dreams*, *North on Evers*, and *Four Corners* was part of an extensive engagement by many independent filmmakers, the revival of Benning's interest in the long-duration shot in the 2000s seems to have been largely a function of his ongoing friendships with Peter Hutton and Sharon Lockhart. Of course, Benning's 1970s films are full of extended shots. Each shot in *One Way Boogie Woogie* lasts exactly a full minute; and the nearly 11-minute sync-sound shot made on the Evanston Express elevated train from its last stop in Evanston to its first stop in Chicago is a warning to viewers that shot length in *11 × 14* will not be predictable. What seems new in Benning's return to the extended shot in the 2000s is an added level of patience that may owe something to Hutton's films of the 1980s and 1990s—Benning has often called Hutton his cinematic brother. Hutton's *Landscape (for Manon)* (1987: Manon is Hutton's daughter), shot silent and in black and white, begins with shots of 25, 27, 11, 27, 18, and 27 seconds, then slows down; midway through the 18-minute film the shots are nearly a minute long—and the silence and relative serenity of Hutton's shots makes them seem even longer.

Each of the three films in Benning's California Trilogy is composed of thirty-five 2½-minute shots, and while most of Benning's earlier extended shots tend to include relatively dramatic action (the shots in *One Way Boogie Woogie* are full of playful elements and cinematic jokes), many of the shots in the Trilogy are comparatively serene. This is true of *SOGOBI* in particular, which is focused on what remains of "wilderness" California, and often alludes to the long history of Californian photography: the framing of Benning's shot of Yosemite Valley recalls canonical photographers from Eadweard Muybridge to Ansel Adams, as well as the many amateur photographers who have recorded Yosemite Valley from the same general position—with one caveat: slowly, as one engages Benning's almost entirely still image, the distant movement of Upper Yosemite Falls becomes gradually (and magically) evident.[11]

Benning has been quite clear about his debt to filmmaker/photographer Sharon Lockhart:

> I should also mention that I was very much challenged by Sharon Lockhart's *Goshogaoka* [1997]. I saw the film right after she completed it and was very taken by her connection to structural film (Warhol's work, and Frampton's, and mine), but I was even more impressed by how she radicalized structure, pushing duration to a new aesthetic level. After I saw *Goshogaoka*, my own work became more radical. (MacDonald 2009: 259)

Benning first emulated Lockhart's use of 10-minute shots in *Goshogaoka* in his diptych *13 Lakes* (2004) and *Ten Skies* (2004). Both films are unusually demanding, but have been surprisingly successful:

> As for audiences, this new strategy is asking them to work harder; you can't experience something subtle if you don't look more closely than we're accustomed to looking, and looking more closely isn't easy. At first I was worried that audiences would be bored, but the contrary seems to have happened.[12]

13 Lakes was inducted in the Library of Congress' National Film Registry in 2015.

Ironically, *13 Lakes* and *Ten Skies* were crucial in convincing Benning to move to digital filmmaking. The rigorously minimal compositional strategy for each of the shots in *13 Lakes* and *Ten Skies* makes any physical damage to the film especially obvious: even the smallest scratch in the emulsion becomes more fully the "subject" of the shot than the often subtle changes in the imagery itself. After a remake of *One Way Boogie Woogie*, *One Way Boogie Woogie/27 Years Later* (2005), and *casting a glance*, Benning bid farewell to emulsion-based cinema with *RR* (2007), evoking the origins of the cinema experience in the railroad journey, as well as the shared mechanical/chemical technologies basic to the locomotive and cinema.[13] Each shot in *RR* begins when a train enters the frame and ends at the moment when the train is no longer visible.

Lockhart and Benning would continue to push the limits of duration, using different technological means. Lockhart's *Double Tide* (2009) appears to be two 45-minute shots, one filmed in the morning, the other in the evening, of a woman clamming in a Maine cove during a double-tide day (actually each of the 45-minute "shots" combines several shorter shots with invisible cuts). *Double Tide* was shot on celluloid and released as a digital film.[14] Benning's *Ruhr* begins with six 10-minute shots filmed in and around Duisberg, followed by a 60-minute shot of a cooling tower used in the processing of the coke necessary for producing steel. Not only did digital shooting avoid the problem with film damage that had so frustrated Benning, it was less expensive and allowed for increased control of sound. And the change in aspect ratio from 16 mm

(4:3) to digital shooting (16:9) seems to have enhanced Benning's interest in making epic landscape shots.

Further experiments with extended duration followed. *Nightfall* (2011) is a 98½-minute single-shot film of a forest scene at dusk: changes in the image are so subtle as to be virtually invisible and throw the sounds of the forest into high relief. In mid-August, 2012, Benning recorded *BNSF* (2013), a 200-minute faux-single-shot of the Burlington Northern Santa Fe rail-lines, "about 8 miles west of Amboy, CA along old Route 66, which is just off frame," from about 4:00 in the afternoon until 7:15 in the evening ("it was about 100 degrees").[15] During *BNSF* an expansive view of the remote desert landscape is interrupted thirteen times by trains moving through the image east-to-west or west-to-east (according to Benning, this is one of the busiest tracks in America: an average of thirty-six trains pass by this spot every day).[16] As in the individual shots in *13 Lakes*, attentive viewing reveals continual subtle changes in the desert landscape, created by the hot breeze and the movement of clouds, as well as obvious differences in the trains that pass by and their cargos. An ever-changing soundscape is created by the quiet of the desert and the more or less regular arrivals of the noisy trains. Like *13 Lakes* and *Ten Skies*, *BNSF* is more engaging than a description may suggest—though it is difficult to imagine Benning extending the single-shot much further than this.

The fact that digital shooting allows extended duration shots to be made easily and inexpensively has sometimes led Benning into self-indulgence. Both *Nightfall* and the more recent *Fresh Air* (2016, a 46-minute shot of three t-shirts on a clothesline blowing in the breeze, accompanied by broadcasts of various news stories involving violence) are less effective than most of Benning's longer films—though the equally meditative *Red Cloud* (2016), an hour-long shot of a drawing of the Oglala Lakota Sioux warrior and statesman, Red Cloud, filmed during the gradually transforming light of sunset (as an LA radio station reports on contemporary events) is engaging and suggestive. Of course, not all the recent digitally shot films demand the level of patience necessary for *BNSF* or *Red Cloud*. *small roads*, a feature-length landscape film made up of forty-seven shots recorded in fifteen mostly western states (individual shots last from around a minute to three minutes), is among Benning's most enjoyable recent films.[17]

Benning's panorama of the American landscape in *small roads* confirms his stature as a major contributor to the history of landscape representation, a modern inheritor of the tradition established by painter Claude Lorrain (1600–82). Whereas Claude used a variety of graphic methods—winding rivers, modulation of light—for carrying the viewer's eye from foreground into deep space, Benning uses roadways (and the vehicles that travel them), as well as inventive composition and careful attention to the soundscape of each shot,

Figure 4 From small roads, *2011. Courtesy of the artist and neugerriemschneider, Berlin*

to create much the same effect. But Benning has the advantage of working with extended duration: each shot in *small roads* creates suspense. At some point in most of the shots a car or truck (in some instances more than one) interrupts the relative quiet of the shot as it passes Benning's camera. Suspense is created as viewers wonder when a vehicle will pass; and after Benning first surprises viewers (in shot 7) by *not* including a passing vehicle, the suspense is doubled: *will* a vehicle pass—and when? Further, as in *13 Lakes* and *Ten Skies*, the succession of shots creates a second kind of suspense: what will the next variation in landscape be; how will it add, visually and sonically, to the variety of what has already been seen and heard?

Cine-Portraits

The switch to digital has also resulted in an expansion of Benning's interest in the cine-portrait that began in his 1970s films. *Grand Opera* includes the portraits of Frampton, Landow, Snow, and Rainer; *North on Evers* includes sixty-four mini-portraits of individuals that Benning met during his trips east and west; and *Landscape Suicide* is, in a sense, a pair of "portraits" of Bernadette Protti and Ed Gein. But it was not until 2010–11 that Benning produced feature-length films made up of portraits in the usual sense of the term. *Reforming the Past* (2010) was made from the sixty-four portraits in *North on Evers*: "I projected *North on Evers* onto the wall and copied the sixty-four portraits with my digital camera. Each was about 10 seconds long. I slowed those portraits down to a little less than a minute each, making a 60 minute silent film" (MacDonald 2017). *Reforming the Past* has sometimes been presented as a performance event: a screening of the film is followed by Benning reading the text of *North on Evers*.

Also completed in 2010, *Faces 1973* uses two 12½-minute extreme close-ups of faces, made for a film (*Ode to Muzac*, 1972), commissioned by the musician Henry Mancini for viewing on his *Mancini Generation* television show. Benning was given the Mancini music "A Shot in the Dark" (from Blake Edwards' 1964 comedy, *A Shot in the Dark*), which was to accompany Benning's film. No fan of the Pink Panther films, Benning responded with a 3-minute tracking shot down Milwaukee's poverty-stricken Third Street into which he inserted six 1-second images of a man shooting up heroin and a prostitute putting on lipstick, including, in the last insert, the close-ups of the two characters (played by Robert Bick and Sharon Sampon) that in *Faces 1973* are rendered digitally in extreme slow motion.[18] *Faces*, a full-length feature made the same year, uses a similar procedure to recycle close-ups of the characters in John Cassavetes' 1968 film of the same name, presented in such extreme slow motion that the changes in the images are barely perceptible. Whether Benning had seen Chieko Shiomi's *Disappearing Music for Face* and Yoko Ono's *Eyeblink* or *Match*—all part of George Maciunas' *Fluxfilm Program* of 1966; or Ono's *Film No. 5 (Smile)* (1968), her portrait of John Lennon—all films in which normal motion is radically slowed down, creating an experience similar to *Faces 1973*—is unclear, though Benning has expressed admiration for Ono's work.[19]

Benning's interest in cine-portrait has also produced two feature films more fully in the mode of Warhol's *Screen Tests* (1964–6). *After Warhol* (2011) is a series of fifteen portraits of the students in one of Benning's classes at CalArts. As the title suggests, Benning was thinking of the legendary informality of the *Screen Tests*:

> I walked into class one day, not knowing what I would be doing and saw one of my students standing against the wall staring into space. I said don't move, got my digital camera and a 16 mm projector for lighting and began to film the class doing screen tests. It was playful and enjoyable. All the portraits were shot on that one day[.]

—like Warhol, Benning gave the students no direction (MacDonald 2017). In *Twenty Cigarettes* (2011) twenty people (old filmmaker friends, colleagues at CalArts, students) are recorded smoking cigarettes. Each is filmed in a different audio-visual environment, and the length of each portrait is determined by the time it takes the individual to smoke the cigarette. The portraits were recorded without Benning present: "I would turn the camera on and leave, so that the smokers wouldn't be affected by my presence or feel any need to interact with me" (MacDonald 2017).

A far more elaborate "portrait" project—roughly similar to *Landscape Suicide*—has developed from Benning's fascination with Henry David Thoreau and Theodore J. Kaczynski ("the Unabomber"). His interest in the two men led him in 2007–8 to construct on his land in the foothills of California's Sierra Nevada Mountains modern versions of the cabin Thoreau built at Walden Pond and the cabin Kaczynski built in Montana. During the following decade these cabins would become the basis for a series of films, including *Two Cabins* (2010): two 15-minute shots of the window in each cabin, filmed from inside (*Two Cabins* is sometimes presented as a two-channel video installation); and two feature films: *Stemple Pass* (2012) and *Concord Woods* (2014).[20] *Stemple Pass* is made up of four 30-minute shots of the Kaczynski cabin (arranged spring, fall, winter, summer), during each of which Benning reads excerpts from Kacsynski's writings (the winter excerpt, originally recorded in code, was decoded by Benning himself).[21] *Concord Woods* (2014) uses two hour-long shots of the Thoreau cabin: the first filmed during summer solstice, and accompanied by Benning's reading from Thoreau's "A Plea for Captain John Brown" (1859); the second, during winter solstice, accompanied by Benning's reading from Thoreau's "Economy," the first chapter of *Walden*. That the two features are meant to be companion pieces is evident in their roughly similar structures and confirmed by their similar length (*Stemple Pass* runs 121½ minutes; *Concord Woods*, 123 minutes), which echoes the roughly similar structures of the two cabins (Kaczynski's cabin was originally based on Thoreau's).[22]

Over the years, the Two Cabins project has taken a number of different forms. At the annual Brakhage Symposium in 2011, Benning presented a lecture on the project, illustrated with *Two Cabins* (2010); and elaborate solo museum shows of films and installations were presented by the Kunsthaus, Graz, Austria from March to June 2014 and by the Kunstverein in Hamburg, Germany from December to March 2015. Both shows are documented in the catalog *James Benning: Decoding Fear*.[23]

There is also *(FC) Two Cabins by JB*, a book produced in 2011 by Benning and Julie Ault, which can be understood as Benning's return to text-based work. *(FC) Two Cabins by JB* is a collage of essays and images that provide something similar, although in book form, to Benning's earlier overviews in *American Dreams* and *North on Evers*.[24] The book includes reprints of Thoreau's "Solitude" and Kaczynski's "Industrial Society and Its Future"; a collage of images, shot by Benning, of the two cabins, inside and out; close-ups of Benning's copies of vernacular paintings by Bill Traylor, Mose Tolliver, Henry Darger, Martín Ramírez, William Hawkins, Black Hawk, Joseph E. Yoakum, and Jesse Howard that hang in the cabins (the Benning copies are seen in close-up while the originals are photographed from books); a listing of the books on the bookshelf in the Kaczynski cabin; Benning's essay, "Twelve

People," mini-biographies of Thoreau, the vernacular painters listed above, and Kaczynski; and finally "Freedom Club," an overview of the Two Cabins project by Julie Ault, and "After Benning, after Math: 12, 13 and counting..." by Dick Hebdige. There is also a bibliography and an appendix of the computer program developed by Benning to decode Kaczynski's journals.

Moving Forward, Looking Back

In addition to alluding to particular films and filmmakers in his earlier work and, in the case of *Grand Opera*, providing portraits of favorite filmmakers, Benning has, in at least one instance, used the work of another filmmaker as part of his own film: for *UTOPIA* (1998) Benning "borrowed" the soundtrack for Richard Dindo's *Ernesto Che Guevara, the Bolivian Diary* (1997) to use as an accompaniment to his visual exploration of the border territory between California and Sonora, Mexico—his way of arguing that Guevara's quest for continued revolution was/is at least as relevant for the United States as for Cuba or Bolivia. In more recent years, Benning has taken to reworking the films of other directors, as well as his own.

In *North on Evers* Benning had already alluded to *Easy Rider* (1968); his motorcycle trips east in that film traverse some of the same territory as Captain America and Billy traverse in the Dennis Hopper film; and in 2012 he produced his own *Easy Rider* to provide a reworking of the film:

> For *Easy Rider*, I wanted to look at Hopper's backgrounds, pay attention to what they "drove by," to make some sense by paying attention to details. Maybe they wouldn't have had to die in the end if they'd done the same. So I did lots of research and found where all of the locations were. Then I replaced the length of a scene with just one shot of the location so the viewer has time to look, listen and think. I'm not re-making the narrative, but I do use some of the dialogue to help connect the locations. (MacDonald 2017)[25]

Benning has also continued to rework moments from his own films. *John Krieg Exiting the Falk Corporation in 1971* (2010) digitally transforms a 17-second shot from Benning's early fictional narrative, *Time and a Half* (1973), that depicts his friend John Krieg exiting the Falk Corporation (where Benning's father worked) into a 77-minute feature.

However, Benning's most elaborate revisiting of his own personal and cinematic past, as well as his most expansive embracing of digital technology and the global mediascape that the digital revolution has made possible is his epic, multi-partite *52 Films*, completed in 2015. *52 Films* was developed for a gallery show where each film would be available on a separate computer. As of this writing (June, 2016), the show has not yet been scheduled, though excerpts from the series have sometimes been shown as interactive presentations: at Hamilton College in 2015 Benning asked members of the audience to choose titles of individual films within the set: after each choice was indicated, Benning showed the film, and then chose one he felt would be interesting to see in relation to the audience member's choice.

For *52 Films* Benning scoured the internet to collect interesting work, much of it produced by amateurs, whom he understands as a new breed of vernacular artists—and he worked at transforming what he found into a collaborative form of personal expression. To make "13 Lakes," for example, Benning tracked down thirteen shots of the same lakes depicted in his *13 Lakes* and arranged them in the same order and within the same textual design. The found shots are generally engaging by themselves, but for those familiar with the original *13 Lakes* and Benning's work in general, particular shots are often amusing in the ways in which they simultaneously confirm and deviate from what Benning did in the original film. Another approach is evident in "1200 hp," where Benning appropriated an online film, then digitally reworked it: first, the audience sees a 5¾-minute, black and white image that Benning has digitally slowed down, of a beautiful young woman riding in a car, the shot accompanied by the Rolling Stones hit "Wild Horses"—at one point during the shot the woman seems powerfully energized by something. The slowed-down footage is followed by the original, 39-second, sync-sound, color shot that Benning found online, which reveals in real time that the young woman's change in demeanor is a result of her being thrilled when the vehicle, using its 1,200 horsepower, suddenly speeds up.

52 Films revisits many of Benning's interests and "remakes" many of his earlier films (including *American Dreams, One Way Boogie Woogie, RR, Stemple Pass, Ten Skies*). In some cases the individual films are brief: "two moments" is just under two minutes; it includes the Zapruder footage of the Kennedy assassination and the footage of Rodney King being assaulted by the LA Police. In other instances, individual films are complex: the most elaborate are the companion pieces, "FUCK ME (green)" and "FUCK ME (orange)," each of which includes eight separate items, arranged, in reverse order, according to the dates when they were originally filmed, beginning in 2015/2015, respectively, and ending in 1957. Together the sixteen items function as a deflected autobiography of Benning, or at least as an evocation of the socio-political context through which the filmmaker has evolved.

There are many re-workings of moments from classic films—the Edison studio's *Kiss* (1896), Pabst's *Pandora's Box* (1929), Lang's *Metropolis* (1927), Hitchcock's *Psycho* (1960), McElwee's *Sherman's March* (1983), Antonioni's *Blow-Up* (1966), Dreyer's *The Passion of Joan of Arc* (1928), Godard's *Weekend* (1967) and Vigo's *Zéro de conduite* (1933)—and references to Hollis Frampton (*HF* is a slowed-down excerpt from R. Bruce Jenkins' *Mutual Interference*

[1976] accompanied by excerpts from the soundtrack of Frampton's *(nostalgia)* [1971]) and Michael Snow ("Wavelength", a gorgeous digital reworking of the Snow film). Benning's interest in text-based cinema is evident in "signs," an 18-minute presentation of twenty cardboard signs made by New York City homeless people, originally collected by Andres Serrano as part of a larger project; each sign is shown for fifty-two seconds (long enough for the audience to read it).[26] Excerpts from news events dealing with racial issues, 9/11, the arms race, wars in many countries are also referenced. All in all, *52 Films* is a major contribution to the long tradition of found-footage cinema.

Digital filmmaking has freed Benning, who has always been prolific, to produce films at a rate that makes keeping up with him an evolving challenge. As he has come closer and closer to mortality, it is as if he hears "Time's wingèd chariot hurrying near," and, more obsessively than ever, buries himself in a frenzy of work. Among the most recent films is *Spring Equinox* (2016), fourteen 5-minute shots made on Mountain Road 56, the road to Benning's property in Pine Flat. Each 5-minute shot is made from a position further up the road (Benning supplies the specific elevation and mile point), so that the differences in what is seen and heard in the successive shots demonstrate the remarkable variety of landscape on this 30.9-mile stretch of road (that the sound of each landscape fades in before the image is seen seems a nod to Harvard's Sensory Ethnography Lab, for which Benning's films have been of considerable importance).[27]

Benning also records the time when each shot was made, from 6:12 p.m. on March 20, 2016 to 8:16 a.m.: that is, as we ascend the road, we are moving back in time. On a literal level, Benning's decision to show the fourteen landscapes in the reverse order from how the shots were recorded reflects the fact that the trip up the mountain at this moment in the year is a movement back toward winter—but there are other implications as well. That so much of Benning's recent work revisits the past, and in many cases is involved in retarding the motion of what he has shot or collected, can be read as a "meta" reflection on his career—and evokes that most American novel, *The Great Gatsby*. Benning, now in his seventies, continues to work against the current of time. Like Jay Gatsby, to paraphrase the final sentence of the Fitzgerald novel, Benning beats on, a boat against the current, "borne back ceaselessly into the past"—as he is endlessly re-born in the cinematic present of his work.

Notes

1. The only instance I'm aware of where Benning crossed the American border to shoot imagery for a film was during the shooting of *UTOPIA* (1998), when Benning crossed into Mexico:

MacDonald: How much time did you spend in Mexico? *Benning*: Just enough to be scared shitless. Less than an hour. Mexicali is a very poor town. I'm not a rich filmmaker, but I look a lot richer than the Mexicalis, and I was alone and fair game. I made it out before the police and the crooks could get to me" (MacDonald 2006: 242).

2. A long-time friend, film artist John Knecht, brought Benning to teach at the University of Oklahoma in 1977–8 and again in 1979–80, where he made *Grand Opera* (1979) and shot imagery for three film installations: *Four Oil Wells* (1978), *Oklahoma* (1979), and *Last Dance* (1981)—all of them depicting oil wells. In the fall of 1978, in between his years at the University of Oklahoma, Benning was visiting professor at the University of California San Diego.
3. My apologies here to David James, whose *The Most Typical Avant-Garde: History and Geography of Minor Cinemas in Los Angeles* (2005) makes a compelling argument that LA should also have been considered a center of *avant-garde* production; but I'm referring to the sense of the *avant-garde* scene and of Benning that we had in the 1970s.
4. *Pascal's Lemma* is dedicated to Blaise Pascal and Frampton.
5. Benning: "I agree with what he [Brakhage] says, basically that you can't see and hear at the same time. It made him decide to work visually, but I concluded the opposite. I wanted to use sound *because* it makes you look at things differently" (MacDonald 1992: 240).
6. Benning's feminist turn was evident at least as early as *I-94* and is implicit in *Landscape Suicide* (in Benning's use of a counterpoint structure to compare the environments of two high-profile murders: Ed Gein's murder of Bernice Worden in rural Wisconsin in 1957 and the "cheerleader murder" of Kirsten Costas in the Bay Area suburb of Orinda, California by her classmate, Bernadette Protti), and in his decision to focus *Used Innocence* (1988) on Lawrencia Bembenek, imprisoned for a murder she says she did not commit. Various issues relating to the exploitation of women, including the issue of "consent" on college campuses currently in the news, are addressed in *52 Films* (2015).
7. Benning:

    "You can't make a crop-duster shot without thinking of Hitchcock. But I wasn't making the shot as an allusion, but because most of the valley is sprayed with chemicals. You see crop dusters there year round . . . I *was* very aware that as soon as you'd see the image, you'd think of *North by Northwest*. That doesn't bother me." (MacDonald, 2006: 249)

    Tanja Vrvilo suggests that the four portraits in *Grand Opera* may be a wry allusion to the faces on Mount Rushmore—an idea I'd not considered. See Tanja Vrvilo (2014: 172). See note 23 for more information on *James Benning: Decoding Fear*.
8. Benning is a habitué of Marfa, Texas, where Donald Judd's outdoor work and the studios housing important works by Judd, Dan Flavin, and John Chamberlain have made the town a destination for art lovers—and in at least one instance, Hollywood film producers: *Giant* (1958, directed by George Stevens) was shot there.
9. In his early epics D. W. Griffith made extensive use of intertitles, including as a way

of footnoting historical research, while Robert Weine and Buster Keaton chose to fashion the intertitles in *The Cabinet of Dr Caligari* and *The General* so that they were visually appropriate for the mood and time-period the films depict (and, in Keaton's case, in order to add a bit of textual humor to the otherwise physical humor of *The General*). On the other hand, F. W. Murnau worked at eliminating visual text from his films—and nearly succeeded in *The Last Laugh* (1924); and Dziga Vertov announced at the beginning of *The Man with a Movie Camera* (1929) that his composite city symphony would be film without text (except, of course, for the text of the announcement!).

10. I'm thinking, for example, of lettrism, visual poetry, the Language Poets, and the widespread interest in the semiotics of cinema.
11. For examples, see Allen (2016).
12. Benning in *Adventures of Perception*: 259. My own experience showing these films, and particularly *13 Lakes*, has confirmed Benning's sense that audiences, especially academic audiences of students, are successful in handling the durational challenges of the films.
13. See Wolfgang Schivelbusch (1986).
14. Lockhart had already pushed duration well beyond the 10-minute shot, in *Teatro Amazonas* (1999), a faux 30-minute shot of a theater audience in Manaus, Brazil, and in *NŌ* (2003), a 32½-minute, faux single shot of Japanese farmers spreading hay on a field.
15. Benning:

    my camera can hold two S x S Cards [Sony 32GB memory cards], each can record about 58 minutes, so I had to reload the cards to get over 3 hours. but I can exchange a card while the other card is recording so that's no problem. but my battery was getting low after about 2 hours so I had to change batteries once, which meant a 10-second break which is hidden by a dissolve, so it's technically two shots but there's no need to admit to this for it's negligible." (Email to the author, August 19, 2014)

16. Email to the author, August 19, 2014.
17. The end credits indicate that *small roads* was shot in Arizona, Arkansas, California, Illinois, Louisiana, Minnesota, Mississippi, Missouri, Nebraska, New Mexico, South Dakota, Texas, Utah, Wisconsin, and Wyoming.
18. Benning:

    In the early 1970s Mancini was looking for new filmmakers to illustrate his music for his TV show. This is before rock videos became a popular form. He contacted a number of film schools (there weren't that many back then) and offered $600 per song. I was one of the only people at the University of Wisconsin making films, so I got a grant. (MacDonald 2017)

    "Mancini . . . was appalled and wanted his money back. My professor, Jim Heddle, refused" (email to author, June 14, 2016).

19. Ono's *Match* and *Eyeblink* and *Disappearing Music for Face* (a close-up of Ono's mouth) were filmed with a camera that could shoot at 2,000 frames per second; the imagery in *Film No. 5 (Smile)* is also slowed down, but not as radically. Benning

has said, Ono is "an artist I really admire. I very much like... Yoko's dream pieces." From unpublished interview with Benning, March, 2016.
20. Benning considers *Nightfall* part of the Two Cabins project—though I am unclear as to why.
21. In these later films, as in Benning's earlier work, the use of text to indicate title and other information (in *Stemple Pass*, the sources of the excerpts Benning reads, and at the end the names and birth and death dates of the three men Kaczynski murdered) is elegant and distinctive—a vestige of Benning's more thorough immersion in textual experimentation in earlier decades.
22. For information about Kaczynski's debt to Thoreau's cabin, see Julie Ault's essay, "Freedom Club" (Ault, 2011): 104.
23. *James Benning: Decoding Fear*, a well-illustrated catalog (with stills from films and paintings, images of the cabins, inside and out) was published in conjunction with the two museum shows as a collaboration of the Kunsthaus Graz and the Kunstverein Hamburg. It includes a forward by Peter Pakesch and Bettina Steinbrügge, the curators in Graz and Hamburg, and the editors of the catalog; essays by Diedrich Diederichsen ("James Benning: Romanticism and Enlightenment") and Tanja Vrvilo ("James Benning: Memories from the Hands"); and "James Benning, the Unabomber, and *Stemple Pass*: An Interview" by Allan MacInnis—plus illustrations of documents relating to Benning's decoding of Theodore Kaczynski's journals.
24. A second book, designed so as to be a companion to *(FC) Two Cabins by JB*, was produced by the Marfa Book Company in Marfa, Texas, as part of the gallery show, "Thirty-one Friends (October)" in 2015. Benning produced thirty-one small artworks—paintings, photographs, small sculptures, framed letters—accompanied by short texts, each referencing one of Benning's friends—and in *Thirty-One Friends (October)* presented as a two-page text/image spread. The friends: Thom Andersen, Julie Ault, Martin Beck, Rhonda Bell, Sadie Benning, Juliette Blightman, Bob Danner, Anna Faroqhi, Jake Fuller, Maia Gianakos, Dick Hebdige, Alex Horwath, Peter Hutton, John Jost, John Knecht, Rachel Kushner, Les LeVeque, Steve Lemon, Richard Linklater, Sharon Lockhart, Scott MacDonald, Gary Mairs, Sarinah Masukor, Zorana Musikic, Michael O'Brien, Peter Pakesch, Lee Anne Schmitt, Deborah Stratman, Joanna Swan, Werner Ruzicka, and Danh Vo. An appendix includes several photographs, including one of Benning, Sadie Benning, and Yoko Ono in 1993.
25. Over the years, Benning's sense of *Easy Rider* has evolved: in 2002 he told me that when the film first came out, "I thought it was kind of heroic, and it made me proud to be a hippie. Then, when I saw it about ten years later, I decided those guys might have gotten what they deserved. [laughter] Just because of their selfishness" (MacDonald 2006: 233).
26. Benning:

> He [Serrano] collected over two hundred of those signs and made a film that shows them very quickly, as a barrage, accompanied by a speech by Martin Luther King and some techno music. I thought what he did in collecting the signs was brilliant, but I thought if

those signs are going to be re-presented, you should have to *look* at them—because normally we look away. I wanted to re-appropriate his signs and show him the way I thought we should see them. (MacDonald 2017: 115)

27. The sound of the landscapes in *Spring Equinox* does not continue after the image fades out.

    The Sensory Ethnography Lab (SEL) evolved during the 2000s, under the leadership of Lucien Castaing-Taylor. One of the notable characteristics of the SEL has been its commitment to the soundtrack, a commitment that is expressed in many of the films that have come out of the SEL by the fact the sound is often heard before image is seen and continues to be heard after the image has faded out.

    Benning's influence on the SEL is evident in *Manakamana* (2013) by Stephanie Spray and Pacho Velez (who studied with Benning at CalArts). Indeed, the structure of *Manakamana* involved a wrestle with Benning's work: *Manakamana* records, in a series of eleven approximately ten-minute shots, six trips by pilgrims to the temple of the goddess Bhagwati on a Nepalese mountain top via the Manakamana cable car, and five trips down. When I asked Spray about Benning's influence, she said: "Benning's films made a strong impression; *13 Lakes* is the first I saw and is a favorite" (MacDonald 2015: 412). Velez explained:

    > We spent a long time figuring out the film's shape, starting from a much more rigid, structural idea of how the film should look. Early cuts featured eighteen rides: nine up, nine down, and for each ride, the camera would switch positions in the cable car: facing forward, backward, forward, backward. It was a very precise and clean edit, without loose ends or mysteries. In many ways, it felt like a Benning film. And that was a problem for us. Somehow, the balance was tilted too much towards conceptual precision and away from small human revelations[.] (MacDonald 2015: 416)

Works Cited

Allen, Jamie M. (2016), *Picturing America's National Parks*, New York, Rochester: Aperture and George Eastman Museum.

Ault, Julie (2011) "Freedom Club," in Julie Ault, (ed.) *(FC) Two Cabins by JB*, New York: Art Resources Transfer.

James, David (2005), *The Most Typical Avant-Garde: History and Geography of Minor Cinemas in Los Angeles*, Berkeley: University of California Press.

MacDonald, Scott (1992), *A Critical Cinema 2: Interviews with Independent Filmmakers*, Berkeley: University of California Press.

MacDonald, Scott (2006), *A Critical Cinema 5: Interviews with Independent Filmmakers*, Berkeley: University of California Press.

MacDonald, Scott (2009), *Adventures of Perception*, Berkeley: University of California Press, 2009.

MacDonald, Scott (2015), *Avant-Doc: Intersections of Documentary and Avant-Garde Cinema*, New York: Oxford University Press.

MacDonald, Scott (2017), "Benning Goes Digital: An Interview," *Found Footage Magazine* 3 (March): 107.

Sitney, P. Adams (1974) *Visionary Film: The American Avant-Garde*, New York: Oxford University Press.

Schivelbusch, Wolfgang (1986), *The Railway Journey: The Industrialization of Time and Space in the 19th Century*, Berkeley: University of California Press.

Vrvilo, Tanja (2014), "James Benning: Memories from the hands," in Peter Pakesch and Bettina Steinbrügge (eds.), *James Benning: Decoding Fear*, Graz/Hamburg: Kunsthaus Graz/Kunstverein.

JOHN BECK

Utah and the Times: *Governing Temporality in* Deseret

James Benning has a longstanding interest in the relationship among Western landscape, history, memory, and the politics of land use, most notably evident in, though by no means confined to, a series of text-and-image films made during the 1990s—*North on Evers* (1992), *Deseret* (1995), *Four Corners* (1997), and *UTOPIA* (1998)—and pursued in the California Trilogy consisting of *El Valley Centro* (2000), *Los* (2000), and *SOGOBI* (2001). The austerity of Benning's approach to landscape and history, with its insistence on allowing image and text (either through the insertion of the written word on screen or through spoken narration) to chafe against each other without overt directorial comment, is especially enigmatic and provocative in *Deseret*, a film concerned with the history of Utah, not least because of the distinctive, and often misunderstood (at least by non-Utahans) nature of the state's relation to the rest of the United States.

Deseret comprises a series of shots of Utah landscapes and a voice-over narration that draws on ninety-four edited extracts from reports on Utah from the *New York Times* from 1852 to 1992. The visual aspect of the film lingers over mountains, prairies, deserts, rivers and lakes; improvised dwellings, church and civic architecture; petroglyphs, industry, and highways. The verbal record covers relations with Native Americans, Brigham Young's management of the Mormon Church, conflict with the Federal Government, statehood, capital punishment, Japanese American internment, nuclear and biological weapons testing, downwinder politics, civil rights, and the culture wars. As this partial inventory suggests, the film delivers a compressed version of 150 years of Utah history (*Deseret* ends with a shot of a billboard celebrating the state centennial—"Utah—still the right place").

The film's simple structure, mimicking the form of an educational or instructional film, nevertheless generates a series of complex questions about the nature of documentary truth (through an investment in and exposure of the limits of the photographic and journalistic record); the tension between verbal and visual representations (the photography sometimes records the sites referred to in the narration, but not always); the relationship between landscape and history (the spaces depicted are generally empty of people while the newspaper accounts are inevitably preoccupied with human activity); and the effectiveness of editing in the production of narrative (the *Times* coverage of Utah is itself selective, focusing on what is considered relevant to the East Coast; the film edits the newspaper accounts; the landscape shots are carefully collated). Together, these preoccupations challenge the viewer to undertake considerable labor in making links between image and text, narrative and pictorial composition, place and history.[1]

Deseret identifies a strange, otherworldly West. It is the West as reported in, and constructed by, the Eastern metropolitan media. It is also the peculiar West of Utah, a state with its own idiosyncratic relationship to the rest of the United States and its own distinctive version of American exceptionalism. *Deseret* allows this strangeness to emerge through the recounting of the historical record while simultaneously presenting a visual account of Utah that gestures toward deeper temporalities (geology, ancient inscriptions, the long life of toxic waste) that are no less enigmatic and ungraspable. The sense of time in *Deseret* is elastic—the stillness of the shots makes the film seem long though the length of the shots is short (and they get progressively shorter); the historical frame is short (merely a century and a half) relative to the age of the place but long in terms of the human transformation of the social and natural environment. The film, then, is very much about the management, or, to use a word with particular resonance in the Mormon vocabulary, stewardship, of time and place—through theological reckoning, government intervention, scientific experiment, historical narrative, and, in the end, through the cinematic structuring of the documentary record.

THE *TIMES*

Benning's background in mathematics and interest in structural film governs the organization of many of his films, including *Deseret*. While he trawled all references to Utah from the *Times*, Benning selected ninety-four and pared each story down to between eight and ten sentences. Shifting language use over the course of 150 years, he has claimed, shrunk the length of the sentences over time, a fact that contributes to a certain accelerating momentum in the film since Benning uses one shot for each sentence in each story, plus one shot between each pair of stories that is presented without narration. These silent shots also get shorter. The result, explains Benning, is that the films speeds up, which, he suggests:

corresponds with the historical realities of journalism. In the early days, stories from Utah wouldn't reach New York for three or four months. If you pay attention to the dates of the stories (the date of each story is superimposed over the first shot in each story), you'll see that, early on, the writers will be talking about something that happened in January in a story dated May: it took that long for the story to get back East. Of course, later the gap becomes a day or two days, and right now it's less than a day. (MacDonald and Benning 2005: 6)

The physical environment, then—the expansiveness of the territory, its distance from the Atlantic coast—is measured implicitly through the length of the delay between event and report, while the acceleration of technological development that shrinks physical distances (railroad, telegraph, telephone, motor vehicles) also clips the length of sentences, as if language seeks to match the efficiency of the machines. In this way, the structure of *Deseret* is to a large extent an index of these effects, the form of the film emerging from a century of shortening journey times and their cultural consequences.

The historical period covered in the film is also carefully structured. The news stories, grouped by decade, indicate that the earliest and the most recent periods predominate—over half of the ninety-four come from the first two and last two decades: twenty-two from the 1850s, nine from the 1860s, eighteen from the 1980s, and eight from the 1990s. This stress on the beginning and end of the 150-year period invites comparisons between them. One final structural aspect of the film worthy of note is that when Utah becomes a state in 1896 the film shifts from black and white to color. This splitting of the film into monochrome and color sections serves to align the first half with nineteenth-century Western landscape photography, which the composition of shots often formally echoes (MacDonald 2001: 441, n. 33). The use of color in the second section underscores the deliberate invitation to read the post-statehood twentieth century alongside the monochrome nineteenth century as two distinct epochs.

The organization of the material in *Deseret*, then, determines the way history is managed and delivered but also produces a specific temporal velocity and steers the viewer toward a comparative reading: history is apprehended as speeding up (through a compressed use of language and shrinking shot length), as amenable to slicing and stacking (there is more of the 1850s, less of the 1870s), and color-coded. The gap between event and its representation is not just there in the film and its relation to history, but also in the press report and its delayed (though shrinking) relation to the event described. The film spatializes time just as the *Times* reports are spatially removed from the Western territory on which they report. The landscape shots depict a seemingly static scene, where contemporary Utah can be made to look like nineteenth-century Utah through the use of black and white and compositional conventions associated with that time, but the modes of representation—the selection procedures, the recitation of print sources, the editing process, the length of shot—all involve a counting off, on different scales and at different speeds, of time passing. This is a film about the times and the *Times*.

Forty-eight of the stories featured in *Deseret* allude to Mormons, and much of the focus throughout the chronology is on struggle, often violent—in the nineteenth century, between Mormons and Indians; Mormons and Indians against the Federal Government (especially during 1857, after President Buchanan, in June, declared Utah to be in rebellion against the US government and sent an expeditionary force to the territory to enforce the law under his newly appointed governor, Alfred Cumming); in the twentieth century, the struggle is increasingly between the people of Utah and the Federal Government's military-industrial presence in the state (nuclear testing, biological weapons development, and toxic-waste sites), and between a socially conservative Utah and, relatively speaking, at least, a more liberal temperament in the east. *Times* stories from the most recent decades not only reveal the persistence of the Church of Latter-day Saints' (LDS) establishment in managing Utah society but are also emblematic of the wider culture wars conducted during the late twentieth century by an ascendant political and social conservatism against the perceived permissiveness of mid-century liberalism. As the film moves toward the centennial year, then, reports from the *Times* note the exclusion of black men from the Mormon church (1978); the excommunication of Sonia Johnson for supporting the Equal Rights Amendment (1980); John Birch Society supporter Ezra Taft Benson's election as church president (1985); Aryan Nation plans to locate its headquarters in Wendover (1989); the Church's excommunication of the only Indian to achieve high standing in the state (1989); the refusal of Utah schools to remove books depicting Indians as "savages" (1988); Utah as the last state to enfranchise Native Americans (1990); and the introduction of tough anti-abortion laws (1991). Stories on polygamy, unsurprisingly, straddle the centuries (1854, 1862, 1890, 1944, 1977, 1979, 1988, 1991).

The cumulative effect of this testimony to a century of resistance to centralized authority positions Utah as, from the outset, out of step with the times (and the *New York Times*), stubbornly fighting a rearguard action against larger forces impatient and indifferent at best to its peculiar history and wayward interpretation of scriptural and national doctrine. The *New York Times* was founded on September 18, 1851, just a year after the establishment of the Utah territory on September 9, 1850. The *Times* positioned itself very much as the paper of record for the country, while Utah explicitly conceived of itself as somewhere outside the establishment. The *Times* and the territory therefore represent two distinct readings of Manifest Destiny, the belief that it was the destiny of the US to expand to encompass all of North America. While the *Times* was invested in progressive incorporation and control from the center, the Mormons in Utah were driven by a determination to remain outside and beyond such control. Neither of these narratives comes off particularly well in *Deseret*, though there is no direct commentary that might nudge the viewer toward a view other than the blank neutrality of the presented material. Nevertheless, the film does, as my discussion of its structure begins to suggest, instantiate—as a sum of the decisions that put it together—a fairly clear measure of Eastern establishment preoccupations and prejudices as well as Utahan stubbornness.

The Shadow State

What is clear from Benning's early selections from the *Times* is that they carry in terse form the entire history of the United States as it struggles to establish cohesion and control over its rapidly expanding territories during the second half of the nineteenth century. One brief extract near the beginning of the film, dated "November 15, 1856," is instructive in this regard. Over shots of open fields, rock formations, horses grazing, desert, forest, and lake, and concluding with a herd of cattle, the voice-over recounts an abbreviated version of a story originally headlined "Law and Order in Utah":

> Brigham Young again boasts of his prowess in holding fast to the Governorship of Utah. President Pierce and his immediate supporters talk loudly of their determination to put down traitors and all who defy the laws but in Utah the laws and authority of the United States, the legality and validity of which are not disputed throughout the Union, are openly defied. Brigham Young's term of service expired nearly four years ago. Pierce promised to remove him. So much for the promise. It turns out that the effort to execute the defied laws of the United States in Utah does not amount altogether to a tithe of that expended in securing the arrest and return of a single slave.

This is a story of boasts and defiance on both sides but little action. Young and Pierce trade words, yet the stand-off continues as Young refuses to recognize the authority of the Federal Government over the territory and his leadership. The *Times* is at pains to stress the exceptional nature of the Utah situation: everywhere else the law and authority of the United States is recognized. The implication is clear that Young is a traitor, though the word is allowed in through the proclamations of the President and his supporters rather than declared directly by the newspaper. The final line, however, expands the scope of the *Times*' assessment of the situation beyond Young's stubborn illegality and Pierce's inaction.

Figure 5 From Deseret, 1995 (I). Shot accompanying the sentence "So much for the promise," November 15, 1856. Courtesy of the artist and neugerriemschneider, Berlin

The single slave the *Times* probably has in mind is Anthony Burns, who escaped slavery in 1853 and fled to Boston, where he was captured the next year under the Fugitive Slave Act of 1850. Pierce, who had supported the passage of the Act and wanted to demonstrate his resolve, sent Federal troops and artillery to Boston to ensure the prosecution of the case after abolitionists attempted to free Burns by storming the courthouse. The court remanded Burns to his owner and he was escorted under heavy Federal guard, watched by a crowd of nearly fifty thousand people, to the harbor where he was shipped back into slavery on June 2, 1854. Policing the case, identified as a turning point that galvanized the abolitionist cause, is estimated to have cost the Federal Government in excess of $40,000.

The final line of the *Times* report of November 15, 1856 used by Benning, then, radically opens the frame, as Pierce's inaction in the face of Young's defiance in Utah is placed within the national political and moral context of the President's willingness to defend, and pay for, the protection of slavery. What is not obvious from the *Times* report, though, is that by November 15 Pierce was entering his last days as President. Eighteen fifty-six was an election year, and Pierce, a northern Democrat, had failed to secure his party's nomination for re-election at the Democratic National Convention in June. Pierce's support for the Kansas–Nebraska Act, which repealed the Missouri Compromise of 1850 and allowed for the possibility of slavery in Kansas under the doctrine of popular sovereignty, not to mention his financially and politically expensive intervention in the Burns case, left him abandoned by his party. By the time the

Times is reporting Pierce's failure to oust Young in Utah, the nation had already elected, eleven days earlier, his Democratic replacement, James Buchanan.

Although Benning edits out of the *Times* report some of the political context for the comments on Young, including references to Pierce's "Jacksonian" determination to put down traitors and the hundred "freemen" languishing in a Kansas jail, also in defiance of "bogus" laws (in other words, jailed for resisting the pro-slavery territorial legislature formed after an election deemed illegal by a Congressional committee), the final sentence on the President's ineffectiveness in Utah remains supercharged. It calls forth the entire history of Westward expansion and the role of slavery in the construction of territorial and state boundaries and governments. It also demonstrates, regardless how distant Utah was from Washington or New York, how the violent and unpredictable contest over the political and moral legitimacy of the United States bound together, like nothing else, centers of power and territorial outposts, including establishment newspapers and antinomian religious sects.

As *Deseret* delivers the *Times*' account of presidential indifference toward Young's resistance to Federal authority while funding military suppression of revolt in Boston, accompanied by images of the benign indifference and pastoral tranquility of the Utah landscape, the film at once reminds viewers of the ways in which politics writes over, and into, places constructed out of it and how the depiction of landscape as unpeopled can serve as a screen to conceal the often bloody struggle for control and ownership. The grazing horses and still waters are, to an extent, manifestations of an achieved destiny that confirms nineteenth-century Federal and Mormon senses of mission. There is no visual evidence of the contested meanings of territorial sovereignty here, of the recent history of persecution that made Young and his church alive to the threat of Federal violence that had driven the sect to Utah in the first place. Nor is there evidence of the ways in which Utah's fate was, from the outset, bound up with the struggle over the right to claim other human lives as the property of free men. Part of the power of *Deseret*, then, lies in the economy with which it alludes to the politics of nation building and the ways in which landscape is the screen upon which ideology is projected and behind which the brutal clamor for meaning is concealed. Once this is registered, no aspect of the film, however innocuous or flatly presented, remains untouched by the histories it contains.

This incendiary volatility compressed into the ostensibly ordinary is as true of the film's title as it is of the verbatim accounts from the newspaper. The name Deseret is not coterminous with Utah, so the choice of the former term as the title of the film suggests a mismatch between the Mormon conception of the state and the Federal US version. Deseret, a word deriving from the Book of Mormon that refers to the industrious honey bees that characterize Mormon collective industry, is a self-designation for the proposed state outlined by

LDS Church leaders in 1849; Utah is the name of the territory as created by the US Congress in 1850. Names and origin stories are important, since the two names of the territory register contesting claims not only on the land but also on the authority that comes to define the settlement built upon it. From the outset, the Mormons knew they had to operate within the context of the Federal Government and its expansionist policies. As early as December 1847, six weeks before the signing of the Treaty of Guadalupe Hidalgo that ended the war with Mexico and left the US in possession of California and most of Arizona, Nevada, Utah, and parts of Wyoming and Colorado, the Church leaders declared their intention to petition for a territorial government in the Great Basin "as soon as circumstances will permit." They made their first move a year later (Crawley 1989: 9).

The LDS Church petitioned Congress to create the "State of Deseret" in 1849, though the US government, preoccupied with the issue of slavery in its newly acquired territories, did not recognize the proposal. Deseret, under the Mormon proposal, encompassed most of present-day Utah and Nevada, large portions of California and Arizona, and parts of Colorado, New Mexico, Wyoming, Idaho, and Oregon. In September 1850, as part of the Compromise of 1850, the Utah Territory was created by Act of Congress. The new territory encompassed only a portion of the northern section of Deseret. On February 3, 1851, Brigham Young was inaugurated as the first governor of the Utah Territory. On April 4, the General Assembly of Deseret passed a resolution to dissolve the state, but in October the Utah territorial legislature voted to re-enact the laws and ordinances of the state of Deseret. In other words, while acknowledging the establishment of the Utah Territory, the Mormons did not relinquish the idea of a "State of Deseret."

While the possibility of creating a state based on Mormonism began to fade after the Utah War of 1857–8, when President Buchanan accomplished what Pierce did not, and the coming of the railroad opened the territory to many non-Mormon settlers, particularly in western areas, the persistence of the notion of Deseret as the true name and true authority of the territory—indeed, the "State"—reveals how deeply Young and the Church elite resisted Federal legitimacy even as their claims were overwritten by national nomenclature. It is this refusal that accounts for Young's unwillingness to step down as governor after his term ended and the *Times*' frustration with Pierce's inertia in 1856. Here, Young is claiming allegiance not only to a higher authority—it is God's will, and not government permission, that justifies his leadership—but also to the doctrine of popular sovereignty that was being used to justify the introduction of slavery into new territories. If the US government conceded that the people could decide whether or not to permit slavery on their land, it made sense for Young to claim the autonomy of his territory in choosing its own leaders (see Turner 2016). The contest over the name of the territory, then, speaks to the question of authority and from which source it is derived. Between 1862 and 1870, under Young's leadership, a group of Church elders ran a shadow government that met after each session of the territorial legislature to ratify the new laws under the name of the "State of Deseret." Attempts were made in 1856, 1862, and 1872 to write a new state constitution under that name based on the new boundaries of the Utah Territory.

The point is that "Deseret" stands as a counter-Utah that overlaps and operates simultaneously alongside the federally recognized state. Deseret is an alternative and a refusal of Federal authority, a double and a shadow that overrides state lines and articulates an alternative, subversive, and irreducible refusal at the core of Utahan identity. "Deseret" marks the difference between how a people might see itself and how it is seen from without. In a sense, Benning's doubling of the photographic representation of Utah with *Times* reportage is an iteration of this split ontology: Utah is what it says it is (Deseret) and what the nation says it is (Utah). There is overlap between the two but they are not synonymous; nor are the congruencies necessarily comfortable. This issue of incommensurate representations—how the camera records a place and how the Eastern establishment has reported on it—is contained within the title of the film, a name that speaks of incommensurability and insubordination inside, but also adjacent to, national narratives of inclusion.

Benning's title, then, recognizes the possibility of an otherness at the heart of Utah that might also, like the expansive borders of a shadow state that is indifferent to official boundaries, encompass more than merely Utah as it is commonly known and extend to include the United States itself. As a faux educational film that delivers a "straight" account of what there is to see and what the *New York Times* says, *Deseret* performs at every level to claim flat, neutral ground. Yet as the choice of title makes clear, there is in all likelihood a shadow to every straight report, another side that speaks aslant while presenting itself unadorned. This is, I think, the case with the narrative voice.

Deseret's deadpan narrative is delivered by Fred Gardner, chosen, according to Benning, for his ability to read the *Times* reports in a neutral tone: "I wanted the language to carry the drama, rather than the *voice*" (MacDonald and Benning 2005: 6). This particular voice, though, does carry purpose. Gardner is well known as an anti-Vietnam war activist and one-time editor of *Ramparts* magazine. It was Gardner who opened the first GI coffeehouse, the UFO, in Columbia, South Carolina in 1967. More recently, he has been a vocal campaigner for the medical use of marijuana and a regular contributor to the *Anderson Valley Advertiser* (AVA), Booneville, California's weekly newspaper. The AVA is more than an average local newspaper; self-described as "America's last newspaper," since its purchase by Bruce Anderson in 1984, the *Advertiser* has focused on environmental and political issues and has a modest national circulation. The paper's masthead borrows from the Industrial Workers of the World ("Fanning the Flames of Discontent') and Che Guevera ("¡Hasta la Victoria Siempre!"—Until victory, always).[2] The voice of the *Times* in the film, then, despite its flat delivery, represents also a particular notion of the press as an activist agent and, via the AVA, of the local newspaper as a means for a grounded challenge to orthodoxy.

While the *New York Times* stands in *Deseret* as the voice of the Eastern establishment, it is a voice inflected in the film with a more engaged conception of journalism as a counterweight to establishment values. As with the latent content of the *Times* reports and the title *Deseret* itself, the narrative voice of the film signifies more than first appears, even—indeed, perhaps especially—when the unspoken, unseen, or unacknowledged clout of that latency remains unclaimed. For while repeated viewing of the film makes it possible to detect the contraction of sentences and shots over time and enables the cross-referencing of word and image to reveal itself, there is no explanation or evidence in the film of the selection process that shaped the text, no account of the title, and no acknowledgment of who Fred Gardner is and why his voice in particular might matter. Certainly, it is possible to view *Deseret* without this information and to develop the same reading—that it is a film about land and sovereignty that stands in an ambivalent relation to the libertarian and radically conservative history of Utah. The decisions made concerning textual edits, the title, and the narrative voice confirm this reading but also underscore how the film is committed to undercutting its own performance of straightforwardness all the way down. There is nothing in *Deseret* without a shadow, however directly it is exposed to light.

SHADOW AS SUBSTANCE

The shift to color once Utah becomes a state operates as a simple visual code to position the territorial era as a kind of prehistory: with statehood comes the full chromatic range of American modernity. This is a kind of *Wizard of Oz* effect, where the monochrome operates as a mode of historical distancing and also of authenticity, while color amplifies the spectacular and also the artificial. The Brigham Young era and the violence of national consolidation are partitioned off by the move to color as definitively past, while the contemporaneity of the color shots secures Utah as an integral part of a recognizable American present. There is more to this realignment than simple updating, though, because as the narrative moves into the twentieth century, Utah emerges as less anomalous within the national polity and instead comes to represent some of the more troubling contradictions of the corporate military-industrial state. The reports from the *Times* increasingly focus on the use of Utah territory for the manufacture, testing, and storage of weapons, environmental despoliation, and conservative social policy. After mid-century, Utah is no longer the outlier in Federal affairs and has instead become representative of the national climate. The shadow has become substance.

A *Times* story of April 26, 1914, describing the Federal withdrawal of 18,700 acres of public land for the Utah National Guard as a "target range and maneuver grounds," prefigures the more radical extent to which the Utah was to become a component of the national security state post-World War II. Like so much of the desert West, Tooele County in northwestern Utah was valuable as a site for activities unwelcome elsewhere. Sparsely inhabited and far from areas of high population density, economically underdeveloped, politically conservative and owned mainly by the Federal Government already, the US military during World War II built the Tooele Army Depot, the Deseret Chemical Depot, and Dugway Proving Grounds (DPG) in Tooele County (Shumway and Jackson 2008: 442–3). Typical of military investment in the West during the postwar period, new bases and facilities in Tooele County provided a welcome boost to the local economy as well as confirming Utah's vital patriotic role in national defense. During World War II, DPG was the key US test site for chemical and biological weapons; though the base was phased out after the war it was reactivated during the Korean War and confirmed in 1954 as a permanent installation. A range of radiation experiments were conducted at DPG during the 1950s and, as Mike Davis notes, between 1951 and 1969 the Army conducted "1,653 field trials of nerve gas which disseminated an estimated half million pounds (or 3.5 trillion lethal doses) of the agent over Tooele County" (Davis 1998: 37). If the beleaguered history of the LDS Church in Utah represents one form of secrecy enabled by the distance of the state from the seat of Federal authority, the militarized West of the Cold War introduced a new mode of federally sanctioned secrecy to the region. While the atomic explosions at the Nevada Test Site delivered a spectacle of US power during the 1950s, promoted by the Las Vegas Chamber of Commerce with calendars containing detonation times and suggested spots for viewing, the chemical and biological work conducted in Tooele County was, and remains, top secret.

It was secret, at least, until 1968, when the death of over six thousand sheep in Skull Valley made the national press. *Deseret* offers an abbreviated account of the incident from the *Times* report of March 24:

> The head of a special investigating team said today that we are as positive as medical science can ever be that nerve gas tests conducted by the Army's top secret Dugway Proving Grounds had killed the 6,400 sheep in Utah's Skull Valley. Senator Frank Moss was told that 320 gallons of a persistent nerve gas agent was sprayed from an airplane. A compound isolated in snow, water,

sheep blood, sheep liver tissue, and in the grass taken from sheep's stomachs is identical to that agent applied by the Army. Replying to the charge, an Army spokesman said that a separate military investigation was continuing and that no definite cause of death had been established. Meanwhile, Dr Kelly Gubler of the Tooele Valley Hospital has written in the *Medical World News* that the testing at Dugway could result in a massive human disaster.

This report is preceded by a shot of vapor rising off the land, followed by a view of the Dugway installation in the distance, a cluster of anonymous low-rise buildings flat below the mountainous horizon. Two shots of snow-covered landscape accompany the third and fourth sentences. A final shot of steam rising from cooling towers nested among rocks concludes the March 24 report. Visually, the nerve gas incident is full of airborne elements either dispersing into the atmosphere or, like the snow, redacting the ground, rocks and trees. Dugway can be plainly seen but the effect of its presence in the landscape is to introduce a disturbing unknowability to the surroundings. What is carried in the vapors that emanate from the land and is expelled from the buildings? Is the snow laced with invisible toxic agents camouflaged as nature? An entry from January 12, 1968 has reported that the CIA "recruits heavily in Utah." On August 21, 1963, President Kennedy, discussing the ban on aboveground atomic tests, avoids addressing a scientific report that has discovered high levels

Figure 6 From Deseret, 1995 (II). Shot accompanying the sentence "The head of a special investigating team said today that we are as positive as medical science can ever be that nerve gas tests conducted by the Army's top secret Dugway Proving Grounds had killed the 6,400 sheep in Utah's Skull Valley," March 24, 1968. Courtesy of the artist and neugerriemschneider, Berlin

of radioactive iodine-131 in Utah children under two years old. By the time *Deseret* gets to the nerve gas incident in 1968, Utah has already been reconfigured as a space of Federal concealment. It is little wonder that even snow is now suspect since the entire landscape has been conscripted as an agent of national security.

The Skull Valley nerve gas incident was a key moment, coinciding as it did with the rise of the environmental movement and the anti-Vietnam War protests, in the exposure of secret military activity in the US, and it led to significant restrictions in the testing of biological and chemical weapons. Like Benning's use of the November 15, 1856 report, the compressed narration of the 1968 story presented in *Deseret* reverberates beyond its local context (as regional news; as a brief segment of the film) to inform and configure the position of Utah in relation to the US, its history and politics, and the shot sequence and five sentences to the rest of the film. Subsequent *Times* reports through the 1980s and early 1990s mark the complex political and environmental challenges faced by Utah as it deals with the ongoing impact of nuclear and other military-industrial activity in the state, from soil contamination and downwinder claims to issues relating to the storage and disposal of chemical agents.

The military Keynesianism of World War II and the Cold War and the social conservatism that emerged at the end of the 1960s, reaching the highest level of government validation with the election of Ronald Reagan in 1980, complemented each other nowhere better than in the American West. Utah's history of suspicion of the Federal Government paradoxically found itself, as the national mood veered to the right, increasingly consonant with mainstream discourse. Yet what is perhaps most striking about the normalization and nationalization of Brigham Young's shadow state, as it has been upgraded into neoliberal, neoconservative consensus, is that the Mormon values of cooperation and collective effort now stand in stark critical relation to the dominant culture of the United States.[3] The Church's communitarian ethos and commitment to stewardship of the environment could not be more at odds with the duplicitous self-interest that characterizes a corporate sector that demands small government and low taxes while building its wealth from Federal contracts. The real shadow state is now, it seems, the corporate elite, which has been able to package reactionary social policy and a deregulated economy as triumphs for individual liberty.

In this regard, the kind of countercultural perspective represented by, say, Fred Gardner's journalism or, indeed, Benning's films, moves closer to Deseret as a refusnik counter-Utah—not the paranoid Deseret of Young's patriarchal theocracy but another version where the ethics of Mormonism's socialistic strain pushes back against the now nationally acceptable version of neocon, neoliberal Utah.[4] As Jan Shipps claims, despite the perception that Utah has always been conservative, throughout the nineteenth century Mormonism "was virtually revolutionary" (Shipps 2016: 74). It is this revolutionary strain in American history that Benning has so often mobilized in order to challenge the normalized reading of American landscape as the iconography of triumphant nationalism and it is often positioned as the latent possibility of alternative readings and dissident forms. In *UTOPIA* (1998), for example, the entire soundtrack of Richard Dindo's 1994 documentary, *Ernesto Che Guevara, The Bolivian Diary*, accompanies images of the southwestern US desert. After building a replica of Thoreau's famous cabin, Benning decided to construct a second, this time a version of the cabin Ted Kaczynski, the Unabomber, lived in (see Ault 2011). As with the doubling of Deseret and Utah—the imagined territory and the official one—the purpose of these jarring combinations is, as Jeffrey Skoller writes in relation to *UTOPIA*, to conjure "potential histories." The focus, claims Skoller, is placed "less on what is possible to actualize than on the complex interplay between events that actually did happen and what can be imagined or desired in relation to them" (Skoller 2005: 101). In *Deseret*, Benning draws out of the Mormon legacy, so effectively undermined by decades of establishment disdain, another, unrealized Utah of collectivist struggle and defiant independence. *Deseret*, then, refuses to allow the conventional narrative of a shared national interest, as captured in the aloof perspective of the *New York Times*, to pass unchallenged. The revolutionary impulse Benning finds in Utah is far from unimpeachable, but it is there, especially during the resistance to Federal Government in the nineteenth century, when the ideological foreclosures of nationalist territorial expansion were as yet incomplete. In the attempt to found an alternative social order and in the refusal to yield to centralized power, Deseret, if not Utah, offered another definition of how it might be possible to live in America, an imagined or desired territory that persists as the shadow of the actually existing United States.

That shadow darkened during the twentieth century, and especially in the years following World War II. The strident anticommunism of Ezra Taft Benson, President Eisenhower's Secretary for Agriculture and later President of the LDS Church, contributed during the 1950s to a conscious disowning of Mormon communitarianism, bolting together Mormon and American exceptionalism in order to claim that America was, as Taft claimed, "the Lord's base of operations" (quoted in Barlow 2016: 108). Yet it is only since 1984 that the state has been steadfastly Republican in state and presidential elections (Shipps 2016: 74).[5] The intuition that there are other histories beyond the official narrative of national consensus, histories that are never entirely buried, is why *Deseret*, I think, never straightens out the strangeness of Utah, never judges its legacy or its peculiarities. In fact, it is precisely Utah's strangeness—its resilience, awkwardness, and its socialistic, utopian willingness to imagine the world otherwise—that makes it essential for Benning, both as a counter-legacy at odds with the familiar narrative of the Western United States as a default conservative heartland, and as a shadow state bent on building another America.

Notes

1. The form of *Deseret* is discussed by Anderson (2011: 117–19) and MacDonald (2001: 338–44).
2. On the *Anderson Valley Advertiser*, see Nazaryan (2015)
3. On the relation between neoliberalism and neoconservatism, see Brown (2006).
4. As a text that imagines the possibility of a dissident West at odds with the dominant national discourse, *Deseret* bears comparison with the kind of environmental non-fiction produced out of Utah by, for example, Terry Tempest Williams (1991) and Ellen Meloy (1999). For further discussion of Williams, Meloy and others in relation to post-World War II military-industrial environmental despoliation, see Beck (2009).
5. At the end of the 1960s, for example, only between 18 and 21 percent of Utahn Mormons described themselves as "conservative Republicans," and loyalty to the Republican Party was no stronger in Utah than elsewhere in the West. The 1976 presidential election marks a turning point, with Utah holding fast to the Republicans while the rest of the country, post-Watergate, swung to the Democrats. During the Reagan era, the Republican hold on Utah hardened; in 1984 three-quarters of Utah voted for Reagan (Campbell et al. 2016: 138–9).

Works Cited

Anderson, Steve F. (2011), *Technologies of History: Visual Media and the Eccentricity of the Past*, Hanover, NH: Dartmouth College Press.

Ault, Julie (2011), *(FC) Two Cabins by JB*, New York: A.R.T. Press.

Barlow, Philip L. (2016), "Chosen Land, Chosen People: Religious and American Exceptionalism among the Mormons," in Randall Balmer and Jana Riess (eds.), *Mormonism and American Politics*, New York: Columbia University Press, pp. 102–14.

Beck, John (2009), *Dirty Wars: Landscape, Power, and Waste in Western American Literature*, Lincoln: University of Nebraska Press.

Brown, Wendy (2006), "American Nightmare: Neoliberalism, Neoconservatism, and De-Democratization," *Political Theory* 34(6): 690–714.

Campbell, David E., Christopher F. Karpowitz, and J. Quin Monson (2016), "A Politically Peculiar People: How Mormons Moved into and Then out of the Political Mainstream," in Randall Balmer and Jana Riess (eds.), *Mormonism and American Politics*, New York: Columbia University Press, pp. 133–54.

Crawley, Peter (1989), "The Constitution of the State of Deseret," *Brigham Young University Studies* 29(4): 7–22.

Davis, Mike (1998), "Utah's Toxic Heaven," *Capitalism Nature Socialism* 9(2): 35–9.

MacDonald, Scott (2001), *The Garden in the Machine: A Field Guide to Independent Films about Place*, Berkeley: University of California Press.

MacDonald, Scott and James Benning (2005), "Exploring the New West: An Interview with James Benning," *Film Quarterly* 58(3): 2–15.

Meloy, Ellen (1999), *The Last Cheater's Waltz: Beauty and Violence in the Desert Southwest*, Tucson: University of Arizona Press.

Nazaryan, Alexander (2015), "The Last (or at Least Looniest) Newspaper in America," *Newsweek* April 12. Available at www.newsweek.com/2015/04/24/last-or-least-looniest-newspaper-america-321646.html. Accessed June 1, 2016.

Shipps, Jan (2016), "Ezra Taft Benson and the Conservative Turn of 'Those Amazing Mormons'," in Randall Balmer and Jana Riess (eds.), *Mormonism and American Politics*. New York: Columbia University Press, pp. 73–84.

Shumway, J. Matthew and Richard H. Jackson (2008), "Place Making, Hazardous Waste, and the Development of Tooele County, Utah," *Geographical Review* 98(4): 433–55.

Skoller, Jeffrey (2005), *Shadows, Specters, Shards: Making History in Avant-Garde Film*, Minneapolis: University of Minnesota Press.

Turner John G. (2016), "Unpopular Sovereignty: Brigham Young and the U.S. Government, 1847–1877," in Randall Balmer and Jana Riess (eds.), *Mormonism and American Politics*. New York: Columbia University Press, pp. 14–31.

Williams, Terry Tempest (1991), *Refuge: An Unnatural History of Family and Place*, New York: Vintage.

NIKOLAJ LÜBECKER

Violence and Landscape in the Films of James Benning

> The more intimate you become with nature, the more you appreciate its beauty. When you live in the woods, rather than just visiting, the beauty becomes part of your life.
>
> The Unabomber[1]

James Benning is often described as a filmmaker who focuses on the relation between human beings and their surroundings. He uses very long takes that allow us to rethink our relation to an environment to which we generally forget to attend. From this description there is only a small step to the idea of a minimalist and contemplative filmmaker; there is only a small step to the notion of slow cinema, and to debates about the ethics and politics of an alternative to conventional narrative cinema. This description is not wrong, but Benning's work is more diverse than it suggests.

Many of Benning's films provoke and challenge the spectator via the subject matter with which they deal. They work with logics of unease and suspense—even when they remain slow, minimalist and discreet. The aim of this chapter is therefore not to challenge debates about the ethical potential of eco- and slow cinema, but rather to show that eco- and slow cinema can also be violent, thematically dense, and politically poignant.[2]

Violence is an important theme in James Benning's diverse filmography. For example, several films raise the questions of how and why violence erupts in a particular individual, and how this violence is related to the environment. With this comes a national dimension: the violence under interrogation, being considered in its specific environment, is American. A relatively early example of such a film is *American Dreams (lost and found)* from 1984. It revolves around Arthur Bremer's failed plans for the assassination of Richard Nixon and the Democratic presidential candidate George Wallace in 1972. Through pop songs, baseball memorabilia, and excerpts from the increasingly unstable Bremer's diary, the film puts together a partial chronicle of recent American history and the important role that violence—not least racial violence—plays in this history. Two years later, *Landscape Suicide* offered another history of violence—two, in fact. The film juxtaposed the murder of teenage cheerleader Kirstin Costas in 1980s California with the infamous Ed Gein case from 1950s Wisconsin. Again, the constellation opens onto reflections concerning American history, violence, and the environment. Many other examples could be mentioned: *Used Innocence* focuses on a murder case, as does *North on Evers*, and the topic of violence and pathological individuals has again been key to some of Benning's most important projects in recent years. For instance, the so-called "cabin projects" about Henry David Thoreau and the anti-technology terrorist Ted Kaczynski (aka "the Unabomber") again raise questions about violence, the environment, and American identity. Even more recently, the video installation *Levee Road* (2015) shows a desert road without ever making explicit that this road runs close to the Corcoran State Prison where Charles Manson is incarcerated. It is therefore true, as Scott MacDonald suggests, that "Violence, past and present, remains, as does race, a psychic frontier for Benning" (MacDonald 2001: 404).

This chapter will seek to understand how and why Benning runs up against this frontier. Drawing on texts by Isabelle Stengers and Félix Guattari (and to a lesser extent Raymond Williams and Gilbert Simondon), it will consider, in particular, the relationship between violence and landscape. In order to do so, it will focus on *Landscape Suicide*, with occasional references to some of the other films just mentioned.

Landscape Suicide: Sociology and Landscapes

As noted, *Landscape Suicide* investigates two murder cases. The first revolves around fifteen-year old Bernadette Protti, who in 1984 stabbed her schoolmate Kirsten Costas to death in a wealthy San Francisco suburb (Orinda). Costas, the popular cheerleader, had bullied the intelligent but insecure Protti once too often. Most of this first section consists of a faux-documentary reconstruction of the testimony that Protti gave to the police when she admitted to the murder a full six months after the events. We see non-professional actor Rhonda Bell, in a fixed shot, sitting in front of a white brick wall. Her account of the events is helped on by questions from an investigator who remains off-screen, a disembodied male voice of authority. Benning highlights the distance between the two interlocutors by recording the investigator's voice in a different room from the one in which Protti speaks; frequently the screen goes black, thereby frustrating our desire to get close to Protti. The effect of these two stylistic choices is to turn Protti's testimony into a monolog rather

Violence and Landscape   57

than a dialog. In this monolog, she struggles to remember the events. What comes across from the interview footage is therefore a powerful experience of detachment and distance: distance between the interrogator and the interrogatee, between the interrogatee and the spectator, between the interrogatee and her story.[3]

A number of elements supplement the interview section. First, we spend three and a half minutes with a woman practicing her tennis serve in the Californian sunlight. Then we watch from the passenger seat of a car driving through Orinda. It is now raining, the streets are empty and the houses seem deserted. On the radio, an agitated preacher speaks about sin. Other scenes present evidence and information linked to the case: photographs, a psychiatric report on Protti, and a truly heart-wrenching letter she wrote to her parents, asking for forgiveness. Toward the end we find another re-enactment scene, this time with the cheerleader. She is lying on her bed, gossiping on the phone. The turntable plays her favorite song, "Memory," from the musical *Cats*. We listen to the song (the sound is non-diegetic), not to Costas' voice. Again, Benning creates distance: from Costas, whom we cannot hear; and between sound and image.

The first section concludes with an eleven-minute long montage of static shots of the suburban environment: houses, fields, pylons, the high school, a used car dealer, the local cinema, and so on. Then a black and white school photo of the murder victim, while a female voice-over (that we hear intermittently throughout the film) lists a number of facts related to the case. For instance, she tells us that in 1984 there were twenty-three juvenile murders in the Bay Area and more than 1,300 across the US; that the mean income in Orinda was $97,842 and that "Memory" was played at Costas' funeral. We also learn the date of Protti's conviction ("March 13, 1985") and the sentence she was given ("second degree murder"). While receiving this information we watch a black and white photograph of a suburban house (presumably Costas'), and, after the end of the voice-over monolog, a black and white school photo of Costas with the dates 1968–84.

It is worth returning to the opening scene with the tennis player. She has no precise role in the narration, we never get to know her identity, but she is part of the environmental set-up. The woman performs the same movement forty times over; the camera doesn't leave her. Benning interjects black frames after every other serve, thereby emphasizing the repetitious nature of the movements, and again preventing us from getting close to the woman. For some time we wonder if we are watching a looped sequence of just two tennis serves; this makes us scrutinize the images. Eventually we realize that the tennis balls are disappearing from the basket by her side. Finally, the camera switches to the other half of the court, covered in balls.

Figure 7 *From* Landscape Suicide, *1986 (I). Courtesy of the artist and neugerriemschneider, Berlin*

This scene brings to mind a scene from Michael Haneke's slightly later film *71 Fragments of a Chronology of Chance* (1994). Haneke's film is also composed of largely static shots and long takes separated by black frames; it is another film investigating a depressing real-life story about the sudden eruption of violence in a distressed individual. Haneke is focusing on a student who in 1993 killed three people in a bank in central Vienna, before turning the gun on himself. In *71 Fragments of a Chronology of Chance* an extended scene shows the soon-to-be killer practicing against a table tennis robot. It sends the ball over the net; he returns it with a forehand, repeating the same movement over and over again. We watch for almost three minutes as the robot turns the young man into a mechanical (but sweaty) body.[4] Haneke is more explicit in his sociological analysis than Benning: he makes the killer play. This suggests a direct link between the various forms of dehumanization that we undergo in Western societies and what the mass media sometimes call "random acts of violence."

At the risk of slightly reducing the complexity of Haneke's film, *71 Fragments of a Chronology of Chance* can be described as a sociological film. Haneke is interested in how certain social structures in modern, capitalist societies produce certain psychological structures. A comparison between Benning and Haneke therefore also helps to bring out the sociological dimension of *Landscape Suicide*. The opening scene in *Landscape Suicide* prompts us to think about the isolation of modern man in the wealthy Californian suburbs, and the disciplining of modern bodies (including the forms of discipline that we engage in quite happily); it stimulates a reflection on how these solitary exercises might link to sudden explosions of violence. There is no doubt that Benning's film offers a socio-political critique. When Benning cuts straight from the fixed shots of the solitary tennis player in the sun, to the tracking shot from a car driving through rainy Orinda while an ecstatic preacher talks about sinning, it is suggested that various forms of religion (working through mass media such as the radio) are happy to exploit the affective deficit of the citizens in the small and wealthy community.

But differences between the two films are also important, and the main difference has to do with the role they give to land- and cityscapes. Haneke shows the motorways surrounding Vienna and the tunnel system linking its various underground stations, but this environment quickly dissolves into sociology: it is yet another expression of Western capitalism. In Benning's film, on the other hand, the suburban landscapes resist such a reading; they refuse to be treated as background. Toward the end of the first part, they get eleven minutes of uninterrupted screen time. We probe them, we look for clues, and we try to integrate them into a narrative about teenage alienation and violence. And we can get quite far with this. For instance, we quickly notice that most of these land- and cityscapes are deserted, and when a human figure does appear, it is generally alone. We also notice that sounds tend to be uncoupled from their source: we hear a siren, but cannot see the ambulance; we hear organ music, but the church seems deserted, its car park is empty; we hear Michael Jackson's *P.Y.T. (Pretty Young Things)* but cannot see anyone in or around the house in which the song is presumably playing. This brings out the ghostly aspect of the suburban environment, and thereby links well to the more sociological themes of alienation and dehumanization. Nevertheless, the environmental shots cannot simply be reduced to sociology: there are too many of them, and they get so much time and space that they interrupt the sociological analysis.[5]

With this insistence on the environment, Benning complicates the idea of social structures producing mental structures, of a socio-economical base producing a mental pathology. Instead, the many suburban landscapes force us to rethink relations between humans and environments in a less anthropocentric manner than we did in Haneke's film. One way to do this is to take a step in the direction of Raymond Williams' famous notion of "structures of feeling" (or, as we shall later see, in the direction of Félix Guattari's idea of three interconnected ecologies—a socio-political, a mental and an environmental). In "Structures of Feeling," Williams critiques what he sees as a particularly schematic form of contemporary Marxism that presents ideology as a stable structure resulting directly from material conditions. Williams argues that in this kind of ideology critique, "what is actually being lived" (Williams 1977: 131) is lost, and that consequently these Marxists are stuck with a fossilized view of the social. Instead Williams introduces the "cultural hypothesis" of "a structure of feeling": "Meanings and values as they are actively lived and felt," and he associates these with "elements of impulse, restraint, and tone; specifically affective elements of consciousness and relationships" (132).

According to Williams, art and literature play a very prominent role in relation to these structures of feeling. Art is a seismograph, capable of registering and expressing mutations in the tectonics of the structures of feeling—and it can do so without reifying these mutations. Art is therefore described as a "living form," a structured formation. Far from simply being determined by economic relations, it can articulate the present as it is lived and felt. For Williams this also means that art and expression cannot be understood at the level of representation alone. In his analysis of the relationship between history, politics, landscape, and literary form in "The Welsh Industrial Novel," he emphasizes the non-representational aspect of this genre: "in mode it [the Welsh industrial novel] is less representation—the common currency of fiction—than rehearsal and performance: a composition primarily governed by the rhythms of speech and song" (Williams 2005: 228).

As we shall soon see, the distance from traditional ideology critique becomes more apparent in the second half of *Landscape Suicide*. However, in the first part already, Benning's emphasis on (suburban) landscapes testifies to his willingness to move beyond sociology and representation; to his desire to explore relations between humans and their environments in such a way that the landscapes could be said to inflect the humans. This is suggested in a significant scene where Benning—through a female voice-over—reflects on the experience of filming the story of Bernadette Protti and Kirsten Costas:

> It's a funny thing about trying to tell the truth. When I began this story I felt the pain of Bernadette so heavily that I overlooked the victim. When I visited Orinda things became more real. The first night I was there, I hallucinated a dark figure in my motel room.

As we listen to the voice-over narration, Benning films a map of the area around Oakland, Berkeley, Orinda, and Walnut Creek. When the "dark figure" sentence ends, the screen goes black; next, we enter the extensive montage of suburban landscapes. The voice-over does not make clear who or what the dark figure was (Costas?), but the swift transitions from this rumination on truth and the real, to hallucination and darkness, and then to the long "slideshow" of suburban landscapes indicate that Benning is interested in the bodying forth of what Williams called "specifically affective elements of consciousness and relationships." And just like Williams, he discreetly relates these affective elements (and their ghostly manifestations) to landscapes and environments.

This distance from conventional forms of sociology grows as the film turns to the famous Ed Gein case that inspired *Psycho*, *The Texas Chainsaw Massacre* and the Hannibal Lecter films. Not surprisingly, Benning's take on this story is less sensationalist than the one found in the more widely known films; more precisely: in Benning's film, the provocation lies in refusing the sensationalist approach. The elements from the first part now all reappear: we have documentary material about the case, a long montage of the wintry landscapes of rural Wisconsin, a car ride with a preacher soundtrack, a deliberately stilted music sequence featuring Gein's last victim, Bernice Worden dancing to *The Tennessee Waltz*. And as the centerpiece: a re-enactment of Gein's testimony.

This symmetry helps to bring out resemblances and differences. First of all, both cases feature killers who cannot remember their crimes—Benning is fascinated by our ability to repress, and by how these repressions allow the murderers to continue their lives in the communities where they committed their crimes. Differences are obvious too: one case is from 1984, the other from 1957, one from suburban California, the other from rural Wisconsin, one is set in an affluent community, the other in a poor community, one involves teenage girls, the other a man and two women, all in their fifties.[6] The main difference, however, is one of tone: the Gein section is more elusive than the Protti case.

The Protti section was halfway between sociology and something else. It differed from *71 Fragments of a Chronology of Chance* by discreetly suggesting how being on site prompted hallucinations that allowed a proximity to the real—and also by giving space to landscapes, which do not dissolve into sociology as they do in Haneke's film. Nevertheless, the opening half of *Landscape Suicide* maintained a strong sociological dimension, evident for instance in the concluding statistics about juvenile murders and mean income. In the Gein section the landscapes are less obviously the expression of socio-political structures. They are rural, barren, and their colors at times are so faded that they look like black and white photographs frozen in time. In the Gein section there are no statistics; instead, we have rumors and the overriding impression that the events escape us.

The film explicitly thematizes the difference between its two parts by returning to the formulation cited above. When Benning attempted to understand the events in Orinda, his female alter ego reflected: "[w]hen I visited Orinda things became more real." Such a successful, environmental tuning-in is not possible in the Gein section. Instead the voice-over now comments: "[w]hen I visited Plainfield, I couldn't get a sense of the murder. But the feeling of a collective guilt still lingers." This time the affective elements—still lingering—do not even take ghostly forms. Perhaps Gein's case is too extraordinary for any form of tuning-in, perhaps the murder lies too far back in time, perhaps Benning's autobiographical link to the events (the fact that he grew up with this story) gets in the way of things "becoming real" (as they did in Orinda)? In any case, it is now even more difficult to map the relations between landscapes, characters, and violence.

We cannot say that the landscapes are insignificant for the Gein story, nor can we say that they are responsible. We have to suspend our desire for causal logics, and search for more fine-grained forms of interaction between individuals, environments, and events. The film's title pushes us toward such alternative ideas about how things happen, and how they relate to one another. "Landscape suicide" was an expression Gein used during the police interrogation. This expression isn't heard in the film and exactly what Gein meant was never clear in the first place. Nevertheless, the title seems to place landscape in a position of agency, and thereby it serves to flatten ontologies. If suicide is "the only serious philosophical question" (Albert Camus), this problem is no longer unique to human beings. Instead the title points to the notion of entropy as it has been theorized by one of Benning's major sources of inspiration, Robert Smithson. Smithson describes entropy as "the hidden aspect of nature. [When the] phenomenon of nature destroys itself through itself" (Smithson 1996: 227). According to Smithson, entropy takes us to the point where "mind and matter get endlessly confounded" (107) [and] we have "a spiraling in on origins" (227). Is it possible that the more and less urban landscapes in Plainfield, Wisconsin, and Orinda, California worked to pull their inhabitants into such entropic processes that they allowed processes of decay to cause minds to collapse? Again: we cannot say the landscapes are insignificant, nor can we say that they are responsible.

In this manner the film's title, and its constellation of violence and landscapes, raise questions about human agency and the various other ways in which things may happen. *Landscape Suicide* challenges our tendency to focus on individual human agency, it challenges ideas about causality, and it invites us to consider the effects that environments (natural and cultural) may have upon the mind. Rather than the fully articulated, sociological discourse (that I believe) we get in *71 Fragments of a Chronology of Chance*, Benning's film drifts toward landscapes, and an undoing of exclusively anthropocentric understandings of how things come to be. With this challenge to better known mechanisms for explaining violence, Benning leaves the spectator hesitant, turning the spectatorial experience into a *practice*. To explain what *practice* means, and why the notion is important, let us briefly turn to the more recent cabin projects.

THE PRACTICE OF BENNING, AND THAT OF HIS SPECTATOR

Since 2011, Benning has made a number of films and installations about two of the most famous cabins in American cultural history: Henry David Thoreau's mid-nineteenth-century cabin at Walden Pond, and the late twentieth-century cabin belonging to the anti-technology terrorist Ted Kaczynski's ("the

Unabomber") at Stemple Pass, Montana. Both Thoreau (two years) and the Unabomber (twenty-five years) spent long periods of time in their cabins; from here they wrote about—and in the case of the Unabomber, sent bombs to—American society.[7] It was crucial for both that they built their own cabins, because this was a first step in the process of re-mediating their relation to the world.

Benning has a house in the forests of the Sierra Nevada. In 2007 he first reconstructed the cabin of Thoreau as faithfully as possible from the descriptions given in *Walden*. He then saw the potential for artistic projects with and around the cabin, and thinking he needed a contrapuntal structure like the one he had used for *Landscape Suicide*, he built the cabin of the Unabomber. He produced paintings for the cabins (copies of works by "outsider" artists), and also reassembled the libraries found in the original cabins (for more detail see Ault 2011, and MacDonald and Panse in the present volume). It was crucial for Benning that he built these cabins himself, because this was a first step in the process of re-mediating his relation to Thoreau, Kaczynski, and the environment. More generally, this is what Benning does: constructs, experiments and through those processes, re-mediates. Literally, in the case of the cabins and their contents; almost as literally when he, often singlehandedly, makes his films.

In his book on *The Senses of Walden*, Stanley Cavell analyses why it is important for Thoreau to reduce the distance between activities such as building a cabin and hoeing a field of beans on the one hand, and writing and reading on the other. In both cases it is a question of making oneself present to the circumstances. Cavell speaks about each "'field' of action or labor [being] isomorphic with every other," and he continues:

> This is why building a house and hoeing and writing and reading (and we could add, walking and preparing food and receiving visitors and giving charity and hammering a nail and surveying the ice) are allegories and measures of one another... This is the writer's assurance that his writing is not a substitute for his life, but his way of prosecuting it. (Cavell 1981: 62)

This closing of any gap between living and making art is clearly communicated in Benning's films, many of which have a very strong hands-on dimension.[8] For *American Dreams (lost and found)*, Benning carefully copied—in his own handwriting—the long passages from the diaries of Arthur Bremer that lay out the reasons and plans for the assassinations of George Wallace and Richard Nixon. These texts roll across the bottom of the screen (transforming the film into a three-channel work in which the spectator desperately tries to keep up with text, sound- and image tracks).[9] In the cabin installations and films, Benning reads excerpts from texts by Thoreau and the Unabomber. Occasionally, he stumbles over the words, but rather than edit out the pauses and mishaps, he is content to make the reading process evident. He also famously takes his students on looking and listening exercises in the area surrounding the California Institute of Arts, where he teaches (or rather, he used to take students for walks until health and safety regulations got in the way). The aim was to "practice paying attention" (Benning 2007: n.p.), and the implications of this practice were clearly conceived as wide-ranging: "[w]e find looking and listening to be a political act, our differences in perception reflecting our individual prejudices" (ibid.). Obviously, there are substantial differences between these various activities, but they are all examples of the many concrete, practical exercises that seep through and inform Benning's filmmaking process.

It is tempting, and to some extent reasonable, to think of such practices as the manner in which Benning seeks to put himself in the shoes of Protti, Gein, the Unabomber, Thoreau, and the others. However, it would be wrong to go too far in the direction of "psychological identification." Rather, Benning explores how we are formed—and how we can be reformed—by the ways in which we interact with the elements present in a specific environment. That Benning isn't aiming for psychological immersion, but for an understanding of practices, seems particularly evident in *Landscape Suicide*, where the narration is given to a female voice-over. The experiences that she is recounting are clearly those of Benning, but it is the experiences that matter, not Benning.[10]

To further understand the implications of this film practice, it is helpful to turn to Félix Guattari's and Isabelle Stengers' largely comparable theorizations of practice. A practice—Stengers writes with a quote from Whitehead—is concerned with "giving to the situation the power to make us think and feel" (Stengers 2005: 185). She emphasizes that practices grow from specific situations, which is why "there is no identity of a practice independent of its environment" (187). Such formulations about the importance of letting a situation work through you resonate strongly with Benning's film practice—and with the spectator's experience of his films. Obviously, this does not mean that we are blank slates when we approach a situation, but it does mean that different situations lead to different practices. This is why Stengers considers the notion of "practice" in opposition to that of "habit" or "norm." Habits are actions that we perform across various situations, and they thereby prevent us from engaging with the specificity of the situation. Practices, on the other hand, are understood as responses tailored to a precise situation. Again, Stengers does not claim that it is possible to avoid habits, nor does she write that all situations will produce practices, but she nevertheless presents practices as an ideal for how to live ecologically.

A similar insistence on the importance of practice—and its potential for redrawing relations—is found in the late work of Félix Guattari.[11] Here the idea of practice goes hand in hand with the theorization of three ecologies: an environmental, a socio-political, and a mental ecology. Just like Raymond Williams, Guattari moves beyond a Marxist model of base and superstructure[12] in order to think and theorize more complex interactions between subjectivities, decentralized socio-political structures, and the environment. Guattari therefore also opens toward "affective ... rhythms" (Guattari 2000: 25) and a "pre-objectal and pre-personal logic" (36) that resemble Williams' "structures of feeling"; and (again like Williams) he gives art and literature a key role in the project of familiarizing oneself with these rhythms. But whereas Williams primarily presented art as what I called a "seismograph," Guattari—closer to an *avant-garde* stance of doing away with any distinction between art and life—aims for art to play an integral part in the project of resubjectification. He insists that subject formation can come to resemble aesthetic practices; and here again, the keyword for Guattari's so-called ecosophy—and its links to Benning's films—is practice. Guattari is wary of the ways in which political structures might territorialize subjectivities, and he insists that specific practices, not least artistic, can help to prevent a fossilization of the subject:

> The principle common to the three ecologies is this: each of the existential Territories with which they confront us is not given as an in-itself [*en-soi*], closed in on itself, but instead as a for-itself [*pour-soi*] that is precarious, finite, finitized, singular, singularized, capable of bifurcating into stratified and deathly repetitions or of opening up processually from a praxis that enables it to be made "habitable" by a human project. It is this praxic opening-out which constitutes the essence of "eco"-art. (Guattari 2000: 36)

The danger for Guattari's "eco"-art is the situation where a subject gets caught in "deathly repetitions," closes in on itself and becomes a solitary tennis robot in the Californian sunshine. In *Chaosmosis* Guattari therefore notes that we must "respond to the event as the potential bearer of new constellations of Universes of reference" (Guattari 1995: 18). A praxic interaction with the situation—a "praxic opening-out" (Guattari 2000: 36)—can allow precisely such a redrawing of the ecological map.

Guattari and Stengers allow us to bring out more clearly the political dimension of Benning's work. Guattari associates this praxic opening-out with "micropolitics." He recommends a series of specific interventions, often discreet rather than loudly revolutionary.[13] These practices must be evaluated according to how effective they are in breaking up existing systems; they must be evaluated in what could be called an aesthetico-empiricist manner: "It will be less a question of taking stock of these practices in terms of their scientific veracity than according to their aesthetico-existential effectiveness" (Guattari 2000: 37). The question is: how well does a specific practice guard us against "deathly repetitions"? Similarly, Stengers' distinction between habits and practices has a political dimension by implying that there is an emancipatory potential in turning habits into practice. One of Stengers' key terms for thinking about how this can be done is "hesitation." Habits are the actions we perform without hesitation; hesitation opens up the possibility of a shift from habit to practice.

Earlier, I mentioned some of the ways in which Benning works as a practitioner, and some of the ways in which his films and other projects clearly bear the marks of this "praxic" dimension. It is hardly surprising that Benning's films thereby also open out to spectators, inviting us to work as practitioners. In the films and projects under consideration here, the "invitation" is extended in a subtly provocative manner. Here, violence—specifically in its combination with landscapes—plays a key role in the production of spectatorial hesitation, and therefore also in the possibility of a reworking of subjectivities through the practice of watching. Benning is breaking habitual viewing patterns, making us hesitate, aiming to create situations that make us think and feel in site-specific ways.

It is helpful to understand the spectatorial position that Benning's films encourage us to occupy along the lines of what Gilbert Simondon calls the "individu-milieu," the "individual as environment" (Simondon 2013: 25). With this idea, Simondon is aiming to distance himself from the many theorisations of individuality that begin with a notion of "the individual." Instead, Simondon proposes beginning with "processes of individuation." As Brian Massumi explains, for Simondon "[m]atter is thus defined in terms of a *form-taking activity*" (Massumi 2012: 31, original emphasis), and different phenomena such as individuals, landscapes, societies, images are all part of that activity. In other words, the form-taking activity results in various impermanent formations; some of these we call individuals, but these are always already superseded by processes that precede and follow them. The individual is therefore the effect of multiple ongoing processes of individuation—never simply "an individual" but always an "individu-milieu." This ontology complicates the distinctions between subjects and objects, between form and matter. As Anne Sauvagnargues explains, to understand Simondon's conception of individuation "we must pass from an ontology of being to an ontology of becoming" (Sauvagnargues 2012: 58).

Benning's films similarly invite us to realize that we are "individuals as environments," or "spectators as environments." And they do so by pulling us into a practice. Many of his films feel a bit like a "DIY kit" (a term that must obviously not be understood pejoratively). Take *Stemple Pass*—one of the Unabomber films shot on Benning's grounds in the Sierra Nevada. It consists of four similarly framed, static shots each lasting thirty minutes. We see the Unabomber cabin in four different seasons. For twelve to fourteen minutes per season, Benning reads from the Unabomber's writings; for the rest of the season we hear what appear to be the diegetic sounds of the landscape. The spectator hesitates: how do the beautiful landscapes relate to the increasingly violent texts? What are the relations between landscapes, terror, technology, and America? How does the Unabomber's cabin relate to that of Thoreau? Am I right to search for strong links between these many elements, and if not, what kind of relations should I be looking for? Benning does not tell us what to make of the violence, nor does he explain the Thoreau–Unabomber constellation; instead he affords us time to hesitate over the answers, and thereby (as Stengers wrote) he "giv[es] to the situation the power to make us think and feel" (Stengers 2005: 185).

This "situation" is neither "pure" nor "unmediated." As Simondon's concept of the "individual as environment" suggested, we are always already caught up in the environment. In *Stemple Pass*, the thirty-minute shots are false long takes: in fact each shot spans a longer period of time, but Benning takes advantage of the digital technology to hide the cuts, and is thereby able to condense time. Furthermore, some of the sounds (that of a helicopter, for instance) were recorded a week prior to filming, while other sounds (of cars) were removed from the soundtrack. The related film *Two Cabins* (2010) goes further: here images from the Sierra Nevada are combined with sounds from Stemple Pass, Montana. Benning argues that these manipulations work to reinforce reality, but they also demonstrate that Benning builds his films (and their landscapes) a bit like he builds his cabins. The point is obviously not that Benning is something like a master-manipulator dominating nature. Rather, the point is that Benning's "eco"-art, his "praxic opening-out," always already works from within the entanglements of nature, subjectivity, and (here) technology. Or better: these entanglements express themselves as film.

A comparable move toward the "praxic" can be found at the end of *Landscape Suicide*. The film began with forty tennis serves from a solitary player, highlighting the habits and routines we put ourselves through in wealthy Western societies. The ending of the film responds with another typically local activity. We are now in snowy Wisconsin, where a hunter is sitting on the ground, cutting up a deer that he has shot. He eviscerates the animal, leaving the warm, bloody guts on the cold white snow; when he has finished, he grabs the animal by its legs, and pulls it out of the frame.

This ending is ambiguous. If we approach it with the idea of habit in mind, the result is chilling: we have previously learned that Bernice Worden was found in a shed next to Gein's house, disemboweled, hanging head down like an animal. This could suggest that Gein's hunting habits drifted from deer to women—it suggests a pathological crystallization in which a subject found itself caught up in—and acting out—"deathly repetitions" (Guattari), quite

Figure 8 *From* Landscape Suicide, *1986 (II). Courtesy of the artist and neugerriemschneider, Berlin*

literally. On the other hand, we can also consider the scene in relation to the film as a whole. Doing this, the result is chilling in a different way. The entire film is about violence, but no violence is shown. It is a film about the repression of violence, about Protti's and Gein's capacity to forget their acts, about communities that somehow allowed (and perhaps even helped) this repression, and therefore ended up living with a killer in their midst[14]—for six months in the case of Protti, for eleven years in the case of Gein. In this context, there is something (chillingly) positive about the last scene. Finally, we may now think, we are confronted with a form of violence . . .; perhaps a process of desublimation can begin . . .; at least there is something to work with . . .

Spectators can debate the merits of the first, the second, or some other reading of the ending and its relation to the rest of the film. But the manner in which Benning pulls out this final scene, and then invites us to place it in the overall film, necessarily turns the spectatorial experience into a practice. Violence plays an important role in this: many events can be left unaccounted for, but murders and other very violent actions cannot. The violence challenges the spectator, and the difficulty in providing an explanation for the events helps to produce hesitation. This hesitation makes us attend to the situation. For instance, it pushes us to reflect on the violence of habits—whether these have to do with how we mechanize ourselves, or with the consequences of this mechanization for the natural environment. But this is not to suggest that violence primarily plays a strategic role in the production of spectatorial hesitation. If violence is present in the films of Benning, it is because it haunts the culture he is filming. Nevertheless, the specific combination of violence and landscapes that we find in *Landscape Suicide* and the cabin projects results in the production of what Guattari called "eco"-art: a critical, praxical investigation of the ways in which ecologies relate, in view of finding a "habitable" space in the relational network.

Considering Benning's investigations of violence and landscapes alongside Stengers' and Guattari's writings thus allows a focus on three important, interrelated issues: ecologies, practice, and politics. In the films studied here, Benning combines an interest in the environment with an interest in pathological subjects (such as Bremer, Protti, Gein, and Kaczynski) and the sociological structures that help to produce these subjectivities (various forms of dehumanization). In this constellation, the environment is not simply a backdrop against which the mental and the socio-political meet; rather these interactions happen *as* environments. Second, it is important to consider the practice aspect of Benning's work. Practice refers to the activities of the filmmaker: how he builds, how he patiently reads, copies (both paintings and diaries), and reworks (earlier films, for instance); how he sets himself a series of very precise tasks, and how such hands-on activities are made palpable for the spectator. Practice thereby also refers to the spectatorial experience: the demand on the spectator to readjust viewing patterns, to work out the relation between tennis serves and the skinning of a deer, to struggle with violence and the different ways in which it is caught up in the three ecologies. The violence interrogated in Benning's films is therefore not only to be considered at the level of representation (for the manner in which it speaks about the American society), it also turns toward the spectator, playing an important role in the production of a hesitation that moves spectators to attend carefully to the situations they are witnessing. To put it too schematically: in the films considered here, violence forces hesitation, and hesitation opens the doors to a practice.

Bringing the ecological dimension and the practice aspect together, it becomes apparent that practice is about understanding and changing the ways in which the ecologies interact. This is what Guattari called "eco"-art, and it takes us to the political dimension of Benning's films: they enter into specific cultural landscapes, and via concrete interventions they aim to redraw relations between ecologies. With this comes also a resubjectivation of the spectator: we are given time to realize that we are (what I called) "spectators-as-environments." This interventionist (or micro-political) dimension is found in *Landscape Suicide*'s highly unorthodox take on the Gein story; and in the various cabin projects as they radically reframe contemporary debates about ecology and technology, and more specifically, post-9/11 debates about terror, American identity, and ideology. In relation to these complex events and debates, Benning reworks refrains, produces hesitation, stimulates thought and feeling in the spectator, making us realize that we are always already caught up in relational webs that extend beyond us and that we must nevertheless seek to understand.

Notes

1. James Benning reads this passage from a 1999 interview with Ted Kaczynski (aka The Unabomber) in *Stemple Pass* (2012) (original in Kaczynski 2010: 406).
2. Julian Ross' (2016) recent article on the "Ethics of the Landscape Shot: *AKA Serial Killer* and James Benning's Portraits of Criminals" also emphasizes (what I have here called) the "poignancy" of Benning's version of slow cinema. Ross' stimulating text presents Benning's ethics in terms of exemplary intersubjective relations, whereas the present chapter argues for the importance of exploring Benning's ethics (and politics) outside the framework of intersubjectivity.
3. See de Bruyn (2014) for a very good analysis of *Landscape Suicide* drawing on trauma theory.
4. Haneke's comments on the length of this scene are also worth citing here:

   > We could have shown the information (that a guy is playing against a machine) in one minute, but because it lasts so long, you understand it differently. The secret is to find the right length in imagining how I as a viewer would react to that. You say okay, then you get bored, then you get angry, you say cut, then after a certain time you start to watch it and feel its pulse. That's the right length, and it's hard to find . . . That's always the secret, and it's a question of music. (Interview with Serge Toubiana, cited in Brunette 2010: 45)

5. Looking back at *Landscape Suicide*, Benning has expressed regret that he did not give even more time to these environmental shots (most of them last for twenty to thirty seconds each). Recent films can certainly be said to stretch such moments—occasionally to the point of becoming feature-length shots.
6. In interviews (and to some extent also in the film itself), Benning explains the autobiographical dimension of the project: he was travelling with his daughter Sadie; she was reading a feature ("Death of a Cheerleader") in a recent issue of *Rolling Stone Magazine*. Sadie, herself a teenager at the time, put down the magazine because the article disturbed her. Benning picked it up, and was reminded of his own unease, growing up with the Gein case in Wisconsin. The *Rolling Stone* cover appears in *Landscape Suicide*. This autobiographical dimension adds another layer to the film, which I unfortunately do not have space to engage with here.
7. Kaczynski, a former mathematician like Benning, killed three people and injured another twenty-three with bombs that he sent to UN-iversities and A-irlines (hence the name "una"-bomber). He remains in prison, and continues to publish his thoughts and ideas.
8. "Maybe I'm ready to stop making films. I don't know. I have been doing installations. They're more fun, they're quicker, and you get to use tools and build stuff" (Benning in MacDonald 1992: 241).
9. The handwritten "subtitles" (and the informational overload) can also be found in *North on Evers*.

10. The fact that Benning lets a woman narrate his experiences obviously also testifies to a desire to subvert gender stereotypes (which Benning himself has remarked upon, cf. MacDonald 1992: 245).
11. Guattari's late ecosophical texts largely predate Stengers' more recent work on the "ecology of practices," but these Guattari texts also contain references to Stengers' early work. There is no need to search for a single point of origin for these ideas about practices and ecology (it would be contrary to the idea of ecology to even try to do this).
12. "[I]t becomes increasingly difficult to maintain that economic semiotics and semiotics that work together towards the production of material goods occupy an infrastructural position in relation to juridical and ideological semiotics, as was postulated by Marxism" (Guattari 2000: 32).
13. For example:

    There will have to be a massive reconstruction of social mechanisms [*rouages*] if we are to confront the damage caused by IWC [Integrated World Capitalism]. It will not come about through centralized reform, through laws, decrees and bureaucratic programmes, but rather through the promotion of innovatory practices, the expansion of alternative experiences centred around a respect for singularity, and through the continuous production of an autonomizing subjectivity that can articulate itself appropriately in relation to the rest of society. (Guattari 2000: 40)

14. It is obviously tragicomic that Costas' favourite song should be "Memory," and that this was the song the entire community listened to at her funeral.

Works Cited

Ault, Julie (ed.) (2011), *(FC) Two Cabins by JC*, New York: A.R.T. Press.
Benning, James (2007), "Life in Film: James Benning," *Frieze Magazine 111*, available at https://frieze.com/article/life-film-james-benning (last accessed September 20, 2016).
Brunette, Peter (2010), *Michael Haneke*, Urbana: University of Illinois Press.
Cavell, Stanley (1981), *The Senses of Walden*, San Francisco: North Point Press.
De Bruyn, Dirk (2014), *The Performance of Trauma in Moving Image Art*, Newcastle: Cambridge Scholars Publishing.
Guattari, Félix (1995), *Chaosmosis: An Ethico-Aesthetic Paradigm*, transl. by Paul Bains and Julian Pefanis, Bloomington: Indiana University Press.
Guattari, Félix (2000), *The Three Ecologies*, transl. by Ian Pindar and Paul Sutton, London: Bloomsbury.
Kaczynski, Theodor John (2010), *Technological Slavery: The Collected Writings of Theodore J. Kaczynski, a.k.a. "The unabomber"*, Introduction by Dr David Skribina, Port Townsend, WA: Feral House.
MacDonald, Scott (1992), *A Critical Cinema 2: Interviews with Independent Filmmakers*, Berkeley: University of California Press.
MacDonald, Scott (2001), *The Garden in the Machine: A Field Guide to Independent Films About Place*, Berkeley: University of California Press.

Massumi, Brian (2012), "'Technical Mentality' Revisited: Brian Massumi on Gilbert Simondon," in Arne de Boever, Alex Murray, Jon Roffe and Ashley Woodward (eds.), *Gilbert Simondon: Being and Technology*, Edinburgh: University of Edinburgh Press.

Ross, Julian (2016), "Ethics of the Landscape Shot: *AKA Serial Killer* and James Benning's Portraits of Criminals," in Tiago de Luca and Nuno Barradas Jorge (eds.), *Slow Cinema*, Edinburgh: Edinburgh University Press, pp. 261–72.

Sauvagnargues, Anne (2012), "Crystals and Membranes: Individuation and Temporality," in Arne de Boever, Alex Murray, Jon Roffe and Ashley Woodward (eds.), *Gilbert Simondon: Being and Technology*, Edinburgh: Edinburgh University Press.

Simondon, Gilbert (2013), *L'individuation à la lumière des notions de forme et d'information*, Paris: Éditions Jérôme Millon Starobinski.

Smithson, Robert (1996), *The Collected Writings*, ed. Jack Flam, Berkeley: University of California Press.

Stengers, Isabelle (2005), "Introductory Notes on an Ecology of Practices," *Cultural Studies Review*, 11(1): pp. 183–96.

Williams, Raymond (1977), *Marxism and Literature*, Oxford: Oxford University Press.

Williams, Raymond (2005), *Culture and Materialism*, London: Verso Books.

Material Environments

COLIN GARDNER

Constructing the Transversal Time-Image: Ecosophy, Immanence, and Corporate "Land" in James Benning's Four Corners *and* California Trilogy

> I think perhaps duration is what helps bring the political back into the shot.
>
> James Benning (Panse 2013b: 66)

In *The Three Ecologies*, Félix Guattari noted:

> Vectors of subjectification do not necessarily pass through the individual, which in reality appears to be something like a "terminal" for processes that involve human groups, socio-economic ensembles, data-processing machines, etc. Therefore, interiority establishes itself at the crossroads of multiple components, each relatively autonomous in relation to the other, and, if need be, in open conflict. (2008: 36)

Applying this principle to James Benning's *Four Corners* (1997) and the California Trilogy—*El Valley Centro* (1999); *LOS* (2000) and *SOGOBI* (2001)—this chapter will explore the ecosophical ramifications of Gilles Deleuze's time-image, specifically the duration of the extended static shot as well as the interstices (the event-generating gaps) *between* shots, as a transversal connectivity between landscape (the perceptual view of the terrain) and the corporate ownership of "land" (with its concomitant exploitation of indigenous people such as the Anasazi, the Navajo, the Zuni and Hopi as well as cheap immigrant labor and the black urban underclass); the transcendent and the immanent, the actual and the virtual.

This "subjectivity without a subject," as Guattari puts it, is an important component of Benning's methodology, which constitutes both a mapping and recording of his own itinerant journeys around the United States—typified by the circular road trip of *North on Evers* (1992)—as well as an attempt to place the autobiographical within a larger, non-linear, and non-contiguous historical and geographical context. According to Benning,

> After completing *North on Evers* I decided I would need only two criteria to keep making work. One, make films that would take me to places where I wanted to be. And two, make work that would put my life in a larger context. Both somewhat selfish reasons, but very workable. In 1998 these criteria would lead me to make *Four Corners* with a desire to write my own history. (Benning 2007: 49)

At first glance, *Four Corners* is a structuralist film *par excellence*, owing a considerable debt to Michael Snow's *Wavelength* (1967) and Hollis Frampton's mathematically axiomatic and serial output, most notably *Zorn's Lemma* (1970). Benning has also admitted a strong artistic debt to the earthworks of Robert Smithson, arguing that "nature is very defined by structure. I mean the Spiral Jetty refers to that—that the salt crystals that grow on the jetty actually grow as spiral growths" (cited in Panse 2013b: 67). It is perhaps not surprising, then, given this predilection for structures and substructures, that Benning should start with the artificial, striated intersection of four state lines (the "cross-hairs" epitomizing the colonizer's need to demarcate territory as exploitable and manageable property, "targeted" within the mappable confines of Utah, Colorado, New Mexico, and Arizona). The number four is then used to structure the interplay of the four narrative sections that compose the film as a whole. Each segment begins with a scrolling text featuring the life story of a specific painter: Claude Monet; Moses Tolliver (an African-American laborer from Alabama who turned to painting in 1968 after being crippled in a work accident); Yukuwa, a fictitious female Native American artist born in AD 142 in Butler Wash, Utah; and finally, Jasper Johns. Reinforcing the mathematical structure, each artist's text is composed of exactly 1,214 letters. Benning then gives us a single take of a representative work by each artist: Monet's *Poppy Field in a Hollow Near Giverny* (*Champ de coquelicots*) (1885); Tolliver's *George Washington* (1989), which is in turn loosely adapted from the president's portrait on the American dollar bill; the Native American rock painting, *Holy Ghost* (from approximately AD 100); and Jasper Johns' *Flag* (1955), a black and white variation on his signature encaustic work.

Each image forms the backdrop for a voice-over read by four different filmmakers: Hartmut Bitomsky, Benning himself, Yeasup Song, and Billy Woodberry respectively.

As if to underline the film's narrative democracy, each voice-over contains exactly 1,186 words and folds biography, art, site, and location into a stratigraphic history of exploitation and marginalization that also encompasses Benning's home city of Milwaukee, Wisconsin. Finally, each section concludes with thirteen static shots (approximately forty seconds each, with ambient sound) of related geographical sites shot in the cycle of the four seasons: Chaco Canyon (summer); the now predominantly black north Milwaukee neighborhood where Benning grew up (fall); Mesa Verde (winter); and Farmington, New Mexico (spring). Book-ending the four sections are two long takes with accompanying music: an opening shot of a bonfire (again with ambient sound) with "Song for the Journey," a traditional Cherokee chant performed by Little Wolf Band, a contemporary Navajo group; and a closing long shot of a Hopi pueblo at First Mesa accompanied by the Last Poets' righteously radical 1970 proto-rap, "True Blues," whose refrain of denigration and racial abuse defies all historical and geographical boundaries:

> I sang the backwater blues, rhythm and blues, gospel blues, Saint Louis blues, crosstown blues, Chicago blues, Mississippi GODDAMN blues, the Watts blues, the Harlem blues, hoe blues, gut-bucket blues, funky chunky blues, I sang the up north cigarette corp blues, the down south sprung out the side of my mouth blues, I sang the blues black, I sang the blues blacker, I sang the blues blackest I SANG BOUT MY SHO NUFF BLUE BLACKNESS!

What starts as an obvious reterritorialization on mathematical and cartographic lines has clearly exploded outwards into a potentially infinite series of deterritorialized subjectifications.

One is fully aware of this spatial push–pull between the centrifugal and the centripetal when actually visiting the Four Corners, which is marked by a plaque on the ground showing where the four state lines intersect. Although it's admittedly great fun to walk in a circle around the plaque and visit all four states in a matter of seconds, this is obviously an extremely reductive approach to space *and* place. Benning introduces a provocative alternative that in many ways explains his *œuvre* as a whole: "I like the idea that when standing on earth, a spot one foot to your left is just that, one foot to your left. But if you choose to get there by going right, it's a 41,851,445 foot journey" (2007: 47). In other words, rather than focus on the "cross-hairs," Benning uses the Four Corners to explore the spatial quadrants as they deterritorialize outwards from their focal point, potentially to infinity, or at the very least via a number of other possible connectivities before returning to "ground zero." Guattari calls this the nonhuman aspect of subjectivity, its resingularization:

> Singularity is not individuality, although it is about being singular. It operates at a pre-personal, pre-individual level [. . .] The resingularization of subjectivity, the liberation of singularities that are repressed by a dominant and dominating mass-media subjectivity, has nothing to do with individuals. (2008: 8)

Instead, it is an entirely aesthetic endeavor, encouraging us to reinvent our lives like artists: construct it, work at it, *singularize* it, not by cultivating a consensus but rather an ecosophy of *dissensus*.

Four Corners achieves this dissensus through a dislocation between narration and image, which in turn provides the basis, as we shall see, for a stratigraphically transverse view of historical time. As Silke Panse points out (2013b), the film's voice-over accounts of the lives of Richard Wetherill (credited with the discovery of Cliff Palace in Mesa Verde and subsequently a homesteader and trader with the Navajo in Chaco Canyon), Benning himself, Herman Dodge "Benji" Benally (a Navajo victim of racism), and the indigenous native American tribes in the Four Corners region are related over images that don't correspond directly to the narration itself. In this sense, the images—whether the chosen artwork or the thirteen static landscape shots that follow—tend to lag behind the ostensible story, forcing us to play catch-up in forging narrative links. For example, the black filmmaker Billy Woodberry's account of Benji's murder in Farmington, New Mexico in 1974, at a time when rolling drunken Navajo outside the city's bars was practically a public sport among whites, is accompanied by Jasper Johns' *Flag*. We are left wondering what the connection might be (an ironic statement on nationalism-as-racism, perhaps?), especially as Johns was born in Augusta, Georgia and grew up in South Carolina. However, his brief textual biography gives little detail of his Southern roots (with its implied racism) or his artistic life in New York, and absolutely nothing about his homosexual relationship with Robert Rauschenberg and the artistic influence of Merce Cunningham and John Cage. Indeed, like the fictional biography of Yakuwa in Part 3, it pays more attention to Johns' upbringing with his extended family, particularly his Aunt Gladys. Instead, the use of Woodberry's voice constructs a far more viable connection with the anti-black racism described by Benning in his account of his Milwaukee roots. "[S]ince Billy is black," affirms Benning, "his voice would connect the blind prejudice of the Farmington Navajos and poor whites to the blind prejudices referred to in the Milwaukee story of blacks and poor whites" (MacDonald 2006: 240). Significantly, Benning's narration is accompanied by Moses Tolliver's portrait of George Washington, which grounds his memoir directly in black visual culture. As Benning notes, "It isn't like it's illustrating it immediately, but you have to reorder the images you see in context with the text you just heard, which is kind of similar to the way *North on Evers* worked" (Panse 2013b: 68). Reading the texts first creates an image in the viewer's mind, which we can subsequently compare to the static images as they unfold. As Panse suggests "Rather than looking outside onto a corresponding landscape, these films generate new, mental landscapes and geographical trajectories" (2013b: 67).

It is important to note that a mental image doesn't necessarily have to be someone's particular thought or even pure thought. As Deleuze notes in *Cinema 1: The Movement-Image*:

> it is an image which takes as objects *of* thought, objects which have their own existence outside thought, just as the objects of perception have their own existence outside perception. *It is an image which takes as its object, rela-*

tions, symbolic acts, intellectual feelings. It can be, but is not necessarily, more difficult than the other images. It will necessarily have a new, direct, relationship with thought, a relationship which is completely distinct from that of the other images. (Deleuze 1986: 198, original emphasis)

It is this new mental-image—where the disequilibrium between text and image, character and place generates a new whole with a very different evolution of relations—that allows Benning also to create a very specific, non-linear image of historical time, what Deleuze and Guattari call *stratigraphic*. They pose the key question as follows:

> What does answering to the requirements of an age mean, and what relationship is there between the movements or diagrammatic features of an image of thought and the movements or sociohistorical features of an age? We can only make headway with these questions if we give up the narrowly historical point of view of before and after in order to consider the time rather than the history of philosophy. This is a *stratigraphic* time where "before" and "after" indicate only an order of superimpositions. (Deleuze and Guattari 1994: 58)

Rather than dig down vertically into the strata of history in order to map the successive layers of time as so much cultural sediment, this stratigraphic trajectory is more of a transverse zig-zagging, bringing old layers to the surface as untimely artifacts, so as to create a new topographic curvature, a truly transversal time-image. This strategy—which is intrinsic to Benning's methodology—is not unlike that of Foucault's genealogy, which dissects various strata of coexistence with different flows, tangents, and dynamic movements. As Deleuze argues:

> One must pursue the different series, travel along the different levels, and cross all the thresholds; instead of simply displaying the phenomena or statements in their vertical or horizontal dimensions, one must form a transversal or mobile diagonal line along which the archaeologist–archivist must move. (1988: 22)

In this way, planes of consistency/immanence are as much historical as they are ecosophical—the two are ultimately inseparable.

By combining the geological, the socio-political, the artistic, and the personal, *Four Corners* constructs a revised version (or, more accurately, deliberate misrepresentation) of official histories, connecting individual biographies to collective history and vice versa. As Benning explains,

> I connected Milwaukee and Wisconsin with the Four Corners because I grew up with the same kind of misunderstanding and hatred for blacks that poor whites and Navajos still have for each other in that area. I liked making comparisons and drawing things together like this . . . I wanted to start my history in Indian culture rather than European culture. That's where America starts. (Benning, cited in Pichler 2007: 127)

By extension, the voice of Yeasup Song is "used for the Native American history because Yeasup is Korean-Asian. The Native Americans originally came from Asia across the Bering Strait" (cited in MacDonald 2006: 240). This incorporation of otherwise marginalized and deterritorialized histories also helps to explain why Benning is perfectly comfortable including the fictitious biography of Yakuwa alongside the more "authentic" texts on Monet, Tolliver, and Johns, especially as it allows him to pursue the likelihood that many of the Four Corners rock paintings were probably rendered by women. Benning admits:

> This is me in defiance of the way that historians work. In all accounts it's assumed that men did this work, but I don't see how anyone can come to this conclusion, especially since many of the same designs first appeared on pottery that those same historians claim was made only by women. (cited in MacDonald 2006: 241)

From here it's only a short step to assert that all history is subjective (and potentially singular): "If I am going to make up my history let me make it up the way I want to," he argues. "If you criticize that, you have to criticize all history not just mine" (Benning, cited in Pichler 2007: 127). This position is reinforced by the film's closing quote from Black Elk: "Sometimes dreams are wiser than waking," which also evokes a famous line from Nietzsche: "Art is more powerful than knowledge, because *it* desires life, whereas knowledge attains as its final goal only—annihilation" (1979: 66, added emphasis).

So how does Benning's transverse time-image work in practice? Let's follow Benning's lead and explore the Milwaukee section in more detail as a specific case study. First, his own voice-over serves to articulate narratives of several interwoven constituencies—whether based on class, race, or national origin—whose histories have generated the city we know today. He starts by tracing Milwaukee's white population to an influx of immigration following the abortive 1848 cultural revolution in the German Confederation, the so-called Forty-Eighters: "By 1900 Milwaukee was in a way a more representative German city than any in the Reich, for no city there had so many Germans from all parts of the empire living together in one place" (Benning 2007: 51). Although Benning's own family had no ties to the old country, many of their neighbors did, and during World War II "Some of them were sending their sons to kill their cousins, and the other way round too" (2007: 50).

Benning then creates a transversal connection between the problem of national kinship and class conflict based on *racial* difference:

> Most of the men worked in the industrial valley that separated Milwaukee into north and south sides, or they worked in one of the 50 local breweries, while the women stayed home raising the children. Twenty blocks to the east

> was Milwaukee's modest black district. The people there worked mostly as unskilled laborers or low-paid domestics. At an early age I was taught to fear that community. (2007: 50)

Significantly, instead of immediately pursuing details of this racial/class conflict (which we would expect given the background image of Tolliver's portrait of Washington), Benning backtracks transversally into a discussion of the area's geology:

> Ages ago this region was covered with water of unknown depth. In time, the water found its way to the sea and a heavy bed of drift formed a plain. A period of erosion followed, cutting the valleys nearly as they are today. Then the ice age leveled the summits and deposited a more varied and fertile soil. Today 150 feet of rich earth covers the Niagara limestone and Cincinnati shale that lie below. (2007: 50)

Pursuing the geological analogy, he then tells of successive waves/layers of cultural colonization: ancient Paleo Indians (triggering a connection to the Chaco Canyon and Mesa Verde sections), French fur traders (1634) and then the consolidation of Anglo-European power with the Declaration of Independence in 1776. Then:

> by 1848, through fraud, retaliation, and sale, the Wisconsin Indians lost all their lands. That same year Wisconsin became a state ... The Black Hawk War of 1832 was the last attempt by the Wisconsin Indians to fight against American encroachment. But within a year, the Indians ceded all the lands west of the Milwaukee River. With a population of 200 the town of Milwaukee was created on March 17, 1835. (2007: 50)

This detour through the history of Native American land expropriation (which is a central theme of Parts 1, 3, and 4, linking the Four Corners region directly to Wisconsin) sets up a renewed (but now heavily recontextualized) discussion of the racial conflict that arose with the postwar emergence of the black ghetto (known as The Core) and its rapid encroachment into Benning's old neighborhood near Washington Park. Instead of seeing the black population as an intrusive other, both racially and as an urban underclass, their transverse connection to the Native Americans makes them as indigenous as any other racial group, serving to reframe the *whites* as invasive outsiders. This innate tension between solidarity and dissensus is clearly designed to work against Darwinian principles of the survival of the fittest and instead promote a more ecosophical solution grounded in Gregory Bateson's three ecologies, whereby "The unit of survival is a flexible organism-in-its-environment" (Bateson 2000: 457). In short, as Guattari argues, "It requires that a plurality of disparate groups come together in a kind of unified disunity, a pragmatic solidarity without solidity; what one might call, for want of a better word, 'fluidarity'" (2008: 10).

It also allows Benning to show that despite Milwaukee's tradition of socialist governments and their advocacy of organized labor and low-cost housing (a legacy of the Forty-Eighters' political radicalism), the unions actually encouraged an exclusionary policy toward low-income blacks:

> Wages increased, but white workers feared their gains would be lost to low-wage black labor. Labor leaders desired to keep Milwaukee white and discriminated against blacks through exclusionary clauses. The small black district remained segregated and poor. (2007: 51)

Although Benning himself marched alongside the city's black population during the 1967 Civil Rights demonstrations, he was beaten unconscious by a group of poor whites, while a childhood friend who had become a city policeman was shot dead by a sniper's bullet. "Every last drop of blood is being drained from the neighborhood's soul," laments Benning. "In time, the poor will be moved out, the few remaining buildings will be razed, and the rich soil will again be exposed and exploited" (Benning 2007: 52).

The thirteen static shots that follow appear at first glance to reinforce this pessimistic view, focusing as they do on the rundown black neighborhoods just to the north of the Menomonee River. However, Benning edits the shots transversally in order to reinforce both a lack of continuity and also evoke different layers of stratigraphic time. Thus the opening shot of a desolate factory on a rundown industrial street is immediately followed by an autumnal scene of a pile of fallen leaves in the woods, as if to contrast contemporary urban decay with the region's pre-industrial (and Native American) past. The next shot, a seedy back alley, whose angles converge at a vanishing point in the depth of the image, seems to evoke a return to shot 1, until we see a squirrel scampering from left to right in the middle distance, as if to refold the city into its rural surroundings, mixing together the two time frames. Benning repeats the effect with shot 11, a frontal perspective of a boarded-up store, followed immediately by a pastoral image of geese on a pond, presumably a reference to Washington Park and the origins of Benning's neighborhood in the annexation of the adjacent farms of Robert Brown and Bill Sarnow. However, rather than end in nostalgia, the segment ends with a street corner church and the feint sound of gospel music, suggesting a predominantly black congregation and a radical spatiotemporal shift from the area's nineteenth-century origins, as if to underline Nietzsche's premise that genealogical history is always untimely, always geared toward the future and "life" rather than a monumentalizing of the past. As Foucault puts, it, and Benning would almost certainly agree:

Figure 9 From Four Corners, *1997. Courtesy of the artist and neugerriemschneider, Berlin*

> Genealogy does not oppose itself to history as the lofty and profound gaze of the philosopher might compare to the molelike perspective of the scholar; on the contrary, it rejects the metahistorical deployment of ideal significations and indefinite teleologies. It opposes itself to the search for "origins." (Foucault 1984: 77)

Although the California Trilogy shares a similar "fluidity" of both social and temporal relations, it eschews the stratigraphic historical approach of *Four Corners* in favor of a more immanent ecosophy, as much virtual as actual. As Benning explains, "After *UTOPIA*, I felt like I had exhausted my interest in text and image, and when I started the California Trilogy, I knew I wanted to completely discard text and work with just image and ambient sound" (MacDonald 2006: 242). Which is not to say that Benning abandons his trademark self-reflexive structuralism, for each segment in *El Valley Centro*, *LOS*, and *SOGOBI* is composed of thirty-five static shots of exactly 2½ minutes. However, unlike in *Four Corners*, where the text precedes and therefore colors our reading of the landscape images that follow, the trilogy works in reverse: explanatory text is limited to a series of descriptive "credits" at the end of each part so that the seemingly neutral landscape is reread as "land" or property after the fact. As Benning explains,

> In the California Trilogy, the credits document what's going on there, what small city it's near and then who owns the land. It's kind of a political reading of landscape itself through ownership, in other words, who makes the profit and who does the hard work. The hard work is in the image and who makes the profit shows up in the credits. (Cited in Panse 2013b: 61)

Thus, far from being an exercise in pictorial and temporal formalism, the three films actually turn out to be a contingent post-structural "container" whereby duration (which, as we shall see, is connected to immanence and life) puts the political back into the shot, so that Benning is able to disclose an ecosophical relation between the corporate wealth of Los Angeles and the irreversible despoliation of Owens Valley, the historical source of its water supply. According to Benning,

> The whole trilogy is basically about the politics of water. In the Central Valley, corporate farms take advantage of two irrigation systems that were built with public money, one with federal money, one with state money. The corporations paid for none of the construction, but they take full advantage of it: 85 per cent of the water in California is used for farming; only 15 per cent is used for manufacturing and public consumption. And, of course, Los Angeles was expanded by stealing water from the Owens Valley. (Cited in MacDonald 2006: 250)

In this way, water—where it comes from, where it goes to, and who owns it—becomes the virtual vector or phylum that ties the films together as an ecosophical project as well as a series of different kinds of time-image that infuse the California Trilogy as a political project in the first place.

The trilogy actually began life as a single film—*El Valley Centro*—which was intended to disclose how water turned out to be a more valuable commodity than gold in forming the basis of the California economy: "farming in the Central Valley each year grosses more money than all the gold that was ever found in California . . . Of course it won't last forever. Irrigation farming

Figure 10 From El Valley Centro, *1999. Courtesy of the artist and neugerriemschneider, Berlin*

over time will ruin all land" (Benning, cited in Panse 2013b: 69). Given this "hidden" economy based on the "liquid" wealth of irrigation, it seems wholly appropriate that *El Valley Centro* should focus on laborers constantly at work but rarely seen. Instead, faceless bulldozers, freight trains, and combine harvesters pass through shots, while a roll call of prisoners at the California State Prison at Wasco is heard off-screen, mingling with the ambient sound of the landscape. Nothing is choreographed—Benning waits for the right moment through careful observation—while the shots' tight framing emphasizes off-screen space while also reinforcing the subjective view of the filmmaker himself.

It then made sense to show who actually benefits from this public largesse, so *LOS* represents the urban companion piece that links the exploitative rural economy to Los Angeles itself. While *El Valley Centro* is composed horizontally, accentuating horizon lines and the shots' central vanishing point, *LOS* emphasizes the vertical, highlighting the textures of glass and concrete as well as geometrical enclosure. *LOS* is also highly eclectic in its focus on racial and class diversity, for Benning makes a point of interspersing community farming scenes with urban workers, churchgoers, and a phalanx of LAPD riot squad at the Democratic National Convention. As we all know from having seen Roman Polanski's *Chinatown* (the thinly disguised story of William Mulholland, the designer of the 233 mile-long Los Angeles aqueduct), the city was effectively built using stolen water from Owens Valley, which in turn destroyed the ecosystem around Mono Lake. Benning's portrait of the city is thus understandably ambivalent, a rich tapestry of corporate buildings, oil refineries, recycling plants, wrecking yards, mini-malls, and heavily irrigated community and private gardens, underlining the economic necessity for water but also its irresponsible wastage on domestic aesthetics.

Part 3, *SOGOBI*, which means "earth" in Shoshonean, appears at first glance to represent a return to the unspoiled landscape, highlighting the classic beauty of the California wilderness: Point Sur, the Tahoe National Forest, Mono Lake, and Yosemite. As Benning explains:

> When I made *Sogobi*, my first idea was to make a film that was purely about nature and about landscape that wasn't encroached upon, almost in a biblical sense, finding real grandeur ... As I went around the US, I realized that it became less interesting to me, the encroachment became more interesting to me than the beauty. (Cited in Slanar 2007b: 170).

Gradually we become aware of human "trespass" in the form of a fire fighting helicopter, zooming into the frame to scoop up water from a lake, and a giant billboard in the middle of the Mojave Desert. Claudia Slanar makes a telling point when she notes:

> Off-screen traffic noise seems to indicate that there is indeed an audience for the largely blank billboard marked only with the word "Available" and a telephone number. The filmic distancing of the object enables a contemplation of the thing in itself and combines with the tangible name of a firm called "Outdoor Systems." This text offers a more direct way of "reading" the image, in consideration of economic realities—irrespective of the humorous pun it presents. (Slanar 2007a: 73)

We also become aware of an increasing level of mechanical "noise" in the film, blurring the difference between the ambient hum of wind and the faint drone of car or airplane engines. In short, nothing is pristine, everything is always already mediated.

Benning tends to associate such mediation with a state of entropy (in Smithson's sense of an irreversible decline within a closed system). With the earth as this closed system—there's only a certain amount of resources to go around—we are easily misled into separating the sublimity of the landscape from mankind's immanent responsibility for its survival. To reiterate Bateson, "The unit of survival is organism plus environment. We are learning by bitter experience that the organism which destroys its environment destroys itself" (2000: 491). Benning makes a similar point, noting that "People living in southern Utah, in one of the most beautiful places in the world, are still dying of cancer from nuclear testing in Nevada decades ago. They became 'down-winders'. A piece of landscape that looks beautiful can become the opposite of beauty" (MacDonald 2006: 234). The cancer victims of the cast and crew connected to Dick Powell's 1956 film *The Conqueror*, whose Snow Canyon and St George, Utah locations were downwind from the Yucca Flats testing grounds in Nevada, are proof positive of Benning's statement. John Wayne, Susan Haywood, Pedro Armendáriz, Powell himself, and half the inhabitants of St George had succumbed to cancer by the late 1980s.

Such mediation is also typical of Benning's tendency to metacommunicate the history of photography and cinema in many of his shots. It is almost impossible to see shot 23 in *El Valley Centro*, which features a crop duster outside of Dixon, without thinking of Alfred Hitchcock's *North by Northwest* (1959), while the image of a container ship passing under the Golden Gate Bridge in *SOGOBI*—which is designed to echo similar shots in Parts 1 and 2—evokes similar sequences in Peter Hutton's *Study of a River* (1997). Similarly, shot 12 in *SOGOBI*, which captures the Bridalveil Falls in Yosemite National Park, inevitably conjures up the classic photographs by Eadweard Muybridge, Carleton Watkins, and Ansel Adams. However, Benning rightly points out that his cinematic rendition is ontologically different because of the very act of duration: "I like that particular shot because it references those classic photographs, but I think it has its own presence because it's time based. And you also have the sound track" (cited in MacDonald 2006: 249).

Time and duration then are key elements in our understanding of Benning's project and its entire ecosophical ontology. This has obvious relevance to Deleuze's notion of the time-image or chronosign, "an image where time ceases to be subordinate to movement and appears for itself" (Deleuze 1989: 335). This is caused by a collapse of the sensory-motor schema associated with the action-image of classical film narrative. As Deleuze explains:

> Time ceases to be derived from the movement, it appears in itself and itself gives rise to *false movements*. Hence the importance of *false continuity* in modern cinema: the images are no longer linked by rational cuts and continuity, but are relinked by means of false continuity and irrational cuts. Even the body is no longer exactly what moves; subject of movement or the instrument of action, it becomes rather the developer of time, it shows time through its tirednesses and waitings. (1989: xi, original emphasis)

In Deleuze's schema, the main vehicle for this genesis is not the interval—the built-in delay that allows action heroes to bide their time within the continuum of the sensory-motor regime, ultimately using the delay to their advantage as the narrative rushes to its transformative climax—but the interstice, the false movement or fissure through which the time-image becomes manifest, much like the dehiscence of blood seeping out through a sutured wound. Thus, instead of being unaware of the cut (as in traditional continuity montage), the edit now draws attention to itself *as* discontinuity. By cutting off the actual/action from its causal motor linkages, the virtual is now able to detach itself from its actualizations and be valid in and for itself. As Deleuze explains, "The two modes of existence are now combined in a circuit where the real and the imaginary, the actual and the virtual, chase after each other, exchange their roles and become indiscernible" (1989: 127). When applied to Benning's trilogy, it's clearly apparent that he relies far more on the interstice *between* shots than the interval across a range of shots, for according to Tom Conley:

> The interstice is the interval turned into something infraliminary in a continuum in which an event can no longer be awarded the stability of a "place" in the space of the image. The interstice becomes what exhausts—and thereby creates—whatever space remains of the image in the sensory-motor tradition. It supersedes the interval and, by doing so, multiplies the happenings of events. (Conley 2000: 320)

Indeed, the trilogy is full of temporal events, not least because the shots are also records of a performance, namely Benning's adventures—in the form of an extended road trip throughout the state—in getting the shots in the first place: "when I made the trilogy, it was really one hundred and five performances: me going to one hundred and five places and recording how I felt at those places at those moments. The trilogy is an accumulation of performance" (cited in MacDonald 2006: 245). Of course we don't actually perceive this latent, spatiotemporal component: it remains virtual, literally hidden in the interstices between shots and made manifest only through our own mental reconstruction. However, it does provide an ontological index for how to read the rest of the trilogy ecosophically, for we are encouraged to look for repetitions as well as differences between and across all three films. It is for this reason that the relatively long duration of each shot encourages the spectator to look carefully at the image (even though not much seems to be happening in terms of a conventional sensory-motor action) so that we can store up information to use later as part of a different vector. "The purely optical and sound situation (description) is an actual image," notes Deleuze, "but one which, instead of extending into movement, links up with a virtual image which forms a circuit with it. The problem is to know more precisely what is capable of playing the role of virtual image" (1989: 47). In this sense, it is the water refrain—or more accurately, machinic phylum in the form of a subterranean flow of pure becoming (Nietzsche) or universal aggregate of action/reaction (Bergson) that flows between the shots and on which they depend—that makes us aware of the necessary audio-visual linkages between the three parts. As Benning explains:

> a lot of what's in the trilogy can't really be perceived unless it is studied. This is true for individual shots, and because there are so many cross-references between the three films. Even the first time through, you might notice that there are cows in all three films, and billboards—you might not remember that they're all from the same company, Outdoor Systems—and aircraft, and trains (a freight train, a commuter train, then a freight train again), and oceangoing ships. There's wilderness in all three. (Cited in MacDonald 2006: 251)

More significantly, there's also an important "bridge" spanning the interstice separating *El Valley Centro* from *LOS* as discrete films, made all the more apparent if we view the trilogy (as Benning himself prefers) in one extended sitting. The former's closing shot is of the Teerink Pumping Station, part of the California Aqueduct at Wheeler Ridge just south of Bakersfield. The opening shot of *LOS* features the Cascades Aqueduct in Sylmar in the North San Fernando Valley. What is not shown (in effect, the interstice's key "event") is the rest of the aqueduct that links the two locations, one drained of its water resources so that the other might be irrigated. As Benning explains, in *El Valley Centro* we see "water being pumped over a mountain to another place to irrigate and then the first shot of *LOS* is water coming down the spillway that was built by Mulholland to bring water to Los Angeles. That's the very first spillway" (cited in Panse 2013: 70). In effect, this radical time-image not only represents the source of Los Angeles' wealth and power but also the historical time (and political shenanigans) that made it possible.

Indeed, this power in and of the interstice—and the series of events that it generates—pervades all three films in the trilogy as each of their opening and closing shots foregrounds water. *El Valley Centro* begins with a winter shot of the Department of Water Resources' spillway at Lake Berryessa in the North Central Valley when the water level is high, and ends with the aforementioned Teerink Pumping Station. *LOS* begins with the Sylmar Aqueduct and ends with a shot of the Pacific Ocean at Puerco Beach, Malibu. *SOGOBI* also opens on the Pacific but ends with another view of the spillway at Lake Berryessa, only this time in summer when the water level is low. This not only encourages the spectator to return perceptually and conceptually to the trilogy's starting point but also suggests an impending ecological crisis if we fail to put a stop to the vicious cycle of exploiting natural resources. As Benning puts it, "The trilogy could play continuously, and you could enter anywhere" (cited in MacDonald 2006: 250).

Benning's use of the interstice is only one temporal (and, by extension, political) weapon in his arsenal. The trilogy is most notable for its use of extended long takes in tandem with static compositions dominated by a vanishing-point perspective and a cone-of-vision placement of the spectator in relation to a seemingly circumscribed landscape. In this sense, Benning's framing resembles classical Renaissance painting, whereby Albertian perspective reinforces both the symmetry of the picture plane and the central dominance of its focal point, much like the composition of Leonardo's *The Last Supper* (1495–8), in which the room's receding architecture privileges the central figure of Christ with the disciples acting as a secondary frame. However, by infusing classical perspective with duration, Benning forces us to see the vanishing point less as an artificial visual nexus and more as a dynamic spatiotemporal conduit, not as a *fixed* pictorial depth but as a potentially limitless abyss that opens out the image-as-container and moves us beyond the strict confines of the *mise-en-scène* (as in the case of the aqueduct, which bridges parts 1 and 2 of the trilogy by entering and emerging from the shots' depth of field). In addition, we are also reminded of the limitlessness of off-screen space beyond the left and right framing edges, whereby each individual shot is now part of a much larger matrix of shots connected via the phylum of water resources. In effect, Benning turns classical space into Baroque space, which is built on a sweeping diagonal that transversally crosses several planes rather than reinforcing static, parallel planar qualities tied to a dominant cone of vision. This forces the spectator's eye beyond the center of the frame to an infinite outside (much like Tintoretto's more revisionist *Last Supper* of 1592–4, where the attending servants vie with the disciples for the spectator's attention, relegating Christ to the margins). Benning thereby generates different pleats of matter that are intrinsically decentred, unleashing "[t]he Baroque fold that unfurls all the way to infinity" (Deleuze 1993: 3).

Throughout the trilogy, Benning generates temporal movement and linkage between and across shots using a number of strategies (which are also pertinent to *Four Corners*). The first is his use of the refrain, particularly birdsong, that adds ambience to a number of shots, as well as wind, the rustling of leaves, and the flow of water. Guattari calls these "mutant centres of subjectivation," a recognizable melodic formula joined with a specific territory, not unlike the existentializing refrain in Proust where the "little phrase" from Vinteuil's sonata has a profound effect on Swann as *the* singular event—a re-creative and profoundly transforming influence. When joined with other refrains—spread throughout the trilogy—they form ruptures that throw us onto other paths and encourage us to form new habits, new readings. This is Deleuze and Guattari's plane of consistency, which is also a heterogeneity. The question then becomes, how do we attain (and re-attain) a modicum of unicity while at the same time re-singularizing ourselves as part of an immanent plane of consistency?

In this sense, the refrain is connected directly to Deleuze's notion of the encompasser as the forger of collective identities, a place where the micropolitical has a broader catalyzing power to forge new, more immanent connectivities. Usually associated with John Ford's Westerns (particularly his use of Monument Valley locations in films such as *Stagecoach* and *The Searchers*), the encompasser is manifested through the landscape as a form of spatiotemporal ambience that both "envelops" and extends its surroundings. Although the landscape may be tightly "framed" within the compositional confines of the filmic shot, we know full well that, like Benning's use of Baroque space, it also extends outside the frame and, through depth of field, potentially to infinity. It is, in short, always in a state of de-territorialization, linking the film's immediate community (the western town, the conflict between homesteaders and ranchers, field workers and foremen) to a wider spectrum of protagonists who are either "yet to come" (the area's future history) or concurrently part of a class- and race-based separation of powers extending to other locations and histories (as in the case of Benning's connection of Farmington to Milwaukee via a common racial divide). In this regard the ultimate encompasser is the sky and its various pulsations, which envelop the immediate milieu and, in turn, the emergent collectivity and its ongoing process of formation.

This is of course the dominant compositional trope of the Chaco Canyon and Mesa Verde sections of *Four Corners* as well as both *El Valley Centro* and *SOGOBI*, which are dominated by horizon lines dividing the screen into land and sky (which in turn allows the shots to be interconnected by sharing a common spatiality). However, this doesn't necessarily preclude the need for an action-hero (single and multiple) to engineer social and political change, for as Deleuze explains:

> It is as representative of the collectivity that the hero becomes capable of an action which makes him equal to the milieu and re-establishes its accidentally or periodically endangered order: mediations of the community and of the *land* are necessary in order to form a leader and render an individual capable of such a great action. (1986: 146, original emphasis)

In the trilogy, Benning uses the encompasser, formed by the containing vessel of the shot, to incorporate and envelop the farm workers (who, through their labor, are directly associated with the presence of the surrounding landscape and the connective tissue of the immanent sky) but also the power of property ownership fueled by the currency of water. In both cases, the (unseen) ecological and economic stakes are much higher than the micro-political context presented on-screen might suggest.

In conclusion, we should also note that the refrain and encompasser in Benning are the very stuff of immanence, which makes his work a fundamentally eco-aesthetic project. This raises a key ecosophical question central to Benning's entire *œuvre*. If, following Guattari, the plane of immanence is pre-subjective, inhuman in its pre-individual singularity, is it still possible for us to carve out an empirical relation—with all the judgment that implies—to what amounts to a condition of chaos? Deleuze insists that immanence and life presuppose one another, for as John Rajchman persuasively argues:

> immanence is pure only when it is not immanent to a prior subject or object, mind or matter, only when, neither innate nor acquired, it is always yet "in the making"; and "a life" is a potential or virtuality subsisting in just such a purely immanent plane. Unlike the life of an individual, a life is thus necessarily vague or indefinite, and this indefiniteness is real. (Rajchman 2001: 13–14)

There is clearly no room for the transcendent in Deleuze's ontology, for the whole idea of a universal subject—to which immanence is attributed through the hegemony of consciousness—tends to denature the very nature of immanence itself. Instead, Deleuze prefers the term "transcendental field": a life that is not dependent upon a being or submitted to a specific act. In other words, immanence cannot be immanent to anything other than itself, it acts as its own container, just as Benning's shots act as containers of their own durational becoming (through which, as potentials, they link to other shots, to other lives, empowered or otherwise). Moreover, as Panse rightly argues, there is no transcendence in Benning's films either: leaves rustle, the wind blows, birds twitter, because they are part of a material presence immanent to an ecosophical world filled with the imperceptible as well as perceptible, including Benning and his camera:

> The term "eco-aesthetics" brings together two separate planes, that of ecological materiality and that of the image. We cannot make images of a burning nuclear reactor from nearby without being affected by its radioactivity. Documentary images are not separated from what is depicted in them; they are part of the world. The immanence of the world to the work and the artist is an ethical and ecological issue. Images are not just visual . . . The filmmaker or artist, the work and the "context" or the "environment," all belong to the same plane of immanence. (Panse 2013a: 44)

It is in this respect that we can label Benning's entire project as innately ethical, in Spinoza's sense of a speculative, practical mode of *living*, a joyful auto-affection involving an inquiry into what a body (and therefore thought) can do in terms of its ability to affect and be affected in turn. "We will say of pure immanence that it is A LIFE, and nothing else," states Deleuze. "It is not immanence to life, but the immanent that is in nothing is itself a life. A life is the immanence of immanence, absolute immanence: it is complete power, complete bliss" (2001: 27). A bliss, in Benning's case, derived as much from the imperceptible—conjured by the virtual, mental image of the active spectator—as from the actual perceptual image itself. The key word here is "active," because Benning's films demand that we pay close attention, they require an investment of our own personal time as well as attention to the passage of time within the diegesis itself. Taking time, like virtue, is its own reward because, as we have seen throughout this chapter, duration not only puts the political (and ethical) back into the shot, it also puts the "land" in an otherwise sublime and purely aestheticized landscape.

Works Cited

Bateson, Gregory (2000), *Steps to an Ecology of Mind*, Chicago and London: Chicago University Press.
Benning, James (2007), "Off Screen Space/Somewhere Else," in Barbara Pichler and Claudia Slanar (eds.), *James Benning*, Vienna: Filmmuseum Synema Publikationen, pp. 47–54.
Conley, Tom (2000), "The Film Event: From Interval to Interstice," in Gregory Flaxman (ed.), *The Brain is the Screen: Deleuze and the Philosophy of Cinema*, Minneapolis: University of Minnesota Press.
Deleuze, Gilles (1986), *Cinema 1: The Movement Image*, trans. H. Tomlinson and B. Habberjam, Minneapolis: University of Minnesota Press.
Deleuze, Gilles (1988), *Foucault*, transl. by Sean Hand, Minneapolis: University of Minnesota Press.

Deleuze, Gilles (1989), *Cinema 2: The Time Image*, transl. by Hugh Tomlinson and Robert Galeta, Minneapolis: University of Minnesota Press.
Deleuze, Gilles (1993), *The Fold: Leibniz and the Baroque*, transl. by Tom Conley, Minneapolis: University of Minnesota Press.
Deleuze, Gilles (2001), "Immanence: A Life," transl. by Anne Boyman, in *Pure Immanence*, New York: Zone Books, pp. 25–31.
Deleuze, Gilles and Guattari, Félix (1994), *What Is Philosophy?*, trans. Hugh Tomlinson and Graham Burchell, New York: Columbia University Press.
Foucault, Michel (1984), "Nietzsche, Genealogy, History," transl. by Donald F. Bouchard and Sherry Simon, in Paul Rabinow (ed.), *The Foucault Reader*, New York: Pantheon Books.
Guattari, Félix (2008), *The Three Ecologies*, transl. by Ian Pindar and Paul Sutton, London: Continuum.
MacDonald, Scott (2006), "James Benning: On His Westerns," in *A Critical Cinema 5: Interviews with Independent Filmmakers*, Berkeley, Los Angeles and London: University of California Press, pp. 228–54.
Nietzsche, Friedrich (1979), "On the Pathos of Truth," transl. by Daniel Breazeale, in Daniel Breazeale (ed.), *Philosophy and Truth: Selections from Nietzsche's Notebooks of the early 1870s*, Atlantic Highlands, NJ: Humanities Press.
Panse, Silke (2013a), "*Ten Skies, 13 Lakes,* 15 Pools—Structure, Immanence and Eco-aesthetics in *The Swimmer* and James Benning's Land Films," in Annette Pick and Guinevere Narraway (eds.), *Screening Nature: Cinema Beyond the Human*, New York and Oxford: Berghahn Books, pp. 37–59.
Panse, S. (2013b), "Land as Protagonist: An Interview with James Benning," in Annette Pick and Guinevere Narraway (eds.), *Screening Nature: Cinema Beyond the Human*, New York and Oxford: Berghahn Books, pp. 60–70.
Pichler, B. (2007), "Into the Great Wide Open: *North on Evers* (1991) to *UTOPIA* (1998)," transl. by Eve Heller, in Barbara Pichler and Claudia Slanar (eds.), *James Benning*, Vienna: Filmmuseum Synema Publikationen, pp. 117–29.
Rajchman, John (2001), "Introduction" to G. Deleuze, *Pure Immanence*, New York: Zone Books, pp. 7–24.
Slanar, C. (2007a), "I'll sneak in the back door: Installations in the Art World: 1978–1985," in Barbara Pichler and Claudia Slanar (eds.), *James Benning*, Vienna: Filmmuseum Synema Publikationen, pp. 68–74.
Slanar, C. (2007b), "Landscape, History and Romantic Allusions: *El Valley Centro* (1999) to *RR* (2007)," transl. by. Renée von Paschen and Eve Heller, in Barbara Pichler and Claudia Slanar (eds.), *James Benning*, Vienna: Filmmuseum Synema Publikationen, pp. 169–80.

SILKE PANSE

Men in Huts in Woods: Independence, Transcendentalism, and Technology in James Benning's Thoreau and Kaczynski Documentaries and Exhibition

> Who can be serene in a country where both the rulers and the ruled are without principle?
> Henry David Thoreau ("Slavery in Massachusetts," 1854)

In times of rising quests for independence of nations and objects, James Benning's exhibition *Decoding Fear* (Kunsthaus Graz, 2014 and Kunstverein in Hamburg, 2015) explores the ethics of individual human independence in a nonhuman, material environment by juxtaposing the hut and the writings of Henry Thoreau, the advocate of *Civil Disobedience* (1849) and nature writer of *Walden* (1854), with the hut and the writings of Theodore Kaczynski, the technophobe eco-terrorist known as the Unabomber. Each had moved into a self-built hut in the woods, Thoreau for two years, two months and two days from Independence Day in 1845 to 1847 at Walden Pond in Concord Woods, Massachusetts and Kaczynski for nearly twenty-five years from 1971 to 1996 in Stemple Pass in Montana, and both advocate a life in the wilderness, independent and self-reliant. Benning has rebuilt and filmed each hut on his own land in Sierra Nevada in California. *Concord Woods* (2014), the video of Thoreau's hut, consists of two static one-hour shots, one at summer solstice and one at winter solstice. *Stemple Pass* (2012), the video of Kaczynski's hut, is divided into four static half-hour shots, one for each season in non-chronological order, alluding to the telescoping of the couple of years into four seasons in *Walden*. Benning reads excerpts from the speeches, manifestos and journals of the previous hut inhabitants to the sound of birds or rain on the soundtrack, leaving time for ambient sound in each shot. There are also plaster replica of each hut in the gallery. In the installation *Two Cabins* (2011), the view from the window of each cabin into the woods is projected opposite of a desk and a pencil for Thoreau and a typewriter for Kaczynski. Benning's meticulously rewritten copies of Thoreau's and Kaczynski's diaries are also exhibited, as are

Figure 11 *Thoreau's cabin in* Concord Woods, *2014. Courtesy of James Benning and neugerriemschneider, Berlin*

his duplications of paintings and drawings by outsider artists, *From the Two Cabins Project (After Traylor, Tolliver, Darger, Ramirez, Howard, Hawkins, Yoakum and Hawk)*, some of which had hung in Benning's replica on his land.

Hut I

In the first shot of his replica of Thoreau's cabin in *Concord Woods*, Benning reads excerpts of Thoreau's speech "A Plea for John Brown" (1859), an abolitionist who independently led an insurrection against slavery in several US states. Brown was hanged for his violent civil disobedience that eventually led to secession—the withdrawal into independence of the Southern states from the Union—a year later, then to the American Civil War (1861–5) and to the independence of slaves. For the American transcendentalists Thoreau and Ralph Waldo Emerson, humans must be independent from the government, from the state, from other humans, from nonhumans—"men are not so much the keepers of herds as herds are the keepers of men" (Thoreau [1854] 1995: 36)—and from objects: "Men have become the tools of their tools" (24). As Thoreau writes in *Walden*: "when the farmer has got his house, he may not be the richer but the poorer for it, and it be the house that has got him" (21). There should be independence of the state from the federal government; of the United States from the United Kingdom; of American philosophy from European philosophy; of the divine from the Church; of the mind from the body; of the slave from the master. Each human their own constitution: "the only right is what is after my constitution" writes Emerson (1841). Slavery is an issue of independence. But while Thoreau argued compellingly against slavery, and while him not paying his taxes because he disagreed with pro-slavery laws is always given as an example of his main act of civil disobedience, he also claimed that he refused to contribute taxes not for any specific reason, but only because of the principle of independence: "It is for no particular item in the tax bill that I refuse to pay it. I simply wish to refuse allegiance to the State, to withdraw and stand aloof from it effectually" (Thoreau [1848] 2014: 21). So against his own anti-slavery beliefs he argued that pro-slave individuals too be civilly disobedient by not paying their taxes to the Union (11). By separating his refusal to pay taxes from a particular issue, Thoreau in effect says that his civil disobedience is not because of his moral conscience. Thoreau is contradictory about the reason for seeking independence. He feels morally conscientious for a specific reason, but also endorses an independence for independence's sake, independent also of a reason: Thoreau's "moral clarity about abolition stemmed less from compassion or a commitment to equality than from the fact that slavery so blatantly violated his belief in self-governance" (Schulz 2015). So for Thoreau, the freedom of independence was more important than what that independence was from. He praised John Brown not necessarily because he sought equality, but because slavery excludes independence.

Benning's rendition of Thoreau's speech is edited. Thoreau writes in a passage about Brown cut from Benning's reading: "He shows himself superior to nature. He has a spark of divinity in him." Thoreau rates civil disobedience through human moral conscience more than nonhuman nature. We only "half express ourselves" (1841), writes Emerson, the rest is divine. The "I" that Emerson claims is part or particle of God does not include his body. Our body is "separate from us" (Emerson 1836: 7), like nature and art. The self on which one is supposed to rely does not include one's own body. According to the transcendentalists, independence defines what is human on the one hand, but on the other, humans are mere dependent passages for the divine: "When we discern justice, when we discern truth, we do nothing of ourselves, but allow a passage to its beams" (1841), Emerson writes in his essay "Self-reliance." When we make a moral judgment and follow this up with an act of civil disobedience, we do not do this independently but merely allow judgment to pass through us. We can only be independent from other humans, but not from what transcends us. When Benning reads the words Thoreau attributes to Brown: "No man sent me here; it was my own prompting . . ." he cuts out how the sentence continues: "and that of my Maker. I acknowledge no master in human form." By editing out the transcendentalist references to the divine, Benning reinforces their claim of independence even more, but leaves the viewer hanging, forcing us into independence also from the transcendentalists.

Benning's images and soundtrack in the videos and the exhibits do not just have something pass through them. Benning reads in a monotonous voice that sounds as though he has to force himself to read. His reading in *Concord Woods* appears pained, as if repeating Thoreau's words hurt him. Benning has previously used the soundtrack of another film, *Che Guevara, the Bolivian Diary* (1994), for his own film, *UTOPIA* (1998), but in *Concord Woods* and

Stemple Pass he himself speaks the words that others have written, thereby bringing the individual—elevated by Thoreau and Emerson—into the repetition with his breaking voice, but adding a material rupture that pauses the transcendence of meaning. The Thoreau hut too breaks up the documentary image of nature with a sculptural presence that emanates material opacity. It looks like the stage for a theater play, in which one waits for a human to exit the hut and enter the nonhuman world. The images of the hut together with the exhibited hut emphasize that the objects are not the same as the images. Unlike the hut in the exhibition, the hut in the image is an opaque object that cannot be accessed. And even the hut in the gallery cannot be used in the same way as the hut it is a replica of. Through duplication, Benning allows the work to be independent from its predecessor. Material replication here works against transcendence—an independence from transcendence.

In *Concord Woods* we do *not* hear Benning read from Thoreau's observations of nonhuman nature from *Walden*, which he wrote when he lived in the precursor of the hut depicted in the image and for which new eco-materialists (Bennett 1994, 2001) and eco-critics (Walls 1995, 2011) celebrate him. For the first shot, Benning chose a speech that is a call to action, or practice, rather than merely a description, albeit of the diversity of nature, and we hear about the exceptionality of a human individual and the independence of their moral conscience while looking at a replica of the hut from which Thoreau wrote about the diversity of nature in a network of nonhuman agents. In the second shot, the mathematician in Benning skips over other sections in *Walden*'s "Economy" chapter to get to Thoreau's lists of doing-it-yourself of life in the woods and the material economy of the savings of self-reliance. With this "bean counting," Thoreau argues for the advantage of a permaculture with as little division of labor as possible and without using animals as tools for the farming of vegetables. Through his reading, Benning underlines Thoreau's economic materialism, which—with its asceticism—is the opposite of the excessive consumerism with which economic materialism is usually equated.

In *Concord Woods*, the ethical in the summer shot (with the praise of independent individual actions) meets the material in the winter shot (by emphasizing dependence on diverse materials through their itemization). Together, the two shots of *Concord Woods* ask us to confront the ethical doings of human individuals and their human practice of making with impersonal nonhuman material diversity and to consider the levels on which ethical contemplations are deliberated. So how to bring the praise of individual human independence in the narration together with the flora and the huts in the images and the exhibition?

Following the political ecologist Bruno Latour, the environmental literary studies scholar Laura Dassow Walls observes how:

> Twentieth-century readers found it hard to connect Thoreau's nature writing with his rampant abolitionism and the political critique of "Civil Disobedience." The more his journal filled with details of animal tracks, fish scales, plant bloomings, and stream depths, the more dry and tedious it seemed ... it seemed Thoreau had become the slave of empiricism, a poet silenced by science. This misreading was itself a product of modernism. (Walls 2011: 102)

After modernism, eco-political thought has been addressing this modernist gap between culture and nature through cyborgs (Haraway 1991), hybrids, morphisms, translations (Latour 1993) and crossings (Bennett 2001). In *Politics of Nature: How to bring the Sciences into Democracy* (2004) Latour opposes a "politics rendered powerless by nature" (Latour 2004: 26) and suggests shifting access to nature away from scientific empiricism, bringing politics into nature through political ecology as an assemblage of politics and nature. In this environment of a political "*single* collective" (29, original emphasis), there is naturally no single individual and no independence. According to Walls, Thoreau is "weaving humans and nonhumans together" (Walls 2011: 103) in an actor-network that "connects nonhumans with the humans who observe" (104). But Thoreau cannot be an embedded materialist environmentalist and be self-reliant. The notion of independence relies on externality. To be independent contradicts being part of, dependent on, and immanent to a network of ecologies.

The two domains that Thoreau engages with—civil disobedience and nature writing—have remained separate. His legacy, shifting between idealism and materialism, fuels confusion. Thoreau has been taken up by deep ecologists who emphasize the inherent worth of nature for nature's sake without the correlation through human self-interest, as well as by eco-critics such as Walls, who suggests that Thoreau takes up "the middle ground" (Walls 2011: 99) of political ecology that Latour advocates. But Latour argues that the idealizations of deep ecology, with its "modern, smooth, risk-free stratified objects" (Latour 2004: 26) where "the producers of this disputed knowledge remain completely invisible" (ibid.), actually prevent political ecology, and that "the distinction between these objects and the political world" remains complete in a "politics rendered powerless by nature" (ibid.). Benning's works take these issues out of the abstractions of literary studies and political ecology, and into the materialities of the documentaries and the gallery. In the two shots of *Concord Woods*, the two sides that Thoreau is noted for—an idealism for which morals and the supernatural are transcending forces, and a detailed materialist empiricism of the natural—are given a platform. The documentaries and the exhibition compel the visitor into this division as they open up a situated ethical practice between independent human morals and material entanglement (Barad 2007).

Being self-reliant implies independence of the self from nature. Only by separating their bodies as nature from the human, independent self as mind can Emerson and Thoreau claim self-reliance. Being self-reliant depends on clear boundaries between the self and the environment on which one is apparently not reliant. The notion of self-reliance contrasts with materialist entanglement and is based on independence from the agency of other subjects or objects. For the transcendentalists, the self is transcendental and not material. The body is part of nature, but not of the self. This becomes apparent from Thoreau's approach to his own body: "There is nothing so strange to me as my own body. I love any other piece of nature, almost, better" (Thoreau 2009: 22). Despite his reliance on "the labor of my hands only" (Thoreau [1854] 1995: 1), Thoreau does not see his hands as part of his material body since he values them as independent tools. And while he industriously breaks down the numbers for the materials for his hut, the same does not apply for when his tailor requests his material measurements (Thoreau did not rely on himself to make his own clothes): "Of what use is this measuring of me if she does not measure my character, but only the breath of my shoulders?" (Thoreau [1854] 1995: 16). The measuring of materiality does not include human materiality.

Much of what Thoreau and Emerson have suggested about relating to nature (such as walking) is now common practice and established as art. But the environment has been modified. The capitalized Nature, of which Emerson wrote that it "refers to essences unchanged by man; space, the air, the river, the leaf" (1836: 7), has changed. Only a few decades into the Anthropocene, Thoreau could observe a nature that was still much more independent of him than it would be today: "Man and his affairs (. . .)—I am pleased to see how little space they occupy in the landscape" (Thoreau 1851). Thoreau's only slightly civilized wilderness would have been more independent of humans than the nature we see in Benning's video. Before humans created much of what previously was regarded as only their natural environment, Thoreau inferred the character of humans from the environment of the objects they made, used, and inhabited: "The most interesting dwellings in this country, as the painter knows, are the most unpretending, humble log huts and cottages of the poor commonly; it is the life of the inhabitants whose shell they are" (Thoreau [1854] 1995: 30). When Thoreau compares a hut to the coat or the shell of its dwellers, he rates the aesthetics of an object not only with respect to its practical use, but also in terms of the morals of their creators and users, and not as independent. A hut is like its maker. In the Anthropocene, nature too can now be seen much more as an extension of human ethics, since so much of it has been affected or produced by humans.

But not only Thoreau deduced the morals of humans from their objects. He himself continues to be judged through his hut as an outpost of his character. While the small size of Kaczynski's hut was presented to the courts as proof of his insanity, the small size of Thoreau's hut exemplified the admirable restraint and moral superiority of its inhabitant. For Thoreau, also inside a hut, the mind of the human inhabitant expands into material space. The problem with the restricted size of the hut is that the mind requires physical space: "One inconvenience I sometimes experience in so small a house, the difficulty of getting to a sufficient distance from my guest when we began to utter the big thoughts in big words. You want room for your thoughts" (Thoreau [1984] 1995: 91). Thoreau tries to remove all that is unnecessary in his life in the hut in the woods and systematically goes through all the things he gladly does without: "Before we can adorn our houses with beautiful objects the walls must be stripped, and our lives must be stripped" (24). *Concord Woods* ends with Thoreau's notorious rejection of even a door mat, making, again, a link between things and ethics: "It is best to decline the beginnings of evil."

In Thoreau's transcendentalist puritanism, aesthetic reduction is cast as ethical gain. "He was a man of Spartan habits," reads Benning from Thoreau's speech about Brown. This can also be applied to Benning's filmmaking. Thoreau's approach of "less is more" is also Benning's. By rebuilding, filming, and exhibiting the huts in his woods and in the gallery, Benning takes the sparseness of the aesthetics of self-reliance in life into minimalism in art. Benning, Thoreau, and Kaczynski all find freedom in reduction, but in contrast to Benning, Thoreau's stripped-down aesthetics are steeped in personal asceticism. Thoreau finds that there is a subjective relation not only between an object and its maker or inhabitant, but also between the observer and the observed: "There is no such thing as pure *objective* observation. Your observation to be interesting, i.e. to be significant, must be *subjective*" (Thoreau 2009: 258, original emphasis). The object should be described "not as if it were 'independent' but 'as it is related to you. The important fact is its effect on me'" (Walls 2011: 104 citing Thoreau 1906: 164–5). What is important for Thoreau is to be found in the relation "somewhere between me and them" (Thoreau 1906: 165). Benning has been influenced by Thoreau in terms of paying attention to what is there (for instance in his famous "looking and listening" classes) and by "the discipline of looking at what is to be seen" (Thoreau [1984] 1995: 72, cited in Benning 2008) that Thoreau develops in *Walden*: "No method nor discipline can supersede the necessity of being forever on the alert" (ibid.). Benning is also regarded as a self-reliant, individualist filmmaker and relates to Thoreau and Kaczynski because he is as misanthropic as they are, as he claims in a post-human manner:

> As I've gotten older, I tend to dislike people more—people in general, not specific people; I think we have a really bad track record ... Even though I'm very social because I teach and travel a lot, I'm trying to find some kind of autonomy in my life, and also solitude, which both Kaczynski and Thoreau were working towards. That's my connection to them. (Dunlevy 2014)

But in contrast to Thoreau, Benning avoids marks of his subjectivity in his work. His practice of filming and of teaching film famously eludes any focus on the subjectivity of the artist in order to be able to look at and listen to what is there. Even though Benning has built the huts and is also the narrator, the images and sounds of *Concord Woods* and *Stemple Pass* are not defined through how he relates to what we look at and listen to. What Benning's camera documents is independent of the filmmaker's relation to it. The effect of what he films on him does not matter with respect to the film. Unlike Thoreau, Benning does not construct himself in his work, or embed himself as himself in it. We do not know more about Benning's life when we see *Concord Woods*.

And what is self-made in self-reliance? Thoreau did not make the ax he built the hut with, but he made the pencils with which wrote. Benning did not make the tools with which he built the huts and he has not made the camera with which he filmed. Thoreau made the sentences, but he did not make the words. Benning made the images, but apart from the huts he did not make the nature that they depict. The self cannot be as easily separated in its relations from the environment as Thoreau would have liked. By showing the self-made replica hut in the not-self-made nature, Benning's documentary images, together with the narrated speech accompanied by diversity in bird song, questions the self-reliance of making an object from its environment, the hut from the woods, and how independent the writer is of the hut and the woods, the self of its environment.

The differences in degrees of self-creation have consequences for the question of how independent documentary can be (and not just in the sense of an "independent documentary"). Documentary is never only self-dependent or self-derived. It has to be in some way a repetition of what it documents, be that materially by taking images of it, or metaphorically by referring to what it documents through words. Documentary images cannot be independent of what they film. But unlike fictional images, who are dependent on their maker, documentary images have to be independent of their taker. What is there has to be independent in order be documented. Benning appreciates discovering things "independently from one another" (cited in Ault 2011: 141). Benning might be more self-reliant in his filming than others, but his documentary images rely on what is not him. His self-built replicas highlight the contradiction inbuilt into the notion of self-reliant transcendentalism. His documentary shots explore these issues through the huts, which, as replicas, are a sculptural "document" as well as independent artwork, first in a natural environment, then in the image, and then in the gallery.

In her essay "Civil Disobedience" (1970), Hannah Arendt takes the stance that the writer of the earlier essay "Civil Disobedience" (1848) was not a civil disobedient precisely because he acted independently and merely as a

Figure 12 *Thoreau's cabin in Kunstverein in Hamburg, Architectural Rendering (*Two Cabins*), 2015. Photo by Fred Dott. Courtesy of James Benning and neugerriemschneider, Berlin*

subject. According to Arendt, civil disobedience is not just a "philosophy of subjectivity" (Puner, cited by Arendt [1970] 1972: 57). She distinguishes civil disobedients (55) as citizens united in their view, from conscientious objectors, who act individually according to "moral imperatives and appeals to a 'higher law,' be it secular or transcendent" (56). For Arendt, Thoreau acted only as a person, not as a citizen, and this retreat to individual conscience made his practice apolitical: "the counsels of conscience are not only unpolitical; they are always expressed in purely subjective statements" (62). Benning's reconstituting of a Thoreauvean awareness through video as *not* subjective, is therefore also political.

BUILDING HUTS, NOT SYSTEMS

The American philosopher Stanley Cavell looks toward the American transcendentalists as a way of exploring an American philosophy that is independent from European philosophy, which had been about building systems. Because there were perceived to be no obligations to a previous history Thoreau and Emerson could develop a do-it-yourself philosophy. Cavell and other film-philosophers such as William Rothman claim that American transcendentalism has fundamentally influenced American cinema, especially classical Hollywood comedy and the observational documentaries of Direct Cinema (which Rothman refers to as cinéma vérité): "Cinéma vérité affirms the reality of the one existing world, the world in which language is a condition of life we call 'human'" (Rothman 1997: 110). Because there is only one existing world that is human and language-based, there is no difference between fiction and documentary, with fiction being the model for documentary: "every cinéma vérité film can be imagined as having been scripted and directed ... as really being a closet classical movie" (111). In contrast to environmental scholars, Cavell reads *Walden* like a fiction film script. For the film-transcendentalists, *Walden* is about the "spiritual quest" of a human (Rothman 2004: 5), not an observation of a material and nonhuman environment, and where eco-philosophers place *Walden* in the slightly civilized wilderness, the film-philosophers have located *Walden* "just outside a major city" (Rothman 2004: 171), in suburbia. "As Cavell points out, Hollywood films usually call this place 'Connecticut'" (ibid.) writes Rothman. The American film-transcendentalists are concerned with the American dream and that "the post-World-War II aspiration [was] the transcendental one of creating the spiritual out of the material, transforming the real Connecticut into the mythical Connecticut, making the dream real" (ibid.). They see materialism merely in the negative sense of consumerism, which needs to be spiritually transcended. Materials only appear as commodities that can and should be relinquished, and are not vital for living.

In the American comedy *It Happened One Night* (1934), one of Cavell's key examples of American film-transcendentalism, Clark Gable's and Claudette Colbert's characters are on the run, without money and hungry. Gable as Peter Warner, a reporter wise to living thriftily, steals carrots for Colbert as Ellie Andrews, a spoilt heiress who does not like them, but eventually submits to her hunger (and with it to Peter). Since for Cavell, hunger is only a metaphor— "hungering is a metaphor for imagining" (Cavell 1981: 6)—eating too is merely symbolic. In the spirit of Emerson, for whom "Nature is the symbol of spirits" (Emerson 1836: 32) and "Words are signs of natural facts" (ibid.), Cavell reads material nature symbolically: "Eating the carrot is the expression of her acceptance of humanity, of true need—call it the creation of herself as a human being" (Cavell 1981: 93). Eating is not for sustaining a human materially, but it has to express something else. Her true need is immaterial and she only becomes human through the immaterial that the material stands for. What makes someone human is immaterial. Any materiality is transcended and not even self-reliance is taken literally since Ellie and Peter are relying on whoever raised the carrots they stole. A carrot cannot just be a carrot. But while Ellie's submission to the eating of the carrot also signifies her submission to Peter, the carrot is not only symbolic, not even in the context of this fiction film. Cavell also writes at length about a blanket being put up in order to prevent the two main characters—who are not (yet) married to one another, but are sleeping in the same room—from seeing each other in bed. For Cavell, the blanket works "as a movie screen" (82). By contrast, the huts in Benning's videos do not symbolize anything else. They did not even symbolize anything else before Benning replicated them. They are huts, not screens, and the video image is neither a hut nor a wood. One does not rebuild a metaphor. Whereas Cavell embraces Thoreau's idealist side, Benning draws out his materialism, and this is also done through documentary.

With respect to film, American transcendentalism, curiously, has only been associated with popular classical Hollywood cinema: "The transcendentalism of Emerson and Thoreau is a central source of popular American movie genres. Their roots in American transcendentalism are essential to what makes American films American" (Rothman 2004: 55). What is transcendental about American cinema for Cavell are its morals and the mood of the characters. This moral outlook is, Rothman writes, "not imposed on movies from the outside . . . but is internal to the stories movies keep telling. It is the American cinema's inheritance of the transcendental philosophy of Emerson and Thoreau" (357). But what is internal to the story of a movie is still external to the viewer. According to Thoreau and Emerson, morals are not an external template to imitate, but rather matters to decide upon always anew and independently. These morals are not expository or prescriptive.

With *Concord Woods*, the viewer is forced into independence in their response to the difficult ethical questions raised, and cannot remain dependent in following a story that has an identifiable moral. *Concord Woods* brings transcendentalism down to earth and asks more uncomfortable questions about independence and even about what is American with respect to terrorism in America. Emerson regards the ability to avoid repetition as a quality of being independent. *Concord Woods*, in the context of *Stemple Pass* and the exhibition, does not come with morals that rely on repeatability. Because it pushes us into independence (since there is nothing we can follow), *Concord Woods*, and its environment in *Decoding Fear*, are perhaps a more appropriate contemporary exploration of American transcendentalism than the film-transcendentalist's fictions, be they in the form of documentary or fiction films.

Hut II

So in the first shot of *Concord Woods* (2014), Benning reads a rousing speech defending violence against humans on grounds of moral conscience from a nature writer who otherwise logs entertainingly about life in the woods. In the first shot of *Stemple Pass* (2012), Benning delivers amusing early journal entries of a life in the woods from of a future serial killer who rejects morals. Hearing both through Benning's voice creates a level playing field where the vectors of a Kaczynskiness of Thoreau and a Thoreauness of Kaczynski can be repositioned.

In the spring shot with Benning's reading of Kaczynski's 1971/2 journals, we listen to a birdwatching Kaczynski report on the clucking of grouse and their mating rituals, and talk about watering and weeding his garden in the wilderness. Kaczynski sounds like Thoreau—and not only literally as both speak through Benning—when he wonders that "no matter how often I look at those wooded hills and walk over them, I still find something exiting and mysterious about them." Kaczynski picks the leaves of yellow violets for salad, and collects leaves from the mustard family: "one of the finest salad plants I have ever eaten. It was slightly succulent and very tender with enough radish flavor to make it spicy, but not so much to make it unpleasantly sharp." In Benning's dry rendition, Kaczynski's travails initially come across as rather comical, and where *Walden* could have been Thoreau's reality TV show about DIY home building (the Wikipedia entry for "Do it yourself" suggests that this is "part of a series on Individualism"), *Stemple Pass* turns into a cooking show. His log on the butchering of a porcupine reports the itinerary of cooking it: "the result was a very tasty soup." This success was, however, inconveniently followed by the vagaries of getting rid of its tapeworm and a gum infection "from chewing the rather tough porcupine meat." We hear Benning relay: "Today, I found I have an infection in the gum. I suspect that this might have resulted from fragments of meat having been jammed in between the gum and the teeth during the process of chewing." Between, around and as part of the meat and the gum and the teeth, Kaczynski is more viscerally and materially enmeshed in his environment than Thoreau, and mindful of how it becomes part of him. Thoreau is more metaphorical in his self-stylizations, which are written for others. Kaczynski reports only to himself. In the fall, winter, and summer shot, we hear how Kaczynski finds his life increasingly mired in what he perceives to be the violence that others commit against his nonhuman environment through technology, for instance through the noise level of machinery that humans bring into the woods. Kaczynski becomes progressively destructive in his apparent defense. Although he struggles more with his conscience regarding the liquidation of nonhuman individuals for gaining food than of humans for stopping technology, he is also deadly for the environment he kills for. Where Thoreau plants beans, potatoes, corn, and peas, Kaczynski forages, steals, shoots, and bombs.

What Kaczynski fears with respect to the systemizing through the "industrial–technological society" (Kaczynski 2008: 59) corresponds with the danger that for the German philosopher Martin Heidegger—who also famously wrote in a hut—lies in the "technical–scientific conquest" (Heidegger 2007: 6)[1] through the ordering system of the standing reserve of technology. In "The Question Concerning Technology" (originally published in 1953),[2] Heidegger criticizes how modern technology utilizes human as well as nonhuman nature for human extraction. Technology becomes inherent to nature, which in turn is used merely as the standing reserve for technology. What is ownmost to technology is enframing. This is not "a shared genus for everything technological" (Heidegger 2000: 30) like treeness is for trees. Treeness is ontological and material. Enframing is systemic. Because enframing is not based on an essential sameness of a kind that can be separated from another, any notion of an independence from technology—such as that Kaczynski seeks—is misguided and would merely reinforce enlisting humans as its standing reserve. Human doing can never directly and independently counter the danger of being consumed and ordered into the standing reserve of technology. There are no independent humans.

While the humans in huts, Kaczynski and Thoreau, have been concerned about their independence from other humans as well as from technology and other things—or, as Benning reads from *Walden*: "the more you have of such things the poorer you are"—the independence of objects like huts from humans and from each other has been a matter of concern for object-oriented ontologists such as Graham Harman. When Heidegger describes the independence of a thing, he uses the German term *selbstständig* (Heidegger 2005: 5). This can be translated into English as "self-supporting", which means that something can rely on its own support. Being self-supporting is not the same as being totally independent from one's surroundings. But while the 1977 translation of "The Thing" uses "self-supporting" as an equivalent to "independent," Harman uses only "independent," thereby editing out the relation between self and support, and emphasizing the independence of a thing from any relation: "As the independent stance [*Selbststand*] of something independent, the jug differentiates itself from an object" (Heidegger 2005: 5 as translated in Harman 2010: 24). In order to make the case that things should be seen as independent from relations, this translation brushes aside the notion that what is self-supporting must have material relations to its environment and that it can only stand on its own and be independent because of its relations; that the independence of a thing lies in its relationality.

Heidegger has often been used for a blanket dismissal of technology as representation in "the general incommensurability between being and representation" (Harman 2002: 301). In Harman's representation of Heidegger, a thing loses its independence by being represented: "something independent can become an object, when we represent it to ourselves" (Harman 2010: 24). Harman employs Heidegger to say about technology that "through en-framing we experience a 'refusal' of world and a 'neglect' of things" (22). Here technology is only interpreted as the standing reserve in the sense that images are merely representations and that things become objects through the technology of the image. According to this line of thought, the things in the world could not be documented through images. Whatever is in a documentary image would always become an object and then vanish "into the objectlessness of the standing reserve" (Heidegger 2000: 19) of its technology.

But independent things do not merely become dependent objects in images and lose what is their ownmost by being enframed through technology. If things always lose their thingness in an image, this would mean that there was an original essence that could be lost. But since things are already not independent of their material environment, they cannot lose this independence (which they do not have) when they exist in an image. A hut does not just stop having an essential hutness, but also gains an image-hutness and a gallery-hutness while retaining being a hut in these diverse environments. The hut cannot be totally independent of its documentary image. It is an image of a hut and a hut in an image, and not an image of anything or just an image. Benning's documentaries do not refuse the world. For Benning and for documentary, things are not only in the image, but also in the world. The depicted environment *in* the image is not merely that *of* the image as the standing reserve of technology. Exhibiting the replicated huts in the image as well as in the exhibition emphasizes their independence from the technology of the image and underlines that what is in the image exists independently of it. Since the huts are made out of similar material to that of their environments in the woods or the gallery—wood in the woods and white plasterboard, wood and metal in the white gallery—their relationalities in heterogeneous environments are further brought to the fore.

What is ownmost to a thing is always more than its relation to humans or its ordering into the standing reserve of human-made technology. What is ownmost to a thing changes according to its relations in its diverse environments, be they of the woods, the image, or the gallery. What is ownmost to the huts of Thoreau or Kaczynski—their hutness—is not an original essence, because then it could be copied. Heidegger challenges Socrates' and Plato's assertion that what is of value—the idea of a thing like a hut—is independent of its materializations and that "the particular actual and possible houses are mutable and ephemeral derivatives of the 'idea'" (Heidegger 2000: 32). He rejects that the idea of something always predetermines every single thing of that kind. What is ownmost to technology is not merely an abstract "idea that hovers above all that is technological" (ibid.). Benning's replica of the huts in wood in the woods in the image, and in plasterboard, wood and metal in the gallery, are not Platonic copies of an enduring original. Benning's replicas in the gallery have not been built as a means to an end and cannot be used as huts. There is more to Benning's huts than to those of Thoreau and Kaczynski.

Freedom without Independence

In *Stemple Pass*, we hear the technophobe's words "I hate the technological society because it deprives me of personal autonomy," spoken by the filmmaker who might be autonomous precisely because he films. But Kaczynski fights violence with violence, blasts with blasts and technology with technology. Using a typewriter, guns, and bombs, Kaczynski employs technology to spread his anti-technological message. Because of the contradictions inherent to Kaczynski's practice, it seems appropriate that Benning uses technology to make a video about this luddite who engages considerably and consistently with the technology of destructive devices in his attempts to destroy technology and its makers and users. Kaczynski uses technology as an instrumentalizing means to an end in a way that Heidegger criticizes. He fights technology as a human through the human means of technology, believing that we could be free from it: "There is only one way to escape from being pushed around, and that is to smash the whole system and get along without it. It is better to be poor and free than to be a slave and get pushed around all your life" (Kaczynski 1985). Heidegger's response to Kaczynski would be that he is chained to technology through his rejection of it in the same way as if he were to embrace it: "Everywhere we remain unfree and chained to technology, whether we passionately affirm or deny it" (Heidegger 1977: 4). Kaczynski cannot be independent from technology. He cannot smash and kill himself out of it. Kaczynski is still part of the standing reserve of technology because his actions are determined through his opposition. Heidegger would have advised Kaczynski that we are neither forced to blindly operate technology, nor "what amounts to the same, to helplessly rebel against it and condemn it as the work of the devil. On the contrary: if we open ourselves to what is ownmost to technology, we find ourselves surprisingly called upon by a freeing claim" (Heidegger 2000: 26). While freedom for Heidegger depends on how humans relate to an environment that includes technology—a freedom *in*—freedom for Kaczynski is a freedom *from*. In this respect, Heidegger shares more with Thoreau than with Kaczynski.

Thoreau and Kaczynski both oppose slavery: Thoreau, that enforced by humans, and Kaczynski, that mediated by human-made technology, *Technological Slavery* (Kaczynski 2008). But while Thoreau's independence is only possible *with* morals, Kaczynski's freedom is only possible *without* morals. A moral conscience is the result of the social conditioning of the system that Kaczynski fights. Morals are normative. We hear Benning speak Kaczynski's words: "I don't pretend to have any kind of philosophical or moralistic justification. The concept of morality is simply one of the psychological tools by which society controls people's behaviour." Kaczynski worked hard to overcome the "uncomfortable" conscience that kept him from killing: "As a result of indoctrination since childhood, I had strong inhibitions against doing these things, and it was only at the cost of great effort I could overcome the inhibitions." Like Kaczynski, Heidegger objects to a systemically predetermined ethics, but for Heidegger it is rather that ethics are prevented through technology. Ethics have become impossible in a world where technological relations have become "the ethical substance of human existence" (Hodge 1995: 21). Ethics cannot develop freely, because they are overdetermined by technology. So despite their different intentions, Kaczynski and Heidegger view ethics as part of the standing reserve of the industrial–technological system.

While Thoreau and Kaczynski imply that independence brings freedom, for Heidegger, humans are not free exactly when they think they are independent. Only those who acknowledge that they are not independent, and only those who look and listen to their own enframing, are free. One can only be free insofar as one "becomes one who listens, not one who obeys. What is ownmost to freedom is *originally* not linked to the will or even merely to the causality of human willing" (Heidegger 2000: 26). Freedom cannot be consciously willed (as Thoreau thinks it can)—or as Joanna Hodge concisely puts it in *Heidegger and Ethics*: "Freedom is revealed to be an ontological condition of possibility, not an ethical characteristic of human beings" (Hodge 1995: 135). Humans cannot decide to be free by being independent: "The freedom of the open consists neither in the independence of arbitrariness nor in the dependence of mere laws" (Heidegger 2000: 26). So while Heidegger would agree with Thoreau that mere obedience to the law constrains freedom, he also opposes the elevation of independence to a quality in its own right, and the arbitrariness of independence for independence's sake. Freedom, for humans, cannot be independent of the condition they are in. Instead, freedom exists in relation to what humans do not determine and to what is not human. There is only freedom *in*, but not freedom *from*.

In the ascetic absence of more direct sensual human relations, both Thoreau and Kaczynski shift their awareness further outwards to senses more geared toward the distance, which are also those employed when watching a film or a video: looking and listening. *Stemple Pass* concludes with Kaczynski's affirmation of nature as enabling perception, an "alertness and openness of one's senses" that allows one to see and hear the diversity of autonomous nonhuman life in relations that exist independently of humans and of technology:

> What is significant is that when you live in the woods, rather than just visiting them, the beauty becomes part of your life, rather than something you just look at from the outside. Part of the intimacy with nature that you acquire is the sharpening of the senses. Not that your hearing and eyesight become more acute, but you notice things more. In city life, you tend to be turned inward. Your environment is crowded with irrelevant sights and sounds and you just

> get conditioned to block most of them out of your consciousness. In the woods you get so that your awareness is turned outward, towards your environment, hence you are much more conscious of what goes on around you.

Benning here suggests, by way of Kaczynski, that the environment generates the perceptions of those who are immanent to it. Through Kaczynski and Thoreau, Benning confronts human liberties with nonhuman aesthetics, concomitantly discounting looking and listening as mere phenomenological sense perception. Nature's beauty "consists not only in sights and sounds, but in an appreciation of the whole thing," Benning reads Kaczynski: "as usual, I was strongly aware of the beauty of the place. It must be understood that this beauty does not consist only in what is seen with the eye and heard with the ear. It is involved with a sense of freedom."

In transcendentalism too the emphasis on experience is not merely phenomenological: "Always scorn appearances" advises Emerson (1841). Given the importance of independent choice for Emerson, he sees no virtue in perception, because it cannot be chosen and is involuntary. Merely seeing something would only be superficial. It needs to be experienced with the heart as well as with the eyes; internally as well as externally: "few adults can see nature. Most persons do not see the sun. At least they have a very superficial seeing. The sun illuminates only the eye of the man, but shines into the eye and heart of the child" (Emerson 1836: 11). The "inward and outward senses" (ibid.), as Emerson calls them, are adjusted to and transcend one another.

In his answer to his question of how does "unconcealing happen, if it is not merely the making of humans?" (Heidegger 2000: 19), Heidegger sounds transcendentalist: "Wherever man opens his eyes and ears, unlocks his heart, and gives himself over to meditating and striving, shaping and working, entreating and thanking, he finds himself everywhere already brought into the unconcealed" (Heidegger 1977: 18). Being brought into the unconcealed as a human does not happen through an objective or a subjective human narrative, but through awareness (Heidegger 2000: 19). This is perhaps where Benning's open-minded mode of looking and listening is less like the individualist observations of Thoreau and more like a Heideggerian unconcealing—even if this is an unconcealing of the individualist observations of Thoreau. We need to look and listen to what is ownmost to technology "rather than merely stare at the technological" (33).

Rather than merely bringing the gallery visitor into the moral standing reserve of an advocacy documentary, she is brought into an assemblage with other human and nonhuman things and objects that is both ethical and material. In the mental and material space between the huts in the images and those in the gallery, and the time that the documentaries allow between the human narration, we are called upon to ask what freedom means in these relations, from whom or from what we need to be independent in order to be ethical and, ultimately, how or if independence and materialism could intra-act. Benning's videos in the context of the exhibition take the question of the ethics of independence into a contemporary environment. They introduce ethics into the gallery and ask us to address responsibility when, not only the context of art, but also the enframing through media technology have detached us from it. When Benning reads that Brown "was more than a match for all the judges that American voters, or office-holders of whatever grade, can create. He could not have been tried by a jury of his peers, because his peers did not exist," this characterization of independence as an independence from representation can be taken as an appeal to think of moral independence more in terms of ethical singularity. Benning's reading of Brown, who practiced his independence in defending the freedom of those who had been denied it, is relevant at a time where independence movements hark back to an imaginary union of the same and are united in directing violence against those who they regard as less than equals. The current recasting of civil disobedience and civil rights as un-American would be much to the chagrin of the American transcendentalists. By juxtaposing the not only heroic Thoreau with the not only mad Kaczynski, *Concord Woods* and *Stemple Pass* ask how ethical independence is, or whether we can only be ethical by being independent.

Notes

1. My translation from *Die Kunst und der Raum* (Heidegger 2007).
2. Since in its only available translation into English (Heidegger 1977) *Wesen* has been translated as "essence," thereby encouraging an inappropriately essentialistic interpretation, I have translated "*Wesen*" as "what is ownmost," and the translations from the German original published in 2000 (Heidegger 2000) are my own. Where the translation is agreeable, I have referred to the 1977 edition.

Works Cited

Arendt, Hannah [1970] (1972), "Civil Disobedience," in *Crises of the Republic*, San Diego, New York, and London: Harcourt Brace & Company.
Ault, Julie (2011), "Freedom Club," in Julie Ault (ed.), *(FC) Two Cabins by JB*, New York: A.R.T. Press.
Barad, Karen (2007), *Meeting the Universe Halfway: Quantum Physics and the Entanglement of Matter*, Durham, NC: Duke University Press.
Bennett, Jane (1994), *Thoreau's Nature. Ethics, Politics and the Wild*, Thousand Oaks, London, and New Delhi: Sage Publications.

Bennett, Jane (2001), *The Enchantment of Modern Life. Attachments, Crossings, and Ethics*, Princeton and Oxford: Princeton University Press.

Benning, James (2008), "Life is Finite," *Wexner Centre for the Arts*, September 30, 2008, http://wexarts.org/blog/more-voices-filmmaker-james-benning (last accessed October 23, 2016).

Cavell, Stanley (1981), *Pursuits of Happiness: The Hollywood Comedy of Remarriage*, Cambridge, MA and London: Harvard University Press.

Cavell, Stanley (2003), *Emerson's Transcendental Etudes*, edited by David Justin Hodge. Stanford, CA: Stanford University Press.

Dunlevy, T'Cha (2014), "RIDM: Director James Benning on the Art of Observation," *Montreal Gazette*, November 12, http://montrealgazette.com/entertainment/movies/ridm-director-james-benning-on-the-art-of-observation (last accessed October 23, 2016).

Emerson, Ralf Waldo (1836), *Nature*, Boston: James Munroe and Company.

Emerson, Ralph Waldo (1841), "Self-Reliance," www.emersoncentral.com/selfreliance.html (last accessed October 23, 2016).

Haraway, Donna J. (1991), "A Cyborg Manifesto: Science, Technology, and Socialist-Feminism in the Late Twentieth Century" [1983] in Donna J. Haraway, *Simians, Cyborgs and Women: The Reinvention of Nature*, London: Free Association Books.

Harman, Graham (2002), *Tool-Being. Heidegger and the Metaphysics of Objects*, Chicago and La Salle: Open Court.

Harman, Graham (2010), "Technology, Objects and Things in Heidegger," *Cambridge Journal of Economics* 34(1): 17–25.

Heidegger, Martin (1977), *The Question Concerning Technology and other Essays*, New York and London: Garland Publishing.

Heidegger, Martin (2000), "Die Frage nach der Technik," in *Gesamtausgabe. I. Abteilung: Veröffentlichte Schriften 1910–1976: Band 7. Vorträge und Aufsätze*, Frankfurt am Main: Vittorio Klostermann.

Heidegger, Martin (2005), *Gesamtausgabe. III. Abteilung: Unveröffentlichte Abhandlungen: Band 79. Bremer und Freiburger Vorträge*, Frankfurt am Main: Vittorio Klostermann.

Heidegger, Martin (2007), *Die Kunst und der Raum. L'Art et l'espace*, Frankfurt am Main: Vittorio Klostermann.

Hodge, Joanna (1995), *Heidegger and Ethics*, London and New York: Routledge.

Kaczynski, Theodore J. (1985), "The Communiques of Freedom Club," http://wildism.org/rca/items/show/10 (last accessed October 23, 2016).

Kaczynski, Theodore J. (2008), *Technological Slavery: The Collected Writings of Theodore J. Kaczynski, a.k.a. "The Unabomber"*, Port Townsend: Feral House, https://archive.org/details/tk-Technological-Slavery (last accessed October 23, 2016).

Latour, Bruno (1993), *We Have Never Been Modern*, Cambridge, MA: Harvard University Press.

Latour, Bruno (2004), *Politics of Nature: How to bring the Sciences into Democracy*, Cambridge, MA and London: Harvard University Press.

Rothman, William (1997), *Documentary Film Classics*, Cambridge, MA, New York, and Melbourne: Cambridge University Press.

Rothman, William (2004), *The "I" of the Camera: Essays in Film Criticism, History, and Aesthetics*, Cambridge and New York: Cambridge University Press.

Schulz, Kathryn (2015), "Pond Scum. Henry David Thoreau's Moral Myopia," *The New Yorker*, October 19, www.newyorker.com/magazine/2015/10/19/pond-scum (last accessed October 23, 2016).

Thoreau, Henry David (1851), "Walking," http://thoreau.eserver.org/walking1.html (last accessed October 23, 2016).

Thoreau, Henry David (1854), "Slavery in Massachusetts," http://thoreau.eserver.org/slavery.html (last accessed October 23, 2016).

Thoreau, Henry David (1859), "A Plea for Captain John Brown," http://thoreau.eserver.org/plea.html (last accessed October 23, 2016).

Thoreau, Henry David [1854] (1995), *Walden; or, Life in the Woods*, New York: Dover Thrift Publications.

Thoreau, Henry David (1906), *The Journal of Henry David Thoreau*, ed. Bradford Torrey and Francis Allen, 14 vols., Boston: Houghton Mifflin.

Thoreau, Henry David (2009), *The Journal of Henry David Thoreau, 1837–1861*, edited by Damion Searls, New York: New York Review Books.

Thoreau, Henry David [1848] (2014), *Civil Disobedience*, LaVergne: Black & White Classics.

Walls, Laura Dassow (1995), *Seeing New Worlds: Henry David Thoreau and Nineteenth-Century Natural Science*, Madison: University of Wisconsin Press.

Walls, Laura Dassow (2011), "From the Modern to the Ecological: Latour on Walden Pond," in Axel Goodbody and Kate Rigby (eds.), *Under the Sign of Nature: New European Approaches*, Charlottesville: University of Virginia Press, pp. 98–110.

FELICITY COLMAN

The Earth as Material Film: Benning's Light Glance Making a Material-Image

> Even the most advanced tools and machines are made of the raw matter of the earth.
>
> Robert Smithson 1968: 101

> Does filming a landscape produce a face of the earth?
>
> Elke Marhöfer 2012: 49

> That's so brilliant, to make a film that would require such concentration that you would notice paint drying. And then to actually feel the way the paint dries, the way light would come off the wall in a different way when it's [wet and dry]: as that transformation comes I think you could learn a lot about light.
>
> James Benning in conversation with Nick Bradshaw 2013, n.p.

At first glance, the films of James Benning appear anachronistic in their scenarios. In the films *Ten Skies* (2004); *13 Lakes* (2005); *casting a glance* (2007); RR (2008); *small roads* (2011); *Twenty Cigarettes* (2011); *Faces* (2010); *Stemple Pass* (2012); *BNSF* (2012); *measuring change* (2016), lengthy durational shots from a fixed camera observe a scene, vista, object, or person, and present a slow-moving landscape photographic portrait of something. *casting a glance* begins with a fixed-camera shot of a body of water. The sound of the water lapping the blue-toned salt crystals is held until the first cut to black, with the the inter-title of "April 30, 1970," followed by another fixed shot, this time pulled back to reveal the location, the Great Salt Lake, Utah; situated by the unmistakable form of Robert Smithson's Spiral Jetty, itself completed in 1970. The birds of 1970 sing sweetly to the viewer, and the affective compression of the future history of this site is heard exquisitely in their song. This shot shares the same color tones as Smithson's own 1970 film *Spiral*

Jetty, where the inexplicable qualities of the Utah landscape emerge through Smithson's Passaic–Manhattan modeling (Smithson 1970). Benning's focus is different; the filming of this form and its temporal states, rather than its milieu (as Smithson's film), reveals its material complexities. Benning addresses the Jetty's on-site conditions; from its inception in 1970 to the time of this film, premiered at Documenta 12, 2007. He visits the site sixteen times between 2005 and 2007. The Jetty is only visible when there is a drought—extreme low tide, which happened around the period of Benning's filming. We observe that Benning's processes of generating these images—through and over the historical period of making—structured by fixed shots, articulates a minimalist elegance, created by the spare framing, restricted color palette, and subtleness of camera movement, the framing, editing, and micro-manipulation of the image. The material elements of crystals, rocks, water, air, sun; animals, insects, plants, and bodies; and their sounds, shapes, and colors are processed into materialized forms, their energy actualized into infrastructural elements and configurations, and they are made to do all the technical work through the lens, filters, and editing of the photographic processes. Combined, all elements cast light, throw shade, and move, enabling us to see the solids and liquids that generate sound audition, and provide a perceptual scale for the human and camera eye. The landscapes under surveillance appear in great detail, with objects picked out in sharp relief by the camera's focal lengths. In *casting a glance*, *BNSF*, and *measuring change*, where human bodies appear, they are either at a distance, or in close range, rendering their predicated gendering immanent to their image. Figures are compressed by these films; scaled-down, and human activities are actualized by the camera into a flat ontology. The human question of why things change is revealed as a false one.

Benning's films begin and end abruptly; their length tied to the durational structuring mechanisms of the site of filming and of the filmmaker's narrative focus. Some temporal patterns may be discernible within the editing rhythms of sound-image (repetition of movements, edited or manipulated patterns), but many are opaque. The temporal lengths of the sound-images are what code the materiality of a particular sound-image, and the viewer waits for the values of that material thing or concept to be revealed. But no instructional, deterministic, or perceptual models for reading are provided; the images simply articulate what unfolds in front of the camera, with no discernable intervention to shape a drama or a story out of the sound-images. Recording freight train movements across North American territory, *BNSF* could pass as surveillance footage. *casting a glance* could be taken as a nature documentary. In contemplating these images, I'm reminded of a phrase from Robert Smithson: "Every object, if it is art, is charged with the rush of time even though it is static, but all this depends on the viewer" (Smithson 1968: 112). But the implicit hierarchy in Smithson's idea that an object may only be affective for a particular kind of "viewer" causes me to question further the attribution of meaning to a film, as an object, thing, form, or idea; rendered through a causal responsiveness of perception; the question is how, not why or what.

At second glance, then, the eye becomes aware of the lustrous landscaping at work. The films engaging the earth glow with light. The light appears. Our first glance was too hasty; these images may use the sun and industrial light sources but they are defining an as yet unknown time-scale. Light is the element from which the image-forms emerge. This is particularly evident in the light conditions as observed in *BNSF* and *casting a glance*. The light colors each frame as it shifts the relationality between molded forms; as it traces and articulates the organic and the nonorganic. Light is the subject, one could surmise; light matter itself, and its radiating energy spectrum. The subject of light is a component of the grammar of the aesthetics of light in film (cf. Aumont et al. 1992; Bozak 2011: 35–49), which can be described with a "painterly" aesthetic in an art historical system (see Landau 2014: 191), but this plastic comparison does not seem adequate to address this type of film form. In terms of the physics of light, which is what the photographer and filmmaker deal with on a practical level, light is the radiation that occurs within an electromagnetic spectrum, visible to the human eye in terms of color hues. Radiation is the energy given off by matter; it can bend, or move in superimposed waves (creating bands of light, observable as colors), or act like particles that jump around, according to the kind of field they are in.

How is a potential change in the consciousness of the situation and sight of an image concentrated in the "perception" of something that continuously moves? Like other forms of radiation, light has been theoretically modeled using diffraction and interference patterns that map spatially the patterns and forms it makes as it travels; through disturbances in known spectra. Moving in waves results in light (like sound or water) making diffractive patterns (Barad 2007: 73–85). In Benning's films, the light subject contributes to the spatializing practice of the image, where superimposed layers of light build an aesthetic of light. In physical terms, such observations could be made and developed, situating the films within another kind of media communication history, one that explores the material ways in which the light registers and the image is rendered. These are not scientific, observational films, although their form brings allusions of that genre. Rather, in their approach to the actualization of the moving sound-images, Benning's films provide us with a modal method of film practice, as art surveillance engaging a mutable light gestalt.

To be rendered as image and perceivable as a modal method at its most base is an actualization of something. Modal thinking is, as Hans Poser argues, "a means to see and transform the world" (Poser 2013: 79). There are many different forms of modal thinking (logical—such as the "logic" of a conflict-resolution narrative genre; semantic—the semiotics of a given genre; material; speculative; etc.), useful for film analysis, and the ways in which we can address the notion of "the image"—as analogically, digitally, or algorithmically produced (Colman 2016). Whatever the technology used to render a particular image, its platform reminds us that there is always a speculative aspect to the contingency of perception; a not-infallible technical, as well as political, modeling that may be as simple as the question of access to a site; the where and how of where a camera can be, before the modality can enable the light to become an image. When films use a material modality to produce images, this materialized image defines both a political zone, and a position within that zone, and is also productive of its own material ontology, which may yet be something outside of an existing classification. The modal operation of the filmic structure waits for the light to actualize something. In *casting a glance* for example, where chronological time indicators are used for scene structuring, the light will produce a material-image of a duration. In the light's materialization of forms and matter—through the technology of film—an openness to wondering within the perception of those material images is enabled further—notwithstanding its recorded time. The image remains unknowable in its entirety at any given point. The glance toward what the light forms enable is an actualization of matter, as an always partially materialized image.

We could discuss a light aesthetic in every film where material elements within a specific scene are made into form by the film's modal schema, new dimensions of singular forms are revealed or made, and a hylomorphic light model emerges. In *casting a glance*, the form that the viewer recognizes as the artwork entitled *The Spiral Jetty* is seen through the focus that is actioned by the camera's attention to light. The light is the modal tool that engages this form, and produces a "perceivable" model in its situation and conditions of light, which change according to the position of the apparatus making the image; the light of and in the film makes the image and makes it visible, revealing as it does the topological features that surround and enable the structure and multiple facets of the form (the Jetty in this case, sheltered by the arm of Rosel Point). The camera enables our glancing to perceive, to strain in the darkness, shadows, the depth of clouds, the sun, opaque water, salt crystals, basalt, and the matter of the surrounding Utah desert (Colman 2006: 170). Benning's camera does not give us a standard "documentary" film view of what this site denotes, although we might recognize the form of site-generated content. The meaning of the matter as film is contingent upon the indexical modeling of the forms-made-images, as made by Benning's time frames.

Light is the key to many films that engage landscapes as their core *mise-en*-scenic elements. In the opening scene of *La Terra Trema* (Visconti 1948),

Figure 13 From casting a glance, *2007 (I)*. Courtesy of the artist and neugerriemschneider, Berlin

Figure 14 From casting a glance, *2007 (II)*. Courtesy of the artist and neugerriemschneider, Berlin

the viewer must wait for the sun to rise to be able to discern the territory into which the narrative titles and the *mise-en-scène*'s audio guide perception. Visconti throws no extra light onto the landscape. The time of waiting in the dark requires viewers to use their other senses, in order to form knowledge of what activities are taking place, and where. Describing each of Benning's films in terms of genre does not advance our understanding of modalities of perception; when it is the light that is designing the topology as it unfolds, or closes in on itself, enabling the activities of the locale to take place (the trains across the Utah desert, the tidal movements of the Great Salt Lake, or in Eastern Sicily, the tidal oceans and the fishermen driving the hapless tuna to shore in Aci Trezza; or the not-so-simple observation of the sun setting). The territorial boundaries of each specific site—prehistoric pluvial lake site, or *frazione*—produces perceptual modalities that lend an *a priori* coherence to the films, as given by their kinship systems (which might provide a more specific epistemology to the images)—revealed by the light on and in its technological platforms. Smithson further reminds us: "Not everybody sees the art in the same way, only an artist viewing art knows the ecstasy or dread, and this viewing takes place in time" (Smithson 1968: 112). Smithson's position, realized in his earth work and film *Spiral Jetty* (1970)—as the subject and object of Benning's films *casting a glance* and *measuring change*—serves as a caveat for the consideration of a producer and/or artist's Archimedean perspective of the affective nature of their making, as one of the multiple elements that come to comprise the materiality of images that we glance toward.

Engaging the terms of "materialism" in relation to a conception of materialist film and image, we articulate the image as an actualization of the experience of matter. That actualization is a coming into being that has been facilitated by a specific power as the agency of a technology. This narrative writes a different one to a film history that would describe *La Terra Trema* as presenting "melodrama" (Rohdie 2015: 126). Genre classifications provide only part of the meaning of an image's actualization through a specific modal situation of the materials of the film works. To situate the material images of *casting a glance* is to take into account the relations produced by the spectatorial conditions (our own glancing), *and* the technological apparatus, *and* the matter being investigated by Benning, whether light, earth, biospheres, infospheres. Together, these three configure the images that comprise a screen ecology that we label a materialist film by Benning. In our glancing, we are thinking with the physicality of the light matter, and machinic optics comprising the image. Benning's images create screen ecologies that articulate how the matter of the world—in this case, light energy—is something that moves diffractively, and is organized as "visible" according to the power apparatus that enable its actualization (in physical and/or as conceptual form). Focusing here primarily on Benning's light as just one of the different kinds of ecologies discernable in his work (for others, cf. Panse 2013; Vrvilo 2014), we perceive that the material image is created by the filmic use of the elements recorded and traced by the camera; where the light recorded disperses perception of the earth as a materialized film. The light dimensions are recorded and mediated by the camera and the postproduction. The resulting material-images—as made by and in the human-traversed environment—give rise to an articulation of the visual grammar that accompanies viewing modes, rituals of exchange, and relations of all kinds. The time paradigms and the situations contribute the ecological elements that enable exchanges to occur within the filmic duration. All of these produce a specific practice of communication, but at the material level we can explore the methods of using the materials of the earth to generate film.

Thinking with Karen Barad, we describe the film image as an image that is made through a diffractive process, which is the result of recorded moments of light particles and waves that move within a specific context—in this case a film's technical ecological apparatuses (content production, camera, the editing process, distributive factors)—to "illuminate" something (Barad 2003: 803)—in every sense of the word. Consideration of the modalities and moving energy of images in this sense presents an alternative approach to theories of the image that might assert a representational "reality" to be found in it, for example, as in the description of an ontology of an image (Bazin 1960), or as the "creative treatment of actuality" in a documentary film (Grierson 1966: 13). However, as Deleuze argues with Foucault, in dealing with the use of light, and the use of language to describe "the visible" and "the articulable," one should bear in mind that these two are different forms that do not correspond (Deleuze [1985] 1988: 48). Yet as their non-correspondence, perceivable light-spaces are brought together into a diffracted plane of light-space in the editing suite by the modal tools of the filmmaker's use of technologies (film apparatuses). Actualized as a light-space, the constitution of the material image is generative of a recognizable film world (which Deleuze describes as a *mondialization* [worldization] [1985] 1989: 59); one that is visible—as light, and articulable—as a space, or site of novelty and creativity, as well as one of repetition and facilitation, and as well as a recording of destruction. With this three-fold conception of the materialist-image, the proposition concerning how a physical optics can produce meaning is tested by our interpretation of a number of levels of making matter. Light, as Barad explains, can behave like a wave *and* like a particle in its movement (Barad 2007: 29), meaning that it produces a range of different forms. The question of difference of course, holds significance for the interrogation of epistemologies of meaning (72). In the context of Benning's material-image making, his work directs us to the partial sight and situation of making images; these are some building blocks, resonant for consideration of screen ecologies. While Benning's stated method is within the manipulative field of an image as "collage" (Benning in Bradshaw 2013: n.p.), the material-image that his films produce engage the diffractive nature of light matter. Light matter offers its own modality on how to consider what Barad describes in terms of the physics of the illumination by diffractive patters of matter of the "indefinite nature of boundaries," which reveal "shadows in 'light' regions and bright spots in 'dark' regions" (Barad 2007: 93). Barad refers her reader to the "material-discursive" nature of matter, as it is made visible by the manipulation of apparatuses (ibid.), and this is the aspect of what I am calling the material-image that we can observe in films that show images of the visible and the (sometimes) articulable. This actualization of a modality, though, is different to an analytic quest to define a specific ontology or label a "reality." As Benning himself points out:

> it's silly to talk about "complete reality." It's always your point of view what you leave out and where you point the camera ... A lot of people want my films to be that, but they've never been that. They've always been a selection, always been colour-corrected, always been highly manipulated with sound. They've always taken a real point of view from what I believe in, and I am full of prejudice. And those prejudices are on the screen. (Benning, in Bradshaw 2013: n.p.)

In film, whenever information is conveyed it is by the distribution of visual, and audio matter, made into cinematic material through production processes of recording, framing, and moving the relational actions of that matter, over time; by forming it into blocks of scenes of time, it is relayed over a durational span that is determined by the projection/ screen device. The finished film, as distributed, thus communicates something of that matter made into material, but the precise nature of that communication is itself reliant upon its own relational spectatorially contextual field—not just a relational aesthetic, but a technical aesthetic of the elements that come together to form the image. Communication of the meaning of matter is thus found through the action of the energy source; in *casting a glance*, this is the sun, which acts in and out of frame and also influences the action in frame, by setting into motion or dislocating all activities on and off screen. Benning's approach provides a number of segues into an appreciation of an earth aesthetics, wherein a politics of experience, rather than a framework for normative "beauty" or art-for-art's-sake, emerges. This kind of approach to film practice can be seen in other artists (Visconti; Smithson; Marhöfer) whose artwork—in this case film work—offers a systematic expression of the modalities of materiality. In Benning, the focus rests on a number of factors of materialicity concerning the intra-actions of matter; the conductors and apparatuses of technology, bodies, attention (material mindfulness), duration, that generate the image.

The materialist aesthetic that Benning invokes then has a specific range, scale, and duration of forms. He draws from a world; his images generally record what are external to his studio, and employ some post-extra-image construction. Benning's camera appears to slow down time-images, but his recording is through the "real-time" of both analog and digital camera. As the field of quantum relays to us, temporal intervals are not stable entities, and the perception of these are in fact governed through light optics (cf. Weibel and Jansen 2006). The system of vision, as we see in film, is one governed by epistemically formed temporal modalities.

The processes of filming actualize matter and generate images. Through the film processes of making the images, light defines forms, and ascribes meaning to matter, creating a materialist-image. Articulation of the aesthetics of the visible; as specific events, things (the intervals between, and scales of things); attention to the matter made into materials for specific uses (cultural and political rituals; vernacular habits); attention to attention itself—as a structure, as a political aesthetic (for example as a way of distributing resources; of matching activities to resources); attention to the management and measurement of matter, and definition of the temporal conditions of matter, are all ways toward overcoming the abstraction of the visible. In describing the issue of the formulation of the abstract notion of time, for example, Whitehead referred to the necessity of distinguishing between the "crude deliverance of sense-awareness and our intellectual theories" in trying to define the experience of the serial nature of time (Whitehead [1920] 2007: 65). While it is frequently argued that time is the key to understanding the shifts in meaning in the cinema—consideration of the materialist aesthetic of duration must refer to the contextual forms of temporality known and expressed in particular historical eras. A form of collaged duration occurs in Benning's films, one that can be distinguished by the image-forms from those of other materialist filmmakers, such as Vertov's kino editorial-style collage-time, or Smithson's Warholian stylized durational semiotic.

At third glance, Benning's films start to compound their cut matter, making formal structures, giving sense to what are otherwise abstracted shapes of the landscape. This process of joining the observed cuts (as intervals of time), takes time. In mapping an "earth aesthetic," we could draw perhaps on the ways of articulating the observable energies of matter in new materialist practices, in relation to film. In this, Benning contributes to investigations into the question posed in materialist film practices, and taken up in film theory, that of: What is the image?

Benning's films can be positioned by the formal qualities of their structural and materialist properties (Holt 2008 provides an historical narrative for this approach), and while these classificatory titles and their systemic implications provide important logistical and quantitative details, they do not concede much about the viewing experience, or the films themselves. Benning works with film and film materials, and the subject matter of his films is concerned largely with a qualitative ontology, as generated by the materials of the world. In this very particular focus, this type of practice engenders a discussion based on the literacy of new materialist thinking. Benning's film glance begins with an explicit connection to technology, because only technological forms can maintain such an unblinking steady gaze. Second, the lifeworld that the technology allows the viewer to see emerges; the content of the film, as the very matter of the word being addressed, and the conditions of its existence. Third, the rendering, or modeling, of this matter by the technological apparatus is determined by a catalog of production of those material conditions, as well as the contingencies of production. It is through modalities of observation, intuition, logics, epistemic, and deontic factors that the films are created. In recording our glances, as Benning himself does as a witness/participant/respondent to Smithson's art work, then the production, which addresses the technology in operation, and the formal components of the film work (such as attention to styles of framing, repetition, sound design, duration, and rhythm, or address of the genres of plot structure or narrative) enable the observations of the camera, the style of filmmaking, and its political potential to be shown and historically articulated.

Films are not representational mirrors of the filmed events and places, but they depict the dynamics of things through a collective temporality made visible through their technological modalities. The durational effects of Benning's images generate experience of the topological conditions under the sight of the camera. In this, Benning's materialist filmmaking style *One Way Boogie Woogie* (1977); *North on Evers* (1991); *Deseret* (1995); *13 Lakes* (2005); *casting a glance* (2007); *RR* (2008); *small roads* (2011) and the California Trilogy of films: *El Valley Centro* (1999), *Los* (2000), and *SOGOBI* (2001), is in direct and indirect conversation with that of Robert Smithson (*Spiral Jetty* 1970), and with Robert Smithson and Nancy Holt (*Swamp* [1969]; *Mono Lake* [1968–2004]), in terms of their respective filmic emphasis on the material duration of seeing the matter of the Earth, and its organization, as its own materialist film site, and in the case of several of the films, a direct territorial engagement with the physical consistency of materials that Smithson dealt with; all now intra-related.

After identifying this form of materialist methodology, we can begin to summarize the modal concepts that are found in this type of film practice. These include temporal modal methods, such as speculation, logics, events, forms of chance, contingency, and epistemology—each constitutive of situated ontological forms of light. In the terms described by Barad, filmmaking (and all photographic practices) are diffractive apparatuses (Barad 2007: 73–4) that create a specificity of entangled matter: all of the elements that comprise the film image, materialized by light.

Light is used in Benning's films as a technological element; it is a diffractive component and also a modal proposition. Light is an informational orienting generator of images emerging from the elements of the earth and its biosphere. Light creates an informatics-aesthetic. Material film practices open an understanding of the concept of technology as not only conducive to enabling the modeling of forms (the two-slit experiment), but also modalizing the elements that the model plays with. Essential to the creation of the moving sound-image, the artwork [film, etc.] is generative of a specific, topologically situated informatics-aesthetic; discernable through the type of attention it gives to the durational information, and conditioning the matter of the event (where event is inclusive of objects, architecture, ecological and human infrastructures: art, food, water and waste systems, accidents, natural and human-made disasters, etc.). In Benning, the event is the light, which makes the image.

Using the key of Benning's sky palette, a narrative-of-the-earth aesthetic begins to take form. Benning patiently builds the conditions of the site of the film. The camera is set at a fixed location; it does not move, rather the light-world revolves around it. Additional postproduction techniques diffuse more light; the velocity of the images may be manipulated (as in *Faces*), or extra time frames are inserted (see Bradshaw 2013). Performing an illusory omnipotence, the camera records identifiable temporal points: vectors where there is a perceptible change in light registration, or where perhaps a different form populates the scene inside the frame. In the color films, the colors of light that are cast by the sky above the earth sites that his camera films create the light palette and its recognizable forms. The films provide names for the matter of these earth films, as a textuality of materiality, which may be indicative of their narrative and/or structuring focus (*Ten Skies*; *13 Lakes*; *casting a glance*; *RR*; *BNSF*). While orienting narratives of a colonialist, ecological, ritualistic, mythic, dramatic, pathetic, comedic, or technological kind could be inserted by the viewer observing and speculating on the range of activities that are shown by the sound-images in the films, such narratives provide only a partial account of the specific crafted screen ecologies of each film.

In glancing, a structural key is discerned. Shots index and organize light into forms; the earth, salt crystals, rocks, water, animals, humans, machines, clouds, the sun. The light organization creates patterns and forms, determining the key for the movement in each film. The editing choices are not apparent in the final films. An emphasis on temporality determines a part of the changes in the key; obvious at first, overdetermined even; but eventually the image movements devise the ways in which the structuring of the materiality of light matter playing out in the recorded images is ordered, edited, and made into a film. Benning's images are highly controlled and the camera does not falter in its registration of the light. The sound-images are registered in a non-hierarchical plane; where the energy of light determines how Benning's viewer can access the sound-images of humans, plants, earth, sky, water, wind—all of the elements in the film's situation. How and for how long the images are able to be sight-audited is down to the modal contingency of the viewer to which Smithson referred. Ordering of these images occurs through the scale of the shot, the camera's depth and distance from an object or situation, and the length of time that those elements are held in shot. This curiously flat spatialization of time occurs through the modality of actualization, which is contingent upon the technology of film in its bringing of light matter onto or into an entity we refer to as a complete film. The action of looking is to anticipate (a modality of futurity) the light coming. Benning's films thus employ this method of film practice as an anticipation of the energy to come into and from the earth: "A great artist can make art by simply casting a glance" (Robert Smithson 1968: 101).

Works Cited

Aumont, Jacques; Michel Marie; Marc Vernet and John Richard Neupert (1992), *Aesthetics of Film*. Austin: University of Texas Press.

Barad, Karen (2003), "Posthumanist Performativity. Toward an Understanding of How Matter Comes to Matter," in *Signs*, 28(3): 801–31. http://humweb.ucsc.edu/feministstudies/faculty/barad/barad-posthumanist.pdf

Barad, Karen (2007), *Meeting the Universe Halfway: Quantum Physics and the Entanglement of Matter and Meaning*, Durham, NC and London: Duke University Press.

Bazin, André (1960), "The ontology of the photographic image," transl. by Hugh Gray, *Film Quarterly* 13(4): 4–9.

Bozak, Nadia (2011), *The Cinematic Footprint: Lights, Camera, Natural Resources*. New Brunswick, NJ: Rutgers University Press.

Bradshaw, Nick (2013), "James Benning," *Sight & Sound* 23(10): 46–50.

Colman, Felicity (2006), "Affective Entropy: Art as Differential Form." *Angelaki: Journal of Theoretical Humanities* 11(1): 169–78.

Colman, Felicity (2016), "Actions of Feminicity on Film; The Materialization of Forms of the Real," Conference paper given at *"The Real of Reality: International Conference on Philosophy and Film,"* Karlsruhe: ZKM.

Deleuze, Gilles ([1985] 1988), *Foucault*, transl. by Sean Hand. Minneapolis: University of Minnesota Press.

Deleuze, Gilles ([1985] 1989), *Cinema 2: The Time-Image*, transl. by Hugh Tomlinson and Robert Galeta, London: Athlone.

Grierson, John (1966), "First principles of documentary" in Forsyth Hardy (ed.), *Grierson on Documentary*, London: Faber & Faber, pp. 145–56.

Holt, Michael Ned (2008), "James Benning: casting a glance, 2007" review in *X-TRA*, 10(4). [Online]: http://x-traonline.org/article/james-benning-casting-a-glance/.

Landau, David (2014), *Lighting for Cinematography: A Practical Guide to the Art and Craft of Lighting for the Moving Image*. New York: Bloomsbury Academic.

Marhöfer, Elke (2012), "Difference Indifference Anti-difference" in *No, I am not a Toad, I am a Turtle*, Berlin: Archive Books, pp. 45–70.

Panse, Silke (2013), "*Ten Skies, 13 Lakes,* 15 Pools: Structure, Immanence and Eco-aesthetics in *The Swimmer* and James Benning's Land Films," in Anat Pick and Guinevere Narraway (eds.), *Screening Nature: Cinema beyond the Human*, Oxford: Berghahn, pp. 37–59.

Panse, Silke (2013), "Land as Protagonist: An Interview with James Benning," in Anat Pick and Guinevere Narraway (eds.), *Screening Nature: Cinema Beyond the Human*, Oxford: Berghahn, pp. 60–70.

Poser, Hans (2013), "Technology and Modality," in Ludger Bühlmann and Vera Hovestadt (eds.), *Printed Physics—Metalithikum 1*, Vienna: Ambra, pp. 71–112.

Rohdie, Sam (2015), *Film Modernism*, Manchester: Manchester University Press.

Smithson, Robert (1968), "A Sedimentation of the Mind: Earth Projects," in *Artforum*, 7(1): 100–13.

Smithson, Robert, (1970), "The Spiral Jetty," in Nancy Holt (ed.), *Robert Smithson: The Collected Writings*, New York: New York University Press, pp. 109–13.

Weibel, Peter and Gregor Jansen (2006), *Light Art from Artificial Light: Light as a Medium in 20th and 21st Century Art*, Ostfildern: Hatje Cantz Verlag.

Whitehead, Alfred North ([1920] 2007), *The Concept of Nature*, New York: Cosimo.

Vrvilo, Tanja (2014), "James Benning: Memories from the Hands," in Peter Pakesch and Bettina Steinbrügge (eds.), *James Benning –Decoding Fear*, Köln: Walther König, pp. 170–83.

Perceptual Environments

TOM CONLEY

A Lake-Event

> Now, my friend, what do you say about who you are when you believe you're telling me who I am?
>
> Michel de Certeau 1982: 99[1]

It was on a warm and lazy afternoon in 2011, in the last hours of "Technologies of the Garden," a conference held in the spacious Music Room of the Museum at Dumbarton Oaks (Georgetown, Washington, DC) when I first encountered James Benning's cinema. Scott MacDonald offered to the public a viewing of 16 mm prints of three distinctly different "garden movies": Kenneth Anger's *Eaux d'artifice* (1953), an eerily enchanting nocturne shot in the Tivoli Estate, Carolee Schneeman's *Fuses* (1964–7), an erotic idyll in a retreat in a rural New York State recalling episodes of *Orlando furioso*, and the seventh sequence of Benning's *13 Lakes* (2004) presenting a view of the shore and rustling waters of one of Minnesota's land (at least according to words embossed on its license plates) of "10,000 lakes." Initially seductive for many, the séance became unsettling, then disruptive and, ultimately, simply annoying. Composed of well-heeled adepts of manicured gardens around Rock Creek and donors to a collection housing rare objects from pre-Columbian America and the Ottoman Empire, the audience was at first carried away in the mix of haunting music and a nocturnal promenade in the dark shadows of the great Italian Garden. Soon after, so it seemed, to the denizens of Georgetown, the sight of the warm and muscular flesh of two nude lovers squirming and frolicking, taking delight in recording their bliss in a *hortus voluptatis*, was too arousing for comfort. Finally, the public found itself at its wit's end when enjoined to behold a ten-minute take, a single shot or *plan-séquence* (roughly, 58:32–1:08.80) of the sight and sound of the gently wafting waters of lower Red Lake in Beltrami County.

After too much came too little. It seemed that nothing was happening. Under a cloudy sky, in a gentle breeze, for what, depending on the viewer's

Figure 15 From 13 Lakes, 2004. Courtesy of the artist and neugerriemschneider, Berlin

disposition seemed to be a passage either of eons or seconds, the screen became a site of molecular convection. Divided by the horizontal line of the lake itself, the screen appeared equally split between the horizon above and what appeared to be a very shallow body of water below. For reason of seeing and hearing lapping water, some participants relieved themselves and, too, their boredom in making off to nearby rest rooms. Others rustled and fidgeted. By the time the shot came to an end much of the room had been evacuated, leaving only MacDonald and a happy few to consider what they had seen.[2]

For this viewer the introduction to Benning was mystical. On this rare occasion, inside a darkened auditorium, adjacent to an idyllic garden in the warmth of spring sun, the whirring fragment of *13 Lakes* demonstrated to those of us who lived with it the nature and quality of an *event*. An event, maybe, but an event of what kind? If not an event, perhaps less an encounter with something unexpected than, slowly and surely, an inward "turn" of experience? An adventure in sensation and perception? It was moment in which, in the cadre of a professional conference in which performance of intelligence is staged and tested, there remained little to say. *13 Lakes* became a place in which we got lost in seeking to fix our bearings. The sequence asked us to consider what we were doing in wishing to "make sense" of it and, along the way, what it means to contemplate duration through duration itself. In this respect as an event the film brought a political charge into the otherwise happy space of the museum in Washington.

Each of the segments of *13 Lakes* belongs to a series of occurrences or happenings whose virtue, thanks to visual composition, may be located in what they tempt us to make of them and, more so, by way of an art that refuses to indicate what it is doing. How so? In an epochal treatment of Jerome Bosch's *Garden of Earthly Delights*, a triptych that would seem to be at the antipodes of Benning's cinema, Michel de Certeau compared the painting in the northern European wing of the Prado to a sibyl casting its gaze upon its spectators:

> The Garden gazes. It's full of eyes that "consider us" (I've counted at least eight or nine). Everywhere the gaze of the other is looking down. The painting gives not an image in a mirror (in Bosch mirrors are rare and diabolical) but a disquieting privation of images organized by what, on the part of the interrogator, comes from it. As if, entirely transformed into a sibyl, its mouth closed, like a sphinx, [the painting] were saying to the spectator, "Now, my friend what do you say about who you are when you believe you're telling me who I am?" (. . .) The aesthetic of the *Garden* consists not in fomenting the new brilliance of an intelligibility, but of extinguishing it. (Certeau 1982: 99)

Any of the sequences could be addressed from a similar standpoint. Hence a privilege given to a learned ignorance: the duration of the landscape lets us take account of how and where we enter it, in what ways we move about and through it, of what it does with whatever words we would use to fashion—or reify—our impressions of its effects over the time of its passage. Whatever knowledge we bring to it does not go by the wayside: rather, it becomes the very register of an invisible relation, the relation itself becoming a chronicle of the "experience" of the lake. The latter is tied to how the event, the shot of the lake in its duration, acquires unsettling political mettle.

The title that Gilles Deleuze places at the head of the sixth chapter of *Le Pli: Leibniz et le baroque* (1988) appears to be an enigma or a motto to which, as in an emblem, the text below is compelled to respond. He asks, "What is an event?" In the first sentence of the paragraph that stands below, he replies:

> An event is not only "a man is crushed": the great pyramid is an event, and its duration during 1 hour, 30 minutes, 5 minutes . . . a passage of Nature or a view of God. What are the conditions of an event so that everything can be an event? The event is produced in a chaos, in a chaotic multiplicity, but only if a kind of screen comes between. (Deleuze 1988: 103)

An event is not merely something that happens, that falls or drops but, rather, something that extends. It can extend so as to become duration itself, but in the chaos of its origin it can be discerned only through a screen or webbing. Having just referred to A. N. Whitehead's suggestive remark that there can be a "passage of Nature" in a given place (99), and having noted when the passage is felt it "appears in the subject as a change of perception" (94), Deleuze soon remarks that chaos can be thought of both as a "sum of possibles" and an agglomeration of depthless shadows [*le chaos serait les ténèbres sans fond*]. The "world only exists folded in the monads, and is unfolded only virtually as the common horizon of all monads" (101). The high degree of abstraction in the words suggests that the printed writing itself makes chaos visible, or perhaps that an implied screen—the screen on which, in ideal circumstances, *13 Lakes* is projected—would be the chaos from which emerges the "folds," pleats, waves, and roiled forms of a cinematic lake- or landscape.

In his paragraphs that follow, three components of the event—here affiliated with the sensation and perception of seepage of time and creation of space in any and all of Benning's lakes—are distinguished. The first, *extension*, is "prehended" (in other words, not grasped or "apprehended" digitally, or simply through tactility, but sensed and shared in a "nexus of prehensions" or multiple sensations on the part of both subject and object or perceiver and perceived), notably:

> when one element extends over those that follow, in such a manner that it is a whole, and those that follow, its parts. A connection of parts-wholes forms an infinite series that has neither a final term nor a limit (if we neglect the limits of our senses). The event is a vibration with an infinite number of harmonics or of sub-multiples, such as a sound wave, a luminous wave, or even an area of space becoming smaller and smaller over a smaller and smaller duration. (Deleuze 1988: 105)

In refusing the temptation of allegory that would make common sense of the image, the spectator of the Minnesota Lake follows a clear and decisive line of demarcation, set midway in the frame between water and sky, that refuses both to dissolve and to indicate a receding perspective. Although of great depth of field, the shot allows water and sky to be discerned as rectangular blocks of approximately equal surface area. Toward the right hand side the line thickens, where an visible mass of land—or merely a thin swath of black—is all that is needed to suggest that the view is of a lake (or at least a body of water into which a peninsula might be projecting) and not a sea or ocean. The mass of cumulous clouds of an equal altitude in the foreground lead into a softer area at the back where, dropping to the waterline, they suggest that rain is falling. In the upper left side area, below where the sunshine could break through the clouds, reflections illuminate the beige tinge of slightly roiled waters over which, in the foreground, a shadow of something unknown is projected. The experienced viewer of extended seascapes would wish to find the line of demarcation very slightly arching downward, thus attesting to the curvature of the globe, in other words, to be assured of a closed totality of our world, where in the time we feasted on comic strips like Milton Caniff's *Terry and the Pirates* we learned how sailors marooned on desert islands saw in the distance a jolly roger fluttering from a mast that seemed to spring not from a boat but from the water itself. Here no one populates the lake-scape, nor does the view yield any sign of the globe or world at large. The straight and flat line, distinguished from those of waves that cut into the frame from the lower right corner, implying a stretch well beyond the two sides of the frame, is continuous. It becomes an attribute of the lake as an event that is both within and exceeds a containing frame.

If there is neither limit nor term to the connection of wholes and parts of the tableau, as the design of the shot implies, the horizon line extends well beyond the frame. If, too, we think of how the gentle breeze is in harmony with waves in the foreground, the scene acquires the second attribute of an event, when the flow of its time (the lapping of the water) and space (the changing patterns of the clouds) qualifies as a force of intension:

> The event is a vibration that carries an infinity of harmonics or of submultiples, such as a sound wave, a light wave, or even a piece of space becoming smaller and smaller over a shorter and shorter duration. For space and time are not at all limits but abstract coordinates of every kind of series, themselves in extension: the minute, the second, the tenth of a second... From there we can consider a second component of the event; ... these are no longer extensions but, as we have seen, intensions, intensities, degrees. (105)

It takes time to discern zones, climes as it were, minuscule differences, tonal variations of air and water. In an almost Lucretian fashion our eyes become inclined to sense particles of atmosphere in motion. A gamut of intensities is felt in what would be the molecular distribution of visibly textured matter. And so also, by way of a sense of layering of surfaces set over each other according to "degrees" of latitude, there would be the presence of a world changing according to the relation that its "zones" (frigid, temperate, torrid) hold with each other. The lake becomes the world on which are floating and drifting ever-changing islands. The lake-event would be the sensation of distributions of intensities, of molar and molecular differences, that our imagination would relate to medieval world maps of thermal zones that isolate masses of land in the flow of water circulating between frigid, temperate, and torrid zones. Where the various lakes suggest different "degrees" of atmospheric differences they are continually "beginning" and "becoming."[3]

In the same breath a third component of the event becomes manifest: the individual. In the film it is the singular and individual lake, taken to be a "creation," or what Whitehead called a "concrescence" of telluric elements. A *prehension*, it becomes the "datum" of another that prehends it, and thus in a field of differences each prehension acquires an "individual unity." Every single thing "prehends its antecedents and its concomitants" (105). As if preferring not to conceptualize the process, the philosopher lets examples take precedence over explication:

> The eye is a prehension of light. Living beings prehend water, earth, carbon and salts. At a given moment, the pyramid prehends Bonaparte's soldiers (forty centuries are contemplating you), and reciprocally. We can say that "echoes, reflections, traces, prismatic deformations, perspectives, thresholds, folds" are prehensions that somehow anticipate psychic life. (. . .) But the datum, the prehended, is itself a pre-existing or co-existing prehension, such that every prehension is a prehension of prehension, and the event, a "nexus of prehensions." (106)

In Benning's film the division of the image between the slightly stormy air and roiled water—a calmer version of the troubled skies above the frothy rivers of Ruisdael's landscapes—suggests that molecules are passing across the horizon line, and that imperceptible "prehensions" are occurring everywhere, not only in the image, but also, for reason of the duration of the shot itself, in what we are making of it. An "individual" sense of "self-enjoyment" results from how the lake is lived, or perhaps how, in concord with the viewer's meditative disposition, the framing and composition draw attention to our experience of time and space. The difficult pleasure of the long take also owes to the absence of any human subject, which makes the event possible. Without human interference—although indications of human presence can be seen and heard in at least six or seven of the sequences—the visibility of the scene becomes palpable.[4]

Three components: extension, intensions or "degrees," and a nexus of prehensions. Where extension, harmonics, degree, and concrescence are a measure of the event, both during and after the viewing of any one of the thirteen lakes, we can feel a latent politics emerging in questions that we unconsciously ask of ourselves: when do we give ourselves a similar amount of time to contemplate a lake? (Almost never.) What are the occasions that allow us to discern the play of molecular aggregation and dispersion? (Practically none.) How can fluvial landscapes be contemplated when urban experience is the mean of life? (In front of a computer-screen or, in greater unlikelihood, in a movie theatre.) What does the long take of ten minutes indicate about our sense of time? (That perhaps media and spectacle have curtailed our span and scope of attention.) What are the effects of the film twelve years after its production, especially in the third sequence in which the image roars when jet-skis zoom along the median line or, in the fourth, where it is slowly traversed by a freighter load with taconite pellets? (Greater concern about the effects of global warming.)

Our encounter with each of the tableaus calls in question both the place that is shown and, from an implicitly psychoanalytical angle, the mental provinces "from where" we look at it. The meditation or "serene state of mind" that each of the takes requires for its appreciation somehow begs us to identify the lake in question. Seeking to discern *where* the lake is found and *why* it might be in an American landscape, jogging through memories of lush and glossy photographs between the yellowing covers of *National Geographic*, we rack our brains for a toponym to match what we see. We turn the unsettling character of a mental landscape into its geographical game of identification. When named in the experience of its duration each lake inspires a gamut of other questions: first, because each body of wafting or rolling water gives way to another. Through their difference and repetition, we tend to imagine each of the takes to be dioramas reminiscent of those in the darkened halls of the James Ford Bell Museum or the American Museum of Natural History that consumed our imagination through our childhood. Intellect tells us that each lake could become a *stanza* (or topical room) of a visual poem. Because of the "degrees" of atmosphere, of latitude and of longitude, and of the explicit serenity and implicit topography, the meditation is both situated and peripatetic.

The emergence of the film's geography could be tied to an implicitly geological or thick "history" of the lakes and their environs. Within the experience of their duration the sequence shots of the lakes can be imagined without having discernible "beginnings." They remind us that in the absence of an inaugural event there can be no historical time, and that without a beginning, history—even geological history—simply cannot be. Some kind of "enunciation" has to begin the beginning (Certeau 2013: 127). But where? The paratactic design of the film has it beginning over and again.[5] Only when it is "begun" to be perceived at a limit of phenomenal time, bereft of reference to an inaugural event, each lake becomes a continuous counterpart. The intervals in black that frame the lakes confirm that they belong to a process of continual recommencement, each tableau coming into view *ex nihilo*.

From this angle we are teased into becoming media-archaeologists wishing to grasp the longer duration of the lake and its environs. A geological occurrence would attribute a cause to the design of what is seen (for the Midwestern lakes: a history of glaciation would explain the flatness and the shallow depth of the waters; for the mountain lakes: the turmoil and thrust of igneous or metamorphic rock would produce the crevasses, rifts and valleys now filled with water). No matter what, with or without the knowledge that would locate the Lake in the history of creation, refusing to let what is seen be turned into a scientific object, we are invited to consider it in a mystical frame. The lake "speaks," it becomes solicitous, it whispers to us through the lapping of waters and thrusts of waves; or, like a silent oracle, the ambient landscape remains still and silent, notably along the jagged line of mountainous backgrounds. It is up to us to invent the relation that through faith we invest in the patience of letting our inner reflections respond to what we see.

The intervals in black that enable us to view the lakes over and again have antecedents in other films, notably in the final shots of *Landscape Suicide* (1986) and, more recently, in the divisions of the four seasons in *Stemple Pass* (2012). In the former—without there being any reference to the grisly handiwork of Ed Gein, a commanding figure in much of the film—a hunter in an aspen grove in Wisconsin in late Fall guts a doe—the crack of gunfire on the sound track has just suggested—that he shot instants ago. It takes a leap of faith (or a nudge of prurience) to associate the hunter kneeling by the felled beast with Gein. In place of pursuing the analogy we are invited to attend to the editing of the footage. Stop-action takes record how he dresses the deer. Armed with a knife and *savoir faire*, the hunter goes about what he has to do: he cuts an incision into the belly, removes the entrails from the cavity of the ribcage, and extracts the liver and heart (edible organs) before setting the bloody viscera on the cover of white snow (see Figure 8, p. 68); finally, he splits the end of the spine before separating the hind quarters. The minimal time-lapses accelerate the operation, which clearly shows that the hunter is an artisan and that what he does requires handiwork that might be comparable to that of editing. In the latter, in *Stemple Pass*, a film whose camera focuses on the somewhat bucolic landscape and retreat in which Ted Kaczynski, another murderer, wrote a chronicle of how and why he manufactured letter-bombs, similar interstices in black connote seasonal change, but not in a cycle of the kind in almanacs or *horæ* that follow the months of the year or, say, the predictable (and tiresome) composition of Garrison Keillor's *Lake Wobegone Days* (1985), in which temporal succession is implied to be both God-given and evidence of divine presence (especially where readers would like to hear in the words they scan the lilt and lull of the preacher's voice heard on *The Prairie Home Companion*).

In the three films—*Landscape Suicide*, *13 Lakes*, and *Stemple Pass*—the cinematic image is simply begun by being "there," each take inventing the "world" afresh, each image bearing no syntactical or locative connection with what precedes or what follows. A condition marking the modern world, the process implies that perception and our will to make sense of things begin in duration. As an event, the lake "takes place" in the micro-perceptions that are felt as infinitesimal punctuation in a continuum.[6] When considered in spatial terms, the punctuation of the three films has affinities with topography insofar as, in the inaugural sentences of his *Geographia*, one of the original world atlases, Ptolemy notes that a landscape or a limited figuration of the world is *not* connected to a whole, and that it is an isolated piece.[7] When applied to *13 Lakes* an implied totality is sensed only when the names of places can be identified, but because minuscule variations in texture and atmosphere become commanding, the locations of the sites tend to float and then dissolve in what might be a mystical geography.[8]

It is for this reason that this paper began with an allusion to Bosch's *Garden of Earthly Delights*, a painting that would seem to be at the antipodes of Benning's film. Like the great panel in the Prado, *13 Lakes* might be a place where we find refuge in getting lost. Or, conversely, in finding one's bearings; it comes as little surprise that *13 Lakes* claims an alcove in the American Registry of Films. Following a simultaneously conscientious and passive viewing of the film in its entirety, the spectator cannot fail to consider the thirteen takes as a geographical essay. Prompting a comparison of sky, texture and atmosphere of the lake-scapes through their juxtaposition with each other, the mosaic aspect of the feature begs the viewer to "map" the ensemble and, as a consequence, to construct and to chart a sensory itinerary. At each of its sites the film begs a variety of questions. What or which lake and why? How have I moved through it? Where have I been distracted, and when did I fell asleep or wake up? If what I have seen is a geography lesson, how ought I connect my impressions of the parts and pieces to gain a sense of a coherent whole? Am I witnessing a document depicting great places belonging to an American patrimony? Thirteen "American" lakes, thirteen instances of America the beautiful, but also, in the presence of jet-skis, jetties and bridges, America under the yoke of industry and development?

It is from the standpoint of the last two questions that the *curieux*, the doubting, intellectually impatient, inquisitive viewer born of the legacy of the Renaissance, the viewer who cannot be done without *naming* and categorizing an object, might hasten to make limited sense of the film.[9] To locate each of the lakes—to confer *names* upon them or to attach them to coordinates of latitude and longitude—would amount to a gesture of symbolization and spatial continuity. Thus pinpointed on an implicit map, the event that had been the lake turns into an object of study. The locative gesture betrays the fact that the experience of the lakes is unsettling, and that the pleasure of living with them can be acknowledged only obliquely, through science and erudition. From this standpoint, for the cause of the mystical character of the experience, a first reaction—or an initial critical gesture—would put the *spaces* that the long takes of the lakes have created into discrete and proper *places*.

This is exactly what is given in the critical reception of the film: alert viewers have identified the names of the thirteen lakes in as many states (as if the cipher might allude to a founding figure, like the colonies, of great American Lakes). Or perhaps, in the spirit of symmetry and spatial logic belonging to the arcana of emblems, the odd and prime number of the title might accord to one of the lakes a secret place, *a mise en abîme* in the whole, when a central lake (Okeechobee?)

in the sum of thirteen is abutted by even units (six) on either side.[10] Or perhaps they are chosen to suggest the perimeters of a space whose cardinal points might be, to the east: Maine (Moosehead) and New York (Oneida); to the north: Michigan (Lake Superior) and Minnesota (Lower Red Lake); to the south, Pontchartrain (Louisiana); to the west, California (Salton Sea) and Oregon (Crater Lake); to the southeast, Okeechobee (Florida); to the southwest, Powell (Arizona); to the west (in the spirit of manifest destiny), Wyoming (Jackson Lake); near the middle, in the sense of an umbilical point, an origin, Wisconsin (Winnebago). Once identified and named, the lakes become part of cartographic puzzle belonging to a pedagogical tradition to which the film refers as if unbeknownst to itself.[11] Along this line *13 Lakes* would have affinities for philately. Several of the images in the very recent "National Parks" collection of postage stamps—notably, Glacier Bay National Park and Reserve, Assateague Island National Seashore, Acadia National Park, Everglades National Park and, to a degree, Mount Rainier National Park—resemble the split-screen format whose implicit duration underscores national (and, for the patriotic American citizen, God-given) serenity and beauty.[12] At the end of a viewing of the film the totality of the experience of viewing thirteen oblong time-images generates a feeling of spiritual cohesion that comes with commemoration.

If a cavalier connection can be made between a few of Benning's lakes and the stamps that the United States Postal Service has issued to show how "[o]ur national parks tell distinctly American stories," or how they might "inspire [us] to marvel at grand vistas" and travel along scenic waterways and winding paths," further comparison with *Stemple Pass* sets the film in the inner pleats of an "American" philosophical topography.[13] The filmmaker is known for having constructed a simulacrum of the cabin that in 1845 Thoreau had built near the shore of Walden Pond. A site from which the philosopher could observe the seasonal rhythms of an untrammeled world, *Walden* became a code-word for durative communion with nature before, today, restored and situated not far from a parking lot, adjacent to the revered towns Concord and Lexington, the cabin belongs to a suburban world of Americana tourists who visit *en masse* and come to swim in the Pond. Benning is known for noting how Thoreau embraced "the discipline of looking at what is to be seen." Yet in the same breath, something remains remiss. When Thoreau's replica stands next to Benning's copy of the retreat in which Ted Kaczynski recorded his manufacture and plans for delivery and detonation of his bombs, like Stendhal's famous pistol shot in an opera, and as implied earlier, a politics intercedes. In *Stemple Pass* the transcending effect given in reminders of Thoreau is undercut through the presence of Kaczynski's cabin.[14] As *Stemple Pass* endures through its four seasons, echoes of the "machine in the garden" muffle Thoreau's presence when the whir of a helicopter has connections with the bomber's words, just as, too, the distant sound of semi-trailers, rolling on a nearby road bring into invisible reaches the routes Kaczynski took to deliver his wares.

The mystical tenor of the "events" of the films owes not only to prehensive extension, harmonics and concresence in duration, but also to the contiguities of unsettling and often unnamable elements that belong to a politics both embracing and questioning myths of the nation in which many of the films are made. In this spirit, in recall of the invocation of Bosch's *Garden of Earthly Delights* in the initial paragraphs and elsewhere in this essay, we might imagine how Benning would go about filming Bosch's painting. Would he begin with a fifteen-minute shot of the globe as it is seen when the triptych is closed? And then would there be, over twenty minutes, stop-action shots of the panels unfolding and revealing the central landscape? Finally, over sixty minutes, there could be a still view of the central panel, that by means of digital erasure, the people and things populating the landscape removed, we are left to gaze only upon the terrain and its strange objects in their unreal colors. As the hypothetical viewing continues over a longer duration of time, our memory of what had been there, of the flesh of delirious fantasy and phantasm, would be set in suspension, leaving in the watery regions of the left and central panels disquiet and delight not unlike what each of the thirteen lakes of Benning's feature had put before our eyes.

Notes

1. Here and elsewhere translations from the French are mine.
2. MacDonald's published essay differs from the presentation. In "Gardens of the Moon: The Modern Cine-Nocturne," he notes that after the initial impact of the Industrial Revolution, gardens became states of mind, spaces "within which the soul could rest and be refreshed, where struggling human beings could, at least for a moment, feel free of their burdens and closer to the divine" (MacDonald 2014: 202). Writing against the grain of Leo Marx's *Machine in the Garden,* offering a panorama of cine-nocturnes in the independent mold, he veers away from Anger, Schneeman, and Benning, briefly praising the latter's *13 Lakes* for its thirteen ten-minute shots of as many "American lakes; each rigorously composed, tripod-mounted shot is framed so that the surface of the lake divides the image horizontally in half." *13 Lakes*, he adds, "is cinema as meditation; it requires and rewards a serene state of mind" (204).
3. The spectator has in mind the tradition of the Macrobian world map, inspired through reverie, in Ambrosius Macrobius, *Commentarii Somnium Scipionis* (Brescia: Bonino de' Boninis, 1483), in which continents, distributed in different thermal latitudes, shy away from the torrid zone, and float in an ocean-sea (see Shirley 1987: 12 (entry 13)).

4. In his study of Patrick Keiller's cinema Daniele Rugo has remarked how "[e]xisting space can be observed only in absence of its inhabitants, and simultaneously, the one who observes can do so only by insisting on his own absence from this space, by turning this absence into the point of view" (Rugo 2016: 274–5). The remark reminds us of when Baudelaire, arguing that our imagination makes the landscape, praises Eugène Boudin's paintings: "strangely enough, in front of this liquid or aerial magic, not once did I lament the absence of humans" (Baudelaire 1976: 660). Rugo's remark about point of view has much to do with what makes events possible: "every point of view is point of view on a variation," and in sum it is "the condition in which an eventual subject apprehends a variation" (Deleuze 1988: 27).

5. Apropos geographies of origin Gilles Deleuze remarks, "in the ideal of recommencements there is something that precedes commencement itself, which takes it up again in order to give it greater depth and to send it backward in time (Deleuze 2002: 17).

6. In *Le Post-moderne expliqué aux enfants* (1986), Jean-François Lyotard notes that parataxis is *the* trope of the vernacular world. Further back, in *Mimesis*, in his treatment of the *laisses* of *La Chanson de Roland*, Erich Auerbach notes how the breaks between each unit of the 4,002-line epic draw attention to the condition of a fragmentary (and, by a short leap of the imagination, cinematic) body of perceptions.

7. Ptolemy puts it like this:

> The end of chorography is to deal separately with a part of the whole, as if one were to paint only the eye or the ear by itself. The task of geography is to survey the whole in its just proportions, as one would the entire head ... Accordingly therefore it is not unworthy of chorography, or out of its province, *to describe the smallest details of places*, while Geography deals only with regions and their general features. (In Ptolemy [c. AD 150] 1932: 26–7, emphasis added)

8. In *Cinéma 2*, Gilles Deleuze notes that the interstice distinguishes the "time-image" from the "movement-image," the latter requiring intervals to obtain a sense of movement and the former the straight or "irrational" cut to invoke duration (Deleuze 1985: 324–5).

9. In his preface to *L'Écriture de l'histoire*, reading Jan Van der Straet's copperplate image of Vespucci discovering America (circa 1624), Michel de Certeau relates how, dressed in armor and carrying a staff and gonfalon, the Florentine voyager represses an unspoken force of attraction he shares with the nude woman who rises from her hammock to welcome him. Foreign to reason, the mystical character in the encounter with alterity (who will be named "America") requires the European to identify the woman through the narcissistic projection of himself onto her nude body.

10. The practice belongs to Ptolemaic cartography. A topographical projection begins from a center from which lines of latitude and longitude are drawn from the vertical and horizontal axes emanating from the point itself. Literature and criticism can be of the same order. At the outset of *L'Espace littéraire* Maurice Blanchot writes that "a book, even fragmentary, has a center to which it is attracted: not

fixed, but a center that moves by way of the pressure of the book and the circumstances of its composition. A fixed center, too, that moves, as if true to itself, by being the same and in becoming ever more central, ever more hidden, uncertain and imperious" (Blanchot 1955: 5, translation mine).

11. See Jacob 2006: 280–97.
12. That, for reason of geography and displacement of time and space, affixed to an envelope, a postage stamp can become a mystical object is almost a *topos* in literature and cinema. Early in *À la recherche du temps perdu* the narrator gazes at a letter from Gilberte. When he sees the address and the postmark, and no sooner when he puts the envelope to his nose, his attraction and anticipation of what it might contain become the very event of the missive before he opens it—in what would be an infinite duration of memory. Viewers of Spanish cinema recall a moment in Víctor Erice's *El espiritu de la colmena* (1973) when the camera holds inordinately on an envelope thrown into a fire, registering the slow, even protracted incineration of a postage stamp bearing the portrait of Francisco Franco. The burning of the letter would simply be paper set to flame, but also, as it happened to be at the time of the making of the film, the anticipated end of what had been an eternity of repression.
13. Celebrating the centenary anniversary of the creation of National Park Service in 2016 (perhaps to raise consciousness about the currently sorry condition of the Parks), the text is from the 2016 United States Postal Service sheet to which sixteen commemorative stamps are affixed. The "park system" aims to "preserve irreplaceable resources for future study and enjoyment, from ancient fossils and fragile ecosystems to an amazing array of artifacts and art," including works by Albert Bierstadt, Thomas Moran, and Helmuth Naumer, Sr. (to which elsewhere some of Benning's images have been compared).
14. For this viewer the effect was double-edged. Experiencing a copy of *Stemple Pass* with Spanish sub-titles drew attention less to the serenity of the landscape in its slow modulation than to the bottom of the screen, where comparison of the voice-over in English with the sub-titles in Spanish turned the film into a study of the art of translation or, broadly, a cultural transfer going *beyond* the "American" character of the film and into an immemorial Iberian world.

Works Cited

Auerbach, Erich (1953), *Mimesis: The Representation of Reality in Western Literature*, transl. by Williard Trask. Princeton: Princeton University Press.

Baudelaire, Charles (1976), "Paysage, Salon de 1859," in Claude Pichois (ed.), *Baudelaire, Œuvres complètes 2*, Paris: Éditions Gallimard/La Pléiade.

Blanchot, Michel (1955), *L'Espace littéraire*, Paris: Éditions Gallimard.

Certeau, Michel de (1982), "Un Lieu pour se perdre," in *La Fable mystique: XVIe–XVIIe siècle*, Paris: Éditions Gallimard.

Certeau, Michel de (2013), *La Fable mystique II: XVIe–XVIIe siècle*, Luce Giard (ed.), Paris: Éditions Gallimard.

Deleuze, Gilles (1985), *Cinéma 2: L'Image-temps*, Paris: Éditions de Minuit.
Deleuze, Gilles (1988), *Le Pli: Leibniz et le baroque*, Paris: Éditions de Minuit.
Deleuze, Gilles (2002), "Causes et raisons des îles désertes," in *L'île déserte et autres textes: Textes et entretiens 1953–1974*, David Lapoujade (ed.), Paris: Éditions de Minuit.
Jacob, Christian (2006), *The Sovereign Map: Theoretical Approaches in Cartography Throughout History*, Chicago: University of Chicago Press.
Lyotard, Jean-François (1986), *Le Post-moderne expliqué aux enfants: Correspondance, 1982–1985*, Paris: Galilée.
MacDonald, Scott (2014), "Gardens of the Moon: The Modern Cine-Nocturne," in Michael G. Lee and Kenneth I. Helphand (eds.), *Technology and the Garden*, Washington, DC: Dumbarton Oaks, Colloquium on the History of Landscape Architecture XXXV, pp. 211–29 (202, 204).
Ptolemy ([c. AD 150] 1932), *The Geography*, translated and edited by Edward Luther Stevenson, New York: Dover Books.
Rugo, Daniele (2016), "England, That Desert Island. Patrick Keiller's Spatial Fictions," *Cultural Politics*, 12(3): 263–78.
Shirley, Rodney (1987), *The Mapping of the World: Early Printed World Maps, 1472–1700*, London: Holland Press.

KRISS RAVETTO-BIAGIOLI

Defacing the Close-Up

> There will be time, there will be time
> To prepare a face to meet the faces that you meet;
> There will be time to murder and create,
> And time for all the works and days of hands
> That lift and drop a question on your plate;
> Time for you and time for me,
> And time yet for a hundred indecisions,
> And for a hundred visions and revisions,
>   T. S. Eliot, "The Love Song of J. Alfred Prufrock"[1]

When confronted by the camera poised to capture his image, Roland Barthes famously reflected: "I instantaneously make another body for myself, I transform myself in advance into an image." For Barthes the encounter of the signifier (the photographic apparatus) with the signified (the face) always results in an inauthentic pose before the camera. These learned body techniques (posing) confront photographic technologies that, as Barthes puts it, dooms us to "always have an expression: the body never finds its zero degree" (1980: 12). There is always already a gesture that makes the body readable not in particular, but in general terms—namely, aesthetics, and their historical, moral, and political associations. In *Twenty Cigarettes* (2011), *Faces* (2010), and *Faces 1973* (2010), James Benning takes a different approach to this encounter. These three moving-image works do not point to the instantaneous yet inauthentic moment in time recorded for posterity, rather they point to the shifting architecture of the close-up, its untimely duration, and the disfigurement of the pose itself. Benning's work demonstrates that the close-up's connection to the pose and with it an always already meaningful expression is contingent on our perception of time. He shows us that, counterintuitively, the duration of the close-up beyond what can be immediately perceived renders identification, and with it empathic projection (feeling for or with the image) increasingly difficult, if not impossible.

Faces 1973 stretches two 2-second close-up shots of a face (one woman and one man) into a 25-minute installation piece. These portraits have been digitally scanned from footage Benning shot on 16 mm in 1973. The scanning process makes these seemingly still portraits change in color and brightness, animating and blurring the features of the faces as it calls attention to how cinema blurs the distinction between movement and time. *Faces*, on the other hand, is an anomaly in Benning's œuvre, because it is comprised exclusively from the found footage. *Faces* is a remake of John Cassavetes' (1968) film by the same name. But in the remake, Benning selects only close-up shots of single faces. The appearance and lingering stillness of each face is made to match the length of time in which each actor or actress was on screen in the original film. Like *Faces 1973* and even Cassavetes' original film, these close-ups stretch and arrest time, revealing hidden gestures as much as they investigate the unique topography of the face. Instead *Twenty Cigarettes* captures twenty people (ten men and ten women of different ages and backgrounds) each smoking one cigarette (a whole pack in total). Each shot lasts as long as it takes the subject to smoke the cigarette, and each sequence is clearly demarcated by a fade to black. Benning's work has often been described as observational cinema—rigorously formal, and deeply aware of its own construction of time and attention to detail. But there is another important facet to Benning's work, one that Scott McDonald describes as "a broad-ranging rebellion against both Hollywood and the perceived 'artyness' of structural film, in the interest of an engagement with such nitty-gritty social issues as race and gender and environmental exploitation" (2000: 300). In this chapter I would like to focus on how Benning also makes us aware of the politics of the face through a complex set of relations—between posing, acting, setting up a shot, shot-consciousness, casting a glance, recording, scanning and reflecting back. I will read his framing of the face as one that resists the conventional use of the close-up, which opens a space for identification, subjectification, and projection, only to unmask this prepared or made up face that is made to signify an idea or an ideal form or to represent an identity, emotion, or individual experience. The faces that linger in Benning's films are not readable in terms of cultural representation and corresponding systems of signification.

After making forty films over a span of four decades (using a 16 mm Bolex camera and a Nagra reel-to-reel recorder), in 2009 Benning switched to high-definition digital video. It is during this period and with the use of the digital format that Benning begins to explore the close-up and with it, uncharacteristically (for him), the human face. The exploration of the face marks a major shift in Benning's œuvre. His previous films have often been characterized as de-peopled: with some notable exceptions the human figure is inaccessible or kept off-screen, yet traces of human activity have always been made present in off-screen sound, the artifacts of labor and signs of inhabitance exposed within the portraits of Benning's landscapes. Humans have haunted Benning's films. This haunting, however, has only served to heighten the spectator's awareness of the absence or spectral presence of the human figure and human activity. But, there is another specter that these films make palpable; that of Benning himself. As Bérénice Reynaud puts it: "we are made subtly aware of the presence [and] the emotion of the filmmaker when composing the shots" (1996: 79). The filmmaker's relation to the images that unfold or fold in around us through an intensely still and steady perspective produce a feeling of place and a complex sense of time. It is this affect, the spectral presence of the film and the filmmaker, that in turn reveals the traces of both the steady gaze of the camera and the contemplative look of the cameraman. Benning's signature aesthetic modality is the long take that is coupled with a static deep-focus shot, which is meticulously framed. *Faces*, *Faces 1973*, and *Twenty Cigarettes* are made and remade in this mode, but their investigation of the close-up and the human face subtly undermines Benning's own trademark style at the same time as they challenge our understanding of the close-up and our ability to read a face on screen.

As Gilles Deleuze argues, "the affect-image is the close-up and the close-up is the face" (1986: 87). But this assemblage (of affect to image, image to close-up, and close-up to face) implies a set of complex relations: between the close-up as a cinematic device that privileges, captures, and magnifies micro-movements; the face as both a space of reflection and an act of expression; and affect, which is rather difficult to define, because it is felt as a fleeting presence of a possible immobile and "eternal unity" (98). Affect-images engage as much as they challenge what Deleuze and Félix Guattari call "the abstract machine of faciality (*visageité*)"—a process of facialization (a making of the face) that imposes significance onto, and subjectifies, people and places by making them legible in terms of inhuman figures like the face, the landscape, or the image (1987: 181).[2] When Deleuze and Guattari declare that "there is something absolutely inhuman about the face," they mean that it is the face as a figure that projects politics onto the flesh, and it is this social ordering that in turn serves as the ground for identification (170). It is not the face that makes meaning: meaning is inscribed on the face. The individual recognizes herself through the face and this social recognition is sustained by the face as a form of representation. The face does not indicate unique individuality as much as it is an interface, a figure that mediates between surface (the white wall that reflects) and depth (the black hole that emotes). The face is "by nature a close-up, with its inanimate white surfaces, its shining black holes, its emptiness and boredom" (171). The pairing of surface and depth, ground and figure, stillness and expression, emptiness and boredom under the rubric of the face, fastens signification (as a system of meaning) to subjectivity (consciousness), and with it the practice of identification.

Unlike the affect-image, facialization becomes a despotic practice of distinguishing and likening: a play of oppositions that identifies self from other, man from woman, child from parent, thereby establishing relations of power (leader and subject, rich and poor, black and white, mine and yours), value judgments (right and wrong, good and bad, normal and suspicious), and a limitation of all possible responses to an either/or axis (acquiescence or refusal, yes or no, this one or that one). Yet for Deleuze and Guattari, this face is not just any face, or the aggregate of all faces as some statistical norm. It is the normalization and measuring up of all faces to the "ordinary White-Man" (176–8). Benning is keenly aware that he wears this face uncomfortably. In works like *After Warhol* (2011) he has fifteen of his students (in his "Acting Bad" class) re-enact Warhol's *Screen Tests*. Benning designed his screen tests as a pedagogic exercise to illustrate to his students how "acting might not be screened the way you acted" (Bradshaw 2013). Screening, he points out, reveals the act of recontextualization—the act of manipulation. While the performance may mimic the discomfort of those performers and famous personas who were originally captured and projected in *Screen Tests*, the studied performances and mimetic gestures of the students are not capable of holding a pose or simply copying past performances before Warhol's camera. All at once, we are made to feel a rather complex set of relations: the recited relationship between Warhol and his subjects; the recontextualized relationship between teacher and student; and the gaze of white men (Benning and Warhol) at their various subjects.

Each student is depicted in a range of shots from medium to extreme close-up with a stationary camera, and each shot is a single take that lasts a few minutes. However, the change in footage from black and white to subdued colors, and the fluctuation in lighting from chiaroscuro to high key (when capturing the various performances) makes the difference or diversity of the subjects more than visible. It is almost as if we can see this measuring up to the socially acceptable norm at work. Differences in lighting reveal the difficulty of capturing dark skin tones as opposed to lighter ones—some subjects seem to be muted or bleached while others are obscured in shadows and darkness.

It is not clear if the extreme close-up of one student's nose and lips references Warhol's fetishization of African-American male beauty or if it is Benning who repeats and doubles this erotic gesture by holding this shot on the screen for more than a minute. On the other hand, there is no standard way of reading the diversion of various subjects' eyes from, or direct address to, the camera. Each face refers to something else, and each face defers to a network of interpretations under the sign of signification—whether it is gender, sexuality, ethnic makeup, weight, age, or complexion. The mechanism of signification already establishes a particular relation to both the camera and the filmmaker, at the same time as it prepares us subjectively to interpret and experience these actors and actresses as images. In the process of watching, we (as spectators) become subjects who feel the presence of the face, and we relate to it through this network of signification. The encounter of Benning with and through the camera exposes the social politics of the face. But there is something in the duration (the long sustained gaze) of these video portraits that allows Benning (and the spectator by proxy) to confront this practice of facialization that projects a face onto Benning and his subjects. As Benning puts it:

> [I]f you hold an image on the screen long enough for our reactions to change about it . . . [then] we will . . . try out various interpretations of the image. But as the shot holds on the screen I think two things begin to happen. We get caught up in the formal aspects of the image . . . And, as we become more aware of these formal elements, I think it releases the significance of the [image] . . . What happens . . . is a kind of evolution, not in the image itself, but in our way of looking at it. (Hank and Lehman 1978: 15–16)

I am not suggesting that Benning can completely escape the practice of facialization—the face of the ordinary White Man that many of his subjects respond to, or the ways of seeing that are embedded in the cinematic apparatus itself—but he makes visible the hidden ground of facialization, and responds with his own politics of defacement.

The suspension of the close-up of the face on the screen may disclose otherwise imperceptible "microphysiognomic details," but these micro-movements do not provide us with those attributes usually associated with subjectivity—a sense of interiority, an understanding of the workings of the heart and mind, or insight into the essential qualities of the human soul. For example, the twenty different video portraits in *Twenty Cigarettes* show that Sompot Chidgasornpongse (the first portrait to appear) is a novice smoker. While he may hold his cigarette between his index and middle finger like almost everyone else, he laboriously puffs away at the cigarette and repeatedly looks down at it in a puzzled manner. The gestures and body language of Dick Hebdige (who appears in the tenth video portrait) indicate that he is a seasoned smoker but here he is clearly repulsed by the cigarette he smokes. He becomes increasingly more nauseated by each puff that he takes (his face blanches and his hand trembles). Norma Turner (the seventh smoker in the series), on the other hand, is someone whose face has been sculpted by many years of smoking (there are multiple lines drawn on her upper lip from repeated inhaling). She seems more annoyed by the intrusion of the constant gaze of the camera that interrupts her cigarette break than she is uncomfortable with smoking. Aside from the "microphysiognomic details" unique to each participant—gestural smoking habits, facial tics, avoidance and direct address to the camera—very little detail is offered about the smokers' identity or the world they inhabit. At the very end of the film we learn the names of each smoker and the location where each portrait was shot. The participants are scattered across the globe—from Bangkok, to Philadelphia, Marfa, Seoul, Los Angeles, Mexico City, Santo Domingo, etc.—but their surroundings are too generic to reveal where they reside or work—some smokers stand in front of brick walls, while others lean against buildings made of plywood or corrugated steel, some are clearly outdoors next to trees, giant rocks, or are set against the blue sky, the rest sit inside homes or offices at tables and desks. The soundtrack also offers little information. We only hear ambient noise. Snatches of on-screen and off-screen sounds mark the passage of time: the smokers inhale and exhale, shift their feet, one man even talks to his dog; airplanes pass overhead, trains seem to move closer and farther away, traffic whizzes by, a gunshot is heard in the distance, birds sing, someone clears plates from nearby tables, television and music play in the background. None of these sounds offers us any critical insight into the inner workings of the subjects' minds. Rather these tiny details produce more questions than they provide answers to any fundamental issue about the subject's identity or emotional state.

Twenty Cigarettes is a performance and a portrait of smoking in an age where we see fewer and fewer people actually smoking or taking cigarette breaks (even in film). Yet unlike the romanticized representations of smoking in film, Benning's video portraits are far from advertisements—the smokers are neither sexualized, nor do they embody the clichéd mediated image of the smoker (as glamorous, suave, cool and sophisticated). This sustained look at smoking creates a unique kind of portrait—it seems to go against our expectations that the portrait should somehow typify a person. Instead, the smoking portrait allows the subject to drift away from such an image or identification of self. As Genevieve Yue points out, with the growing concerns about health risks, the subsequent restrictions on smoking in public spaces, and the pressure to perform in the workplace, the smoking break has all but vanished:

> Despite the differences in the smokers, who vary not only by age, race, and gender but also by their puffing styles ... each gets lost at some point in thought, in a look, the two often indistinguishable in such moments of idle drift. The cigarette is then snubbed, tossed, or otherwise extinguished, and the camera cuts to black, the smoker presumably gone back to work. (2013)

While the cigarette break may seem like idle time, smoking is not idle. It is presented as habitual and ritualistic but also as a very unseemly practice—taking place in empty landscapes, alleyways, back streets, and in the confines of private spaces. Smoking, however, seems to make space for a contemplative type of wandering. The gestures of the participants are repetitive—they bring their cigarettes to their mouth, take a drag, inhaling and exhaling—but their eyes wander across the frame rather than staying fixed on a single spot. Their faces change expression but reveal little emotion, making it difficult to know what they are thinking. More than simply observational or reflexive, these portraits ask us to think less about the person smoking and more about the cigarette break, specifically, what constitutes a pause from work, everyday routines, various modes of sociality, or even from thought itself. The cigarette break was itself a controversial issue in the US, fought by organized labor in the 1940s against the mass-production industry that banned cigarette smoke on the job. Workers pursuit of their smoking habit created a space of "autonomy and rest within the rigidity and monotony of their work" (Wood 2016: 11). In Benning's film we may be spared from the secondhand smoke, but we are made to experience time as both conspicuous consumption (the whole pack of cigarettes) and an untimely drifting between pausing, thinking, looking, and passing time that cannot be quantified or qualified in terms of value. But we are also reminded by Benning that with the rise of high-quality digital imaging, the ubiquity of surveillance cameras, and massive data storage capacities, capturing and recording the cigarette break in its entirety (even in remote or obscure locations) has also become part of our daily routine. We are never really out of reach of the camera that chronicles, analyzes, and data-mines our daily habits.[3]

As opposed to Béla Balázs who posits in his seminal work on the close-up that the face on a screen provides the viewer with a sense of intimate proximity and privileged access to the interior workings of the person behind the face (1970: 43–5), Mary Ann Doane explains: "cinema does not represent or present the face—it becomes a face . . . The cinema as face faces the spectator, and the intensity of an intersubjective dream is unveiled" (2014: 117). It is the dream of intersubjectivity that confuses the close-up for the face. In face-to-face encounters, the face may very well function as an entity that distinguishes each person individually, that socializes and denotes social roles, as well as one that communicates by establishing relations. We may get the impression, in *After Warhol*, we can read the faces (the poses, feelings and expressions) of the students as they perform for, and react to Benning and his camera. But what are we to make of the screen that faces us; the one that organizes and presents us with two illusions, one of subjectivity and the other of intersubjectivity? While we may be able to read defiance on the face of some of Benning's performers who directly address the camera with their fixed look, or feel anxiety when one subject turns her face away from the camera, diverting her eyes from its impervious stare, we are no longer interpellated as subjects (as Althusser once argued). The face of the screen places us in the position of the reader rather than the "I" of the speaking subject or the "hey you" of interpellation. And with films like *After Warhol* and *Twenty Cigarettes*, we scan less for meaning than to be mesmerized by the face of the screen. This indulgence in affect is in itself also a trap—one that fetishizes feeling. Affect is only part of an assemblage that decouples the point of view of a subject from human observation, giving us the face, the pose, the sustained look at the camera, the sustained gaze of the camera, the structure of relations, and the experience of intensity.

It is the cinematic close-up (not affect alone), as Deleuze argues, that undermines the functions of the face, by turning the face into something untimely and uncanny—a phantom, a vampire, a shadow that extends to infinity, a boiling point, a point of condensation or coagulation that suspends individuation. Therefore, affect cannot be readily legible (consumable) as emotions like defiance, anxiety, or shame. Benning's film *Faces 1973* radically changes how we behold the close-up of a face by prolonging two 2-second clips shot on 16 mm at twenty-four frames per second into 12½ minutes each of HD. The first image to emerge is that of a woman, shot in such a tight close-up that we can only see her face from the tip of her nose. The top of her head is left out of frame, as is her right ear. Her dark hair, the outer part of her cheek, and her left ear are already out of focus. She is poorly lit, making her skin take on a reddish hue that is just a few shades lighter than her lipstick. This ruddy cast accentuates the fact that the whites of her eyes are bloodshot and streaked with a web of tiny capillaries. Aside from this play of white against red, her eyes are so dark they are almost indistinguishable from the shadows that envelop them. But they glisten with tears and reflect the light from a single source that lies somewhere in front of the actress. Her face is a surface, a map, a landscape of features—displaying facial traits, lines, pores, and the cavities of the nostrils. The eyes and the mouth reveal only slightly more detail than Deleuze and Guattari's black holes on a

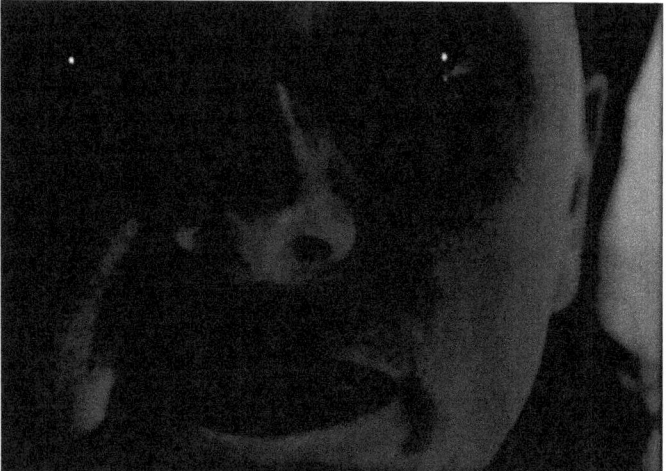

Figure 16 From Faces 1973, *2010. Courtesy of the artist and neugerriemschneider, Berlin*

white wall. The face may be abstracted, but it no longer holds the intensity of expression nor the power of a particular quality (those attributes that Deleuze ascribes to affect-images).

It is less the attention to detail that makes this sustained image so uncanny than it is the sense of movement it generates. The woman blinks and moves her lips. We catch a glimpse of the inside of her mouth, which glistens in the dim light, and finally we see the bottom row of her teeth before her mouth closes once again. But unlike in the chronophotography of Georges Demenÿ, which was meant to animate speech, we cannot read her lips, nor can we actually see her lips move (Kittler 1987: 135–8).[4] The movement is so slow that we only recognize the difference in the image. Instead of perceiving movement (even indirectly as the cinematic illusion of twenty-four still frames per second) we must rely on our memory to understand that her mouth opens and closes again. This insignificant gesture has profound effects on the topography of her face: the way that light and shadow are cast reshapes its architecture, and muscle movements stretch the flesh and draw lines on the surface of the skin. While we cannot see the movement of the face, there are many other movements present in the image that we do see. Tiny artifacts from the transfer of film to HD appear, there are faint shifts in lighting which emerge in pixelated blocks that transit across the frame creating zones of indistinction, floating blemishes, particles of dust, and strange convergences of skin and textures (digital, film, and flesh). These artifacts rub up against the flesh and the scratches on the original film's surface, seemingly mimicking the pores of the skin and the lines on the face. Digital artifacts, scratches, and facial lines present us with a complex layering of time all moving at different speeds—facial lines indicate habitually repeated movements and gestures that carve their path onto the face, the scratches on the film point to the wear and aging of the original medium, and the digital artifacts are evidence of the process of transferring one medium to another. Paradoxically, the image is constantly moving, even if the figure of the woman is not. But even more surprising is the seemingly subtle expansion and contraction of the image of the static face. It looks like breathing. But it is unclear just who is breathing. Is it the woman performing before the camera; the breathing of the cameraman that is embodied in the recorded image; me as the spectator who breathes and projects my own breathing on to the image; or is it the image itself that somehow breathes through all of these layers of time?

Benning has spent his career preoccupied by the encounter of the ever shifting present with memory, recollection, and narrative or meaningful interpretation:

> We experience time in the present but the present is a point on the line, and since lines have no dimension . . . we are stuck at this dimension zero and as

the future becomes the present and the present immediately becomes the past ... we can only perceive it as a memory ... For example, if a car passes with its direction indicator on, the blinking light can only be "seen" in memory because the light isn't blinking at all—it's either on or off ... In fact, this applies to all bodies in motion. (Benning and Zuvela 2004)

This encounter of different dimensions of time is made manifest in *Faces 1973* with the blink of an eye. The woman's blink presents us with something that is completely opposed to its rhetorical insinuation. What is normally over in a fraction of a second (the bat of an eye), is in the film stretched over the length of an entire minute. Yet it is difficult to determine precisely when the blink starts and when it ends. But the cinematic registering of fluttering eyes on HD produces what C.W. Winter describes as "multiple single diaphanous frames that are suspended on the screen, in trios and in clusters—groupings of images appearing, mutating, and dissolving, like Bergson's sugar cube, in extended decay-time" (2011). In the process of layering and sustaining one image over another we see the time of the present (the real-time of projecting and viewing the film) literally overlap with the past, presenting itself as a future image on top of an already past present. This image of time troubles what we understand as chronology—the ordering of time as past, present, and future. It is this convergence of time that disfigures the face. That is, no figure of the face survives to capture, grasp, or ground as an image. So what is it there in this image that faces us? Figure-phantoms that are constantly interrupted by a prefigurative duration, sentencing them to the order of serial potentiality, a mediated return and decay.

These figure-phantoms populate Benning's remake of Cassavetes' *Faces*. Benning's film asks us to think about a rather complex set of relations: how difference is coupled with repetition; how cinema is always a reproduction or a copy (what Benjamin called "art in the age of mechanical reproducibility"), how the act of presentation in cinema is always a remake; how the remake or the reanimation of actions through images affects the spectators' memory; and how memory requires recognition on the part of the spectator, therefore, suggesting memory's relation to a repetition of images. *Faces* is both a partial and a literal copy of Cassavetes' film: Benning copied the original film with his digital camera, but he captured only a selection of the individual faces shot in close-up, calculating how much air time was given to each character in a scene and dividing the time up if there were more than one character on screen at any given time. Benning's film repeats both the structure (the length of each scene) and the running time of the original. He explains:

> In *Faces* ... I used a stopwatch to add up the screen time each character had [in a scene], and I would have to average that time if more than one person was

in the frame. I determined that Gena Rowlands is in [the third] scene half the time and the other two characters are in it a fourth of the time. I would find a close up of Gena Rowlands, be it a second long or three seconds long, and stretch it to the length of screen time she had. If the scene was 20 minutes and she had half of it, then I would have to stretch the three seconds to ten minutes. (Lim 2013)[5]

This stretching of the presence of an image to include the images of the past and future simultaneously produces multiple figure-phantoms. A good illustration of such figure-phantoms can be seen in the opening shot where Dickie (played by John Marley) wags his cigarette between his lips as if to command the off-screen female hand holding a lit match to enter the frame. The movement of his cigarette creates waves of after-images that trace paths of movement, rippling across the screen. But the appearance of this hand is so subtle that it would be almost rendered invisible if it were not for the ever shifting penumbra of light from the match that proceeds from its fingers. The refraction of the light in addition to the scanning of the film image to HD allows us to see the approach of the hand even before it occupies any space on screen. An aura of itinerant lines (lines that look like the transmission of old-time television) indicates the imminent movement of the flame, the match and the hand. The bleeding of light and shadow along vertically oriented lines of transmission transforms the way we understand the index as having "a privileged relation to time, to the moment and duration of its inscription" (Mulvey 2006: 9). Unlike the Peircian index, which actualizes the thing it represents, the moving lines of light and darkness that proceed the hand with the lit match become an index of a future movement. The close-up of the assemblage of hand-match-fire does not arrest time or present us with a mimetic image of an actual hand. Instead this assemblage moves, and thereby disfigures and blurs each of the figures within the assemblage, as well as the space between the flame and the cigarette. The index becomes abstract movement itself, or rather movement as the index disfigures the thingliness[6] of the hand, the match, the flame, and ultimately the face.

By cutting out all of the images between his own selections of close-ups, Benning's film does not reproduce the same sense of a situation created by the sexual hierarchies and tensions present in Cassavetes' film. Yet it does present us with an assertive type of facialization—one that brings the face to the surface in what appears to be the two-dimensional flatness of an icon. Benning has two separate approaches to the close-ups copied from *Faces*: with some close-ups he intervenes and cuts out the faces of Gena Rowlands, John Marley, Lynn Carlin, Fred Draper and others, placing them onto a black background, yet with other close-ups he reveals how Cassavetes fails to distinguish the face from the background. While the first tactic isolates the face, the second makes it difficult to distinguish the plane of the face from that of the milieu. But neither approach provides the face with any sense of depth or interiority. This flatness makes it seem as if the close-up functions like an icon, resembling the face and grounding the image. As Deleuze and Guattari point out, the "face is the Icon proper to the signifying regime . . . The signifier reterritorializes on the face. The face is what gives the signifier substance; it is what fuels interpretation," allowing us to read a face as having an expression, and therefore, signifying meaning (1987: 115). Such signification is always facialized. Benning's suspension of these faces in time, however, does not make them graspable as forms of likeness or resemblance (the function that Peirce attributes to the icon). That is, the process of slowing down the projection of the close-up does not render the face static, holding it still so that we (as spectators) can contemplate the meaning and features of the face. The face becomes a two-dimensional plane of features (pock marks, scars, textures, make-up, hair follicles), plays of light and shadow, and unexpected movements (the blink, the breath, the clenching of the jaw). Yet these two-dimensional planes are planes without a compass or sense of direction—our eyes are free to scan the frame but we do not know where to look.

As a result, the sustained focus on the face does not end up immortalizing it by "snatching it from the flow of time" (Bazin 1967: 9) (as André Bazin argues when he compares cinema to the death mask [1967] or Georges Didi-Huberman to the Turin Shroud [1984]).[7] Rather than seeing the face as face (as a whole or a unity that reflects an intensity or an idea), we scan the frame for autonomous micro-gestures. In the place of profound ontological or emotional truths, we surprisingly find small mechanical gestures that populate the image with noise, acts of transmission, digital scanning, and uncanny gestures of the face that emerge due to the manipulation of the rate of projection of the moving image. We are made to sense the practice of facialization in the act of capturing and projecting the close-up. This is not simply an exercise in camera consciousness or making us feel the cinematic apparatus at work. It is the unmaking of the face.

Homay King points out that in the original *Faces* the camera "comes to function like a face; it looks and reacts to facial expression . . . The enunciating position is thus contaminated by, and implicated in, what it observes: no longer is there a discursive distinction between the camera-reporter and what it reports on" (2004: 134). But Benning's skipping from close-up to close-up reveals its own contaminations and implications, its own making present of the facializing process—one that concentrates on the scanning and circulation of faces. Even though the phantom-connections (actions and reactions) remain embedded in these close-ups, the situations that emerge from each of Cassevetes' scenes have been transformed. As in *Faces 1973*, we see Dickie blink and move his lips, but by slowing down the rate of projection the aggressive machismo that typifies his character is radically altered. In the opening sequence of *Faces* (Cassavetes), Dickie does not bother to acknowledge the welcoming of his three female assistants who stand up to greet him. He curtly brushes away one of them who approaches him with correspondence that needs to be signed, telling her not to bother him and adding "you look lousy," and then when asked if she can do anything for him, he responds, "I will give you a list of my maladies." In Benning's remake, the possessor of the hand and target of Dickie's insults—one of his female assistants, who automatically brings him a cigarette—remains unseen but the hand takes on a greater role, making a visible connection to Dickie through the lighting of the cigarette he holds in his mouth. For a minute we see the flame bridge the match and the cigarette. This bridge is sustained by the white light of the flame. Dickie's drastically sloweddown movements appear languid and gentle—he looks up to the off-screen subject of the hand with what appears as intense, mute, reverence rather than dismissive contempt. This prolonged look upwards is suddenly cut as the flame is just about to be extinguished, only to be replaced with the image of a different female assistant whose eyes are cast downward. The juxtaposition of these two close-ups changes the power dynamic of the original scene. Now it appears as if Dickie is the one who looks up to the women who work around him and they face him with downcast eyes. It is a gesture that becomes more ambiguous when the close-ups are juxtaposed, for it is not clear whether the woman's expression is submissive, dismissive, ashamed, or repulsed.

By juxtaposing one close-up to another, Benning mimics the filmic convention of shot-reverse-shot (which is not present in the original): when Dickie looks up to the left his female assistant looks down to the right, only to raise her eyes and look at something or someone off screen. There is then another

Figure 17   From Faces, 1968. Courtesy of the artist and neugerriemschneider, Berlin

sudden cut to a man who also looks to his right—seemingly turned away from the woman but toward Dickie. This generates a circulation of looks—of man to woman, woman to man, and man to man—associating the characters' spatial coordinates with eye-line matches. But as King adds, these shots "rarely tell us anything about what a character is thinking or feeling, only where he or she stands in a geometrical relation to [one] another" (2004: 119). In Benning, it is the relation itself that produces a sense or situation—a being with others, which includes a being with the camera, and the various acts of facialization that seem to intervene in and contaminate the circulation of looks.

But facialization is also confronted head on in this circulation of looks. The sense (affect-image) that emerges out of the circulation of images, faces, and acts of facification cannot be articulated as the expression of one particular face or set of faces nor can it be controlled by the intervention of the film editor. As Daniele Rugo points out this sense (or affect) produced by the circulation of images is always unstable:

> [T]he creation of sense happens primarily as circulation. One could say that the articulation of the givenness of the world (familiarity) starts with an articulation with and of others . . . It is for this reason that sense can never be closed or assigned once and for all; for its referentiality to work, [it] must be open again. This, however, means that something shows itself as incommensurable to any specific assignation of sense. (Rugo 2012: 185)

There is an inherent madness to this circulation that does not reaffirm collective engagement as much as it invites an opening, a becoming other, or more precisely a becoming with others. King suggests we think about this sense generated by assemblages, collectives, and group dynamics as "deviant affect." In the case of Benning's work we also need to qualify this collective and open-ended deviance as one that is accompanied by a deviant sense of time—stretching the circulation of images, faces, and looks beyond the *mise-en-scène*, montage, or simple reaction to the screen that faces us.

In remakes like *Faces* and *Faces 1973*, time-images circulate: images of the scanning, transfer and transmission; references to other texts, films, advertisements, poses and persona, double and redouble, only to be shuffled and recontextualized; glitches emerge in the form of noise (both visual and aural), digital artifacts, scratches in the surface of the film, lines on the face; and the encounter between present, past, and future of the image appears simultaneously, splitting into different registers of time, replaying, accelerating, and slowing down. Consequently, Benning's remakes also display a deviant practice of facialization—a practice that works against the many attempts to "temper the madness which keeps threatening to explode in the face of whoever looks at the [image]" (Barthes 1980: 117). Benning's practice of deviant facialization reveals another type of madness, the madness of systems of signification that try to domesticate and fix the face as close-up (something that can be observed and grasped in its entirety) and the close-up as an affect that can be read as an emotional expression or a reflection of a general idea. While Barthes distinguishes the hallucinatory ("ecmnesic") madness of the photograph from the ("oneiric") illusion of cinema, Benning's work on the close-up challenges such distinctions because they are attempts to harness time by separating it into two modes—the hallucinatory "ecmnesic" present and the illusion of an ideal, dream time that is never here and now but always a past or an endless future. Benning's work demonstrates that these "two modes, for all their profound distinctions in mood and structure, are the two faces of the same fundamental experience of time" (de Man 1983: 226).

The close-up of the face is always an effacement—the irruption of the present into our dreams of organizing reality, and the projection of the inauthentic dream on the prefigurative present. Various attempts to domesticate the close-up and with it, the face, end up disfiguring it. What are we to make of such acts of defacement? "If dismantling the face is a major affair, it is because it is not simply a question of tics, or an amateur's or aesthete's adventure. If the face is a politics, dismantling the face is also a politics" (Deleuze and Guattari 1987: 188).[8] For Deleuze and Guattari the politics of defacialization involves the practice of "becoming-clandestine"—a practice they describe as "eluding the organization of the face," which reproduces the ordinary White Man, the cinematic apparatus that faces us with the desire for meaning in the form of the close-up (171). In Benning's case, in this becoming of the face, the close-up and affect, there is nothing left to hide. What Benning brings to the surface is the politics of interface that buries itself in the features of a face, fixing the face as if it were untimely—an icon, a pose, a meaningful expression, an interface or index that connects some internal essence of the soul to an external reality. With his slow sustained examination of the face he peels off these various assemblages that attach themselves to it. But in Benning's work this assemblage lets go of its content and form (its many layered facializations) and becomes incomprehensible.

Notes

1. Eliot 1934: 4.
2. In *A Thousand Plateaus*, Gilles Deleuze and Félix Guattari explain the process of facialization:

   > A single substance of expression is produced. The white wall/black hole system is constructed, or rather the abstract machine is triggered that must allow and ensure the almightiness of the signifier as well as the autonomy of the subject. You will be pinned to the white wall and stuffed in the black hole. This machine is called the faciality machine because it is the social production of face, because it performs the facialization of the

entire body and all its surroundings and objects, and the landscapification of all worlds and milieus. (1987: 181)

3. Benning's portraits present us with a series of paradoxes: *Twenty Cigarettes* is comprised of twenty individual takes, the length of which is determined by how long it takes each individual smoker to smoke a cigarette but these individual acts of smoking are also presented as the film's collective act (together these twenty people smoke a whole pack of cigarettes); smoking is shown to be both a form of escape (a break, or moment of rest) and an act of defiance particularly in an age where the cigarette break has all but disappeared, and smoking has become the subject of various political debates and social regulations; this act of escape or defiance, however, is not clandestine, rather it is painstakingly performed and recorded where it can be observed and analyzed in excruciating detail.
4. Kittler describes Georges Demenÿ's experiments on visualizing speech through photographs as follows:

> A human mouth opened, expectorated the syllables "Vi-ve la Fran-ce" and closed again, while the camera dissected, enlarged, stored, and immortalized its successive positions, including the "fine play of all facial muscles," in component parts with a frequency of 16 Hz. To contemporaries, "many of these oral movements appeared exaggerated because our eye cannot perceive fleeting movements such as these, but the camera makes them visible by bringing motion to a standstill. (1987: 136)

5. Benning concludes "They each have the exact amount of screen time in each scene. In both of these remakes [*Easy Rider* and *Faces*], I was very much interested in using the actual structure of the original film to determine the structure of my film" (Lim 2013).
6. See Heidegger (1975: 28). For Heidegger, 'Thingliness' is a way of thinking about what makes things what they are, rather than simply attributing other characteristics.
7. See also, *Camera Lucida*, where Barthes argues that the photograph "cannot signify except by assuming a mask" (1980: 34).
8. This is a politics that involves "real becomings, an entire becoming-clandestine. Dismantling the face is the same as breaking through the wall of the signifier and getting out of the black hole of subjectivity" (188).

Works Cited

Balázs, Béla (1970), *Theory of the Film*, transl. by Edith Bone, New York: Dover.
Barthes, Roland (1980), *Camera Lucida*, transl. by Richard Howard, New York: Noonday.
Bazin, André (1967), *What Is Cinema?* Vol. 1, transl. by Hugh Gray, London and Berkeley: University of California Press.
Benning, James and Danni Zuvela (2004), "Talking about Seeing: A Conversation with James Benning," *Senses of Cinema*, 33, http://sensesofcinema.com/2004/the-suspended-narrative/james_benning/ (last accessed on May 15, 2016).

Bradshaw, Nick (2013), "James Benning," *Sight & Sound* 23(10): 46–50. Available at www.bfi.org.uk/news-opinion/sight-sound-magazine/interviews/sight-sound-interview-james-benning (accessed July 9, 2016).
Deleuze, Gilles (1986), *Cinema 1: The Movement Image*, transl. by Hugh Tomlinson, Minneapolis: Minnesota University Press.
Deleuze, Gilles and Guattari, Félix (1987), *A Thousand Plateaus: Capitalism and Schizophrenia*, transl. by Brian Massumi, Minneapolis: Minnesota University Press.
De Man, Paul (1993), *Blindness and Insight*, London: Routledge, 1993.
Didi-Huberman, Georges (1984), "The Index of the Absent Wound," *October* 29: 63–82.
Doane, Mary A. (2014), "Facing a Universal Language," *New German Critique*, 41(2.122): 111–24.
Eliot, T. S. (1934), *The Waste Land and Other Poems*, New York: Harcourt.
Hank, Stephen and Lehman, Peter (1978), "11 × 14: An Interview with James Benning," *Wide Angle* 2(3): 12–20.
Heidegger, M. (1975), "The Origin of the Work of Art," in *Language, Poetry, Thought*, trans. Albert Hofstader, New York: Harper Colophon, 1975.
King, Homay (2004), "Free Indirect Affect in Cassavetes' *Opening Night* and *Faces*," *Camera Obscura 56*, 19(2): 104–139.
Kittler, Friedrich (1987), *Gramophone, Film, Typewriter*, Stanford, CA: Stanford University Press, 1987.
Lim, Dennis (2013), "An interview with James Benning," Museum of the Moving Image, podcast, http://bombmagazine.org/article/7046/first-look-james-benning, www.movingimage.us/programs/2013/01/04/detail/first-look/ (last accessed on January 9, 2017).
MacDonald, Scott (2000), "The Filmmaker as Lone Rider: James Benning's 'Westerns,'" *Western American Literature*, 35(3): 298–318.
Mulvey, Laura (2006), *Death 24× a Second: Stillness and the Moving Image*, London: Reaktion Books, 2006.
Reynaud, Bérénice (1996), "James Benning the filmmaker as Haunted Landscape," *Film Comment*, 32(6): 76–9.
Rugo, Daniele (2012), "Contrapuntal Close-up: The Cinema of John Cassavetes and the Agitation of Sense," *Film-Philosophy*, 16(1): 183–98.
Winter, C. W. (2011), "Time Overlaps Itself: James Benning's John Krieg and the act of sustained recollection," *Moving Image Source*, www.movingimagesource.us/articles/time-overlaps-itself-20111007 (last accessed on July 5, 2016).
Wood, Gregory (2016) "The Justice of a Rule That Forbids the Men Smoking on Their Jobs: Workers, Managers, and Cigarettes in World War II America," *Labor: Studies in Working-Class History of the Americas*, 13(1): 11–39.
Yue, Genevieve (2013), "Smoke Break: Work and Idleness in the Age of the Great Recession," *Social Text*, 28, http://socialtextjournal.org/periscope_article/smoke-break/ (last accessed on 16 June 2016).

DANIELE RUGO

The Adventure of Patience: James Benning's Films as Perceptual Environments

BLACK LEAVES FALLING

One of the most striking passages in James Benning's film *Ruhr* (2009) shows a forest framed from a low angle against the light. Throughout the 18-minute fixed shot, the black silhouettes of the trees in the foreground contrast with the bright blue sky in the background. The scene is almost silent, apart from a distant and constant hum. No wind agitates the leaves and it is difficult to detect any sign of movement. One minute into the shot the sound of an engine, initially faint then more and more pronounced, announces the passage of an airplane, which appears and quickly crosses the top half of the screen. As the plane leaves the frame, the drone of its engine becomes fainter and the scene returns to its quasi-stillness and quiet. Fifteen seconds after the exit of the aircraft, the silence is disturbed again by a mounting rustle that anticipates the oscillating movement of the branches, followed by the swinging of smaller trees until black leaves start falling, crossing the screen from the top left to the bottom right. After this brief but intense disturbance the scene returns to its relative stillness and silence, until the passage of another airplane, flying in the same direction via a slightly different path, produces a new excitement of branches and leaves. For eighteen minutes the audience witnesses these drops of experience, interactions between an aircraft and a forest, in which each one expresses itself to the other in singular ways and manifests its singular patience. In this sequence Benning seems to invite us to pay attention to a new, expanded sense of the word "aesthetic." Alfred North Whitehead captures this when he writes that feeling, rather than being a human faculty, should be attributed "throughout the actual world" (1979: 177). Each being has its own aesthetic, singular manners of receiving (being affected) and expressing. These singular ways are always already sharing each other out, extending beyond themselves, infected by the environment that they are embedded in and that they express.

Figure 18 From Ruhr, 2009 (I). Courtesy of the artist and neugerriemschneider, Berlin

For Whitehead each occasion in the world is at once significant and patient (1979: 192), expressive and receptive. Insisting on this framework, the present chapter shows how Benning's work produces a demand for perceptual transformation, call it an adventure of patience.

Ruhr is Benning's first film shot outside of his native America. The locations, all in the Ruhr Valley in Germany, include landmarks as well as industrial landscapes, a mosque, and a residential street. The first shot frames the Matenastraße Tunnel in Duisburg; the second takes place inside HKM Steelworks in the same city; the third (described above) is in the proximity of Düsseldorf International Airport; in the fourth Benning positions the camera at the back of a group of men praying inside the Merkez Mosque in Duisburg; the fifth shows a man using a pressure washer to remove graffiti from Richard Serra's sculpture "Slab for the Ruhr" at Schurenbach; the sixth records the minimal activities of a residential street—Fritzstraße; the seventh documents the cooling process at Thyssen Krupp's Schwelgern coke plant.

The shots are dense and rich, but very little can be extracted to provide an accurate definition of what they are about. It is equally difficult to isolate a specific moment whose significance rises above and claims independence from the sequence as a whole. Nonetheless in each shot a little something, a fleeting detail, emerges that seems for a moment to stand out. In the Matenastraße Tunnel for instance, after having witnessed a number of cars, vans, and lorries driving in both directions, a man can be seen riding a bike away from the camera. Inside the steelworks, while there is no sign of human labor, two men in white helmets walking in the background briefly interrupt the mechanical movements of the machinery that lifts, nudges, and deposits incandescent steel tubes. At Schurenbach, one becomes aware of the slight mist produced by the water bouncing off Serra's sculpture. On Fritzstraße, a tune tentatively executed on a piano at the beginning of the shot provides a strong aural dissonance in a film dominated by the hums and thuds of machinery. Whatever it is that triggers our attention, none of these details seem to be more significant than the overall experience of the film as a passage of time in a specific place. One could say that every detail is a function or a consequence of the attention that the film as a whole demands and of the time it takes for something to happen.

In this sense, and despite the change of setting, the film offers formal strategies and thematic concerns similar to works such as the California Trilogy (*El Valley Centro* [1999], *LOS* [2001], *SOGOBI* [2001]), *13 Lakes* (2004), *Ten Skies* (2004), *RR* (2007), *Nightfall* (2009), *small roads* (2011) and *BNSF* (2013). Formally these works use wide durational shots, framed by a fixed camera and accompanied by direct sound that is often, but not always, in sync.[1] Thematically they all seem to be variations of Benning's thesis that, as he puts it, "place is a function of time" (MacDonald 2007b: 430).

These films pose a challenge and it is the testing nature of the experience of making and watching them that structures their unfolding and replaces dramatic tension and narrative arc. It is this challenge that sets both the condition of the films and the adventure to which they entrust the maker and the viewer. Benning's adventure is one conducted with patience, that is to say, with a passion capable of enduring, without consuming, whatever it commits itself to. With Benning's images one has to be willing to commit oneself to the adventure of patience, call it the giving of attention, an attention that is meant to survive beyond the films. The event of the film, what the film makes visible, is a solicitation to ways of experiencing beyond the limits of the frame and beyond the duration of the take. In an interview with Scott MacDonald, Benning says:

> I do think people want to know more about things after they learn how to really hear and see. Yes, I do hope they will go on to interrogate not only what I show in my films, but what they see and hear in their everyday lives. Paying attention can lead to many things. Perhaps even a better government. (MacDonald 2009: 265)

These films are also undoubtedly the source of frustration; call it boredom, the insistent pressure produced by tedium.[2] This frustration, I believe, derives from our assumptions that cinematic works should deliver more than just a vista, but also from our presuming always a little less than the world actually delivers. Another way to put this would be to say that the source of our frustration derives from the impossibility of demarcating the eventful from the uneventful in these films. While the eventful describes a compression of time for the sake of maximum significance, the uneventful designates passage itself *as* significance. This frustration has a flipside: seen from this point of view the whole world becomes significant, its significance incessantly modulated by subjects that are diverse, diffused, and at once independent and dependent, equipped with singular modes of receptivity and expression. The world is significant as such and this significance expresses itself in demanding a kind of attention that implies a loss of control. Watching Benning's films one has a sense of what this loss might amount to, since the works constantly force the acknowledgment of how, despite our designs, we can't quite eliminate the recalcitrance of the world on screen, its willingness to move of its own accord, to avoid our sense of choreography, to anticipate it or to align with it at the wrong time, when our patience has worn out.

The films mentioned above are also difficult to qualify. This indeterminacy, the fact that one does not quite know what to call them (landscape films? political films? documentaries? visual poems?) is due neither to hesitations on the side of the director nor to the insufficient descriptive power of the categories at our disposal. One could in fact use each one of them and each would correctly identify one or more features of the films. And yet something would still be missing. Benning's films are structured around something that both encompasses landscape, politics, documentary, and the peculiar poetry of the visual, and exceeds them. The difficulty in reducing them to categories produces a margin of indeterminacy. This margin is a product of the demand Benning casts on himself and on the audience, it is the site where the challenge, set up with mathematical precision,[3] begins to produce an adventure. In other words these films appeal to and for an experience, an experience of space and time, and can therefore be determined only once the experience has run its course. This determination moreover does not resolve itself in more accurate categories, but concerns the assessment of what the experience has produced. Satisfaction, if any, comes from enduring the experience, from the learning that this endurance affords. It is worth noting that Benning submits himself to the very appeal he makes to the audience. Discussing *13 Lakes* the filmmaker emphasizes how the "tension in the frame between the golden, lapping water and that violent sky ... captures aspects of the uniqueness of that place and of my experience of it" (264). The experience of being in and filming these places (the discomfort of working for a relatively long time in trying weather conditions: snow, heat, wind) is also part of what is passed to the spectator. Benning himself is the one captured by the experience he offers and it is in this sense that he understands his work: "I have a very simple definition of an artist; the artist is someone who pays attention and reports back. A good artist pays close attention and knows how to report back" (MacDonald 2009: 264).

The simplicity and directness of Benning's images show more than one can see, because what is shown solicits the audience to renegotiate its relation to the world beyond the act of spectatorship. Benning understands his films in close relation to the practice of paying attention that he has formalized in the "Looking and listening" class he offered to students in California and elsewhere. Of this he said:

> each week 10 or 12 students and I go somewhere to practice paying attention. We spend a whole day crossing an oilfield, an early morning watching the sky gain light, ten hours on the local buses or a night along 5th Street in the homeless section of downtown Los Angeles. We find looking and listening to be a political act. (2007: 38)

The tuition offered by the class and the one solicited by the films are part of the same project, operate in the same margin, and aim to generate the same kind of perceptual (and political) shift. The images thus aim to trigger a mode of relating to the world that is not unnatural, meaning not exclusive to cinema. What Benning demands is not acquaintance with a concept or a particular way of thinking about the aesthetics of cinema (not even the structural school, which he always, implicitly or explicitly acknowledges). What Benning demands is what Whitehead calls "instinctive faith." Whitehead invokes this faith when he writes: "we are instinctively willing to believe that by due attention more can be found in nature than that which is observed at first" (2016 20). It is worth noting that by "nature" Whitehead intends not the opposite of culture, but what "we observe in perception through the senses" (2). To think otherwise means to produce what Whitehead calls "the bifurcation of nature into two systems of reality, which, insofar as they are real, are real in different senses" (21). We must discard the distinction between the hidden reality of nature (described by physicists) and experiences of it (those human and nonhuman ones described by common sense), which are purely psychic additions. Since for Whitehead "our experiences of the apparent world are nature itself" (2007: 62), this faith in the world, the awareness that more can be found and that this more should concern us, does not come from high up. For Whitehead:

> [it] springs from the direct inspection of the nature of things as disclosed in our immediate present experience... to experience this faith is to know that in being ourselves we are more than ourselves; to know that our experience, dim and fragmentary as it is, yet sounds the outmost depths of reality. (1967: 18)

This deeper faith is present in each act of knowledge, since for Whitehead "that which is known is actual occasion of experience, which refers to a realm of entities which transcend that immediate occasion" (1967: 158).

If we pay attention more will be found (more world, more nature) in Benning's films than we are aware of at first sight.

THE SPIRIT OF LANDSCAPE

Writing on *13 Lakes* and *Ten Skies*, Scott MacDonald remarks that "no filmmaker has been more involved with exploring and documenting the American landscape and cityscape than Benning" (2007a: 220). In significant ways all of the films mentioned—and the list should extend to include at least *One Way Boogie Woogie* (1977) and its two remakes, *Landscape Suicide* (1987), *Deseret* (1995), *Four Corners* (1998), and *UTOPIA* (1998)—can be accessed as representations of landscape. Benning himself has often discussed the relation his films entertain with landscape painting, describing *One Way Boogie Woogie* as a "tribute to Piet Mondrian and Edward Hopper" (MacDonald 2009: 265). He has also expressed his familiarity with the Hudson River painters Frederic Church and Thomas Cole. MacDonald couples this remark on Benning as a landscape filmmaker with the assertions that these films can be read in terms of "contemplation," "spiritual sensibility" (2007a: 218) and "spiritual health" (231). The long history of landscape representation in Western art, going back to the early Middle Ages, is in fact traditionally associated with the practice of contemplation and with ideas of spiritual transcendence. Benning's relation to these practices is one that needs to be examined more closely, since his work seems constantly to solicit a more engaged commitment to the experience of this world here, rather to than suggest a healing process. The patience Benning demands is neither a device for appeasement nor preparatory work for disclosing higher truths.

The philosophical underpinning of the association between landscape representation and transcendence can be traced back to the influence that Neo-Platonism exercised on scholastic philosophy. It is with Plotinus' emanatist ontology that the idea of art's symbolic nature receives a comprehensive formulation. For Plotinus the work of art stands as a material reference to a higher reality, the cosmic harmony upon which individual experiences of beauty depend. In the remarks dedicated to beauty in the *Enneads*, Plotinus sets out to answer these questions:

> What then is this something that shows itself in certain material forms? . . . What is it that attracts the eyes of those to whom a beautiful object is presented, and calls them, lures them, toward it, and fills them with joy at the sight? (1969: 56)

For Plotinus it is symmetry that first attracts the eye. However the initial answer only provides a foothold for a series of regressive movements, so that symmetry is said to owe its beauty to a "remoter principle" (57). Plotinus then insists on the affinity between beauty in this world and "the splendours in the Supreme" (57). The principle thus postulates that "all the loveliness of this world comes by communion in Ideal-Form" and continues by stating that material things become beautiful "by communicating in the thought that flows from the Divine" (58).[4]

Christianity imported many features of this framework and the earliest pictorial representations of landscape identified particular natural objects as metaphors of divine qualities. The painted scene becomes an allegory of the divine sense of the world. Natural landscapes are understood as a confirmation of the divine order and compositional strategies used by painters have to reflect and champion this ideal. In this configuration an appreciation of images of landscape is used as a metaphor for the contemplation of the created world. Since the created world is a book written directly by God—*scriptus digito dei*—the composition and interpretation of these landscapes is largely derived from the multi-layered exegesis used for the scriptures, or as Hugh of Saint Victor expresses it: *scriptura explicat quae creatura probat*. God presents itself first in the book of nature. Already at the outset of its history then the representation of landscape shows itself as a "readable text" (Pugh 1990: 3) and can be described, in the words of Mitchell (1994: 5), as "a natural scene mediated by culture." Contemplation of nature and of its representations was therefore a way of connecting with the divine, and partook of a transcendental project that reinforced the spiritual/material, interest/disinterest binary. Contemplation thus signals an attempt to move beyond this world here, a world of appearances or at best of divine signs, in view of access to the world that these appearances both bear witness to and conceal. It is interesting in this context to note that even when allegories made way to less obviously symbolic renditions of nature, the turn stayed within a religious horizon. What Panofsky aptly called the "total sanctification of the visible world" (1971: 142) depends precisely on the permanence of ideas. An instance of this is the *devotio moderna*, a form of everyday mysticism that became popular in the Netherlands from the fourteenth century onwards.[5] The *devotio* was a meditative life ideal of pious citizens who nonetheless took an active part in trade and professions and sought to celebrate the holiness of everyday things. The renewed interest in the visible world and the stress on concretization and actualization in the Flemish painters of this time is in many ways an expression of this movement.

This understanding of landscape as having a transcendental, but also therapeutic quality continues during the Renaissance. As Gibson writes (2000: 78) "from the contemplation of nature as a means of relaxation, as therapy for both mind and body, it is but a short step to the contemplation of nature's surrogate in art." Leon Battista Alberti's comments sustain such a view. In his *De Re*

Aedificatoria (completed in 1452), Alberti associates landscape with restorative benefits by suggesting: "we are particularly delighted when we see paintings of the pleasant countryside or harbors, scenes of fishing, hunting, bathing or country sports, and flowery and leafy views [...] Paintings of springs and streams may be of considerable benefit to the feverish" (1991: 299–300).

Closer to Benning one still finds echoes of this transcendental project in Thomas Cole. In his "Essay on American Scenery" Cole, the most prominent advocate of a vision of America as Eden, writes that scenes of nature immediately conjure the image of "God the creator," since "they are his undefiled word, and the mind is cast into the contemplation of eternal things" (1965: 102). As Barbara Novak explains, the artists that established American landscape painting attempted to "retain God and nature in any combination that seemed workable" (1980: 5). Cole's followers, Church and Moran in particular, extended his assumption that wild nature was essentially divine—God's original creation. This led to what is referred to as the "Great Picture." As Scott MacDonald writes "for these painters the divinity of American landscape was obvious in its grandeur" (2009: 200).

This brief and limited excursus reveals how the representation of landscape is often predicated on the idea of a subject standing away from its object. The very idea of contemplation rests on this ability to wrest oneself away from the world framed in the image and it thus effects a clear separation of the subject from the world. The former consolidates its own "subjectivity" in the act of looking, while the second acts as the inert counterpart for such consolidation. The lyrical beauty of the pastoral, the classicist composure of the picturesque, the monumentality of the sublime all assume a world enjoyed from a privileged point of view as a reserve of images and ready-made metaphors, projecting and promoting theistic, humanist, bucolic or romantic ideals. The world is validated through its ability to materialize our conceptual frameworks. Even the more recent occurrences of landscape in narrative cinema do little to help describing what Benning is after. In the group of films under analysis here, of which *Ruhr* is the most representative example, Benning dodges both the existentialization of place and its explicit politicization. The former strategy enfolds the landscape in a series of subjective projections, while the latter makes it the function of a political discourse. Benning is as distant from the treatment of place in films such as Antonioni's *L'Avventura* (1960), Tarkovsky's *Stalker* (1979) or Ceylan's *Winter Sleep* (2014) as he is from Huilliet and Straub's *Trop tôt/Trop tard* (1982) or Rocha's *The Age of the Earth* (1980). The individual and collective subjectivity that these films presuppose seems to run counter to Benning's specific challenge.

Benning's films shift emphasis in their very construction: what is important is not whether the subject apprehends the object accurately, but what affective traces the encounter produces. One could borrow Adam Sitney's terms to describe how in these films we accompany the "surprise and excitement at the disjunctions and the meshings of the rhythms of the world and the temporality of the medium" (2003: 125). The truth of the works is the interest in the world that they elicit. It is not that Benning abandons the sphere of the aesthetic—he rather extends it beyond aesthetic judgments; as Whitehead says, feeling is throughout the world. Another way to capture this would be by way of reference to John Dewey, who writes:

> to grasp the sources of aesthetic experience it is necessary to have recourse to animal life below the human scale. The activities of the fox, the dog, and the thrush may at least stand as reminders and symbols of that unity of experience which we so fractionize when work is labor and thought withdraws from the world. (1958: 18–19)

The sense of the aesthetic that moves Benning and that is at work in his films also entails a concept beyond the human scale, invoking as it does meteorological, atmospheric, industrial processes, but also a mode of perception that sidesteps the centrality of the human subject. This decentering of the rational subject is not however in view of a return to innocence. The transformation is not toward innocence lost, but toward maturity[6] gained, a politically aware interest in the world, an "educated hope" (Bloch 1998: 340). The kind of experience Benning is advocating is one that breaks away both from disinterest and appreciation.[7] The ambition of Benning's films is precisely to remove the audience from a state of disinterest and to make their aesthetic experience pass from a judgment to a practice. In this Benning is much closer to a political filmmaker than to a landscape painter, but the politics is that of an encounter, a relational process. The subject, as well as the object, does not precede, but emerges from the encounter.

THE POLITICS OF "THE TIME IT TAKES"

The question that remains to be asked is what tools Benning uses to achieve the perceptual agitation that his films seek. Those films that provide no commentary and no explicit advocacy of a particular cause seem best suited to show these tools at work. The tools are the attention and patience Benning demands. As Benning himself says "duration puts the political back in the shot" (Panse 2013: 66). While *Landscape Suicide*, *Deseret*, *Four Corners*, and *UTOPIA* still provide some (however minimal) narrative thread and expository element—whether on-screen text, voice-over, or interview—with *El Valley Centro* Benning begins to rely exclusively on the power of images and of ambient diegetic sound. The shots become longer, from 2½ minutes in the

California Trilogy to the 193 minutes of *BNSF*,[8] and tend to focus increasingly on the morphology of places, their elemental qualities, the infrastructures that mark them (roads, railways, airports, aqueducts, spillways, oil rigs) and in some cases the activities that shape them. Farming, transport and steel making are preferred subjects, and human beings are at times entirely excluded from the frame.[9] *El Valley Centro* is an aesthetic engagement with issues of water management, land use, and industrial farming in the Great Central Valley, including the kind of labor carried out and the kind of laborers who carry it out. However what makes *El Valley Centro* a political film is the attention and time it takes to see this. Similarly *Ruhr* (and the one-shot film *Pig Iron* [2009]) can be understood as a study of a steelmaking region and its community, a kind of companion piece to the ones Benning has devoted to his native Milwaukee.[10] In *Ruhr* and *Pig Iron* we see, among other things, the repetitive nature of labor, which parallels the rigorous automatism of worship and the dominance of technology (in the form of heavy machinery) over human craft. The subject matters become accessible and "visible" only once we pay attention. The tool of this politics is the patience one needs to see what is already there, on the surface, the attention demanded and given, our interest rekindled and sustained. Since we can't become absorbed in the narrative, we become taken by the experience. One can neither settle for the right distance (the durations would ultimately repel one from the film), nor for penetration (the camera never moves across or through places). One is rather drawn in by *the time it takes*. It is in this experience that one finds the most forceful political point of the film. If this patience at times feels and looks like a contemplation, it is neither for the sake of reaching over beyond the world to the source of appearances, nor to derive from these appearances enjoyment or satisfaction, but to change the ways in which we relate to them. In this sense one can call Benning's films "perceptual environments." They should be paid to attention to "in their affirmative importance" (Stengers 2011: 516). Once Benning's films are reduced to formal reflections on the representation of landscape, their demand for a perceptual transformation is domesticated.

So are Benning's films not landscape films after all? Yes, but only inasmuch as what is presented becomes the foothold for a perceptual transformation. The "aesthetic" in Benning's films becomes the mark of a renewed interest and concern for the world. While the lived experience of those places would yield a more intense result, Benning deliberately uses the rules of spectatorship (a certain captivity, disposition to reception and film's ability to intensify expression by restricting the field of view)[11] to force patience and attention. Speaking about his one-shot film *Nightfall* (2009) Benning says: "the actual experience is much stronger than the experience of watching the film... but if I took you to that mountain top you would have difficulty looking at this for one hour and a half, so I am hoping that this is part of what the film teaches: we need discipline to pay attention" (2012).

The lack of forward movement in the films, the absence of drama and narrative are the formal strategies Benning uses to achieve this. They are replaced by a different structuring principle: the demand for attention and patience. As MacDonald writes in his discussion of *13 Lakes*:

> by the third shot it has become clear that the film will be an extended sequence of ten minutes' duration, and further, that these durations will be . . . unusually minimal: almost nothing will be happening. Once this realization has come, viewers must decide either to leave the theatre or to accede to Benning's durational challenge. (2009: 257)

It is a willingness to see our ways of perceiving the world disrupted toward patience that keeps us interested, or else. This transformation does not restore us to health, it rather produces a violent break, and Benning's interest in the tradition of American antagonism (Thoreau) and the figure of the psychopath (Arthur Bremer, Ted Kaczynski) is contiguous with this practice.[12]

If these films are documentaries, Benning documents in order to foster a certain mode of receptivity: his objectivity is a call for attention, not for truth. Something is going on and this something matters. In these films the audience has to work harder, but this means at the same time being able to simply endure, to do nothing. These films demand from both director and audience at once responsiveness and relinquishment, thus blurring the lines between activity and passivity. Take for example the shot that occupies the final hour of *Ruhr* (2009). The frame shows the upper half of a coke-processing tower

Figure 19 From Ruhr, 2009 (II). Couresy of the artist and neugerriemschneider, Berlin

in Schwelgern against the background of a changing sky. Industrial processes and meteorological phenomena meet and blend. The clouds pass by and other elemental features, which at first seem mere background, become more important as time goes by. In the passage of the clouds from right to left we become aware of the wind, of its direction and of its impact on the environment we are witnessing. All this becomes even more evident once, two minutes into the shot, a dense cloud of steam begins to grow from the tower. From then on, every few minutes, the sound of a screeching and looping siren announces that water has been poured down onto the base of the tower. This creates a curling column of steam leaking through the steel-latticed structure and then contracting and dissipating into the atmosphere. The light is subject to rather drastic changes, not only because darkness slowly conquers it, but because the rays of the sun tint the cloud of steam with yellow, orange, pink, gray, and blue hues, producing a temperature shift in the overall light that the image emits. At this point however we have abandoned the position of the spectator who knows where to look and are drifting and hovering on the image, wondering what we should be looking at. We become then familiar with the strange, but not in the sense that we explain it away, but as that which we offer ourselves to. The more we pay attention, the more evanescent and vivid the images and the world they frame become and the more partial our grasp on them becomes.

Before communicating anything about their subject matter or their "aesthetic" value, Benning's films offer an experience of patience, the time it takes to see the pervasive aesthetic (as in sensory) character of the world, the presence of feeling throughout. Thus Benning echoes Whitehead's idea (1979: 189) that there is no meaning outside of experiential meaning. Whatever we take from Benning's films, whatever construction we deduce or invent from putting together the signs and references on the screen, whatever meaningful design or aesthetic plan we come to attribute to his films, nothing will take the place of the adventure of patience these films force upon the audience. There is no shortcut; apart from this adventure: "there is nothing, nothing, nothing, bare nothingness" (167).

The significance of the world, its mattering for us, stands therefore always in an inextricable relation with patience. For Whitehead one of the world's characteristics is that it "exhibits about itself also the fact that it is apprehensible by consciousness" (1922: 12). Whitehead calls this the world's own patience. Whitehead's argument is based on the idea that the status of each occasion (factor) in the world (fact) is revealing of it thanks to the world's patience. For Whitehead each factor is embedded in an all-embracing fact. It is this characteristic that causes each factor to be significant for the world as a whole. At the same time, "correlative to the significance of each factor for fact, there is the patience of fact for each factor." This patience, Whitehead adds, "must exhibit itself as a systematic uniformity within fact" (9). The significance of each aspect of the world—its ability to express the world as a whole—is the correlative of the world's patience for each of its aspects, for their self-expression. Significance could not be expressed if it didn't find a mode of receptivity, an infinite patience. The world allows each of its occasions (a cloud, a color, a gesture, the movement of a leaf, a kiss, a tear, a stone, a drop, a wave, water poured down a cooling tower) to be significant for and representative of its creative passage out of an infinite patience. There is no significance in the world without patience. As Whitehead writes elsewhere, patience is the general metaphysical character of the world (1979: 192). The whole world is significant-patient.

THE DEPTH OF THE WORLD

Benning's challenge and the adventure that ensues are not in view of spiritual health, but seek to engage this double character of the world. The lack of camera movements in Benning's films, which hints at the limitation of human agency, should be read in this direction. The disclosure of detail after detail in Benning's shots create a spatiotemporal framework within which the audience experiences subtle changes, but more importantly shifts in their own perceptual abilities. Without this openness to patience one misses out on the significance of these works. Benning transforms the audience by modeling a more perceptually active and at the same time more passive sensual awareness of the world. Passive, because we are asked to relinquish control in favor of the moment-by-moment disclosure of the world, its self-presentation, its patience. Active, because as Benning says, this strategy asks the audience "to work harder; you can't experience something subtle if you don't look more closely than we're accustomed to looking and looking more closely isn't easy" (MacDonald 2009: 259). In this aesthetic indictment, which strives for the impossible picture of perfect attention, resides Benning's adventure. This adventure is neither in view of confirming a cosmic order, nor in view of finding oneself, of embarking on a spiritual journey, but rather of losing oneself, feeling oneself completely lost, lost to the strangeness of the world. Losing oneself is disobedience to a false ascent, an invitation to conversion or transfiguration of the everyday. Benning's films begin in wonder and when they have run their course, what remains is a renewed passion for wonder (which can lead even to "a better government"). What Steven Shaviro says of Whitehead's thought can be applied to Benning: his work has "important consequences, but it does not offer us any firm conclusions" (2012: 144). If we meet the challenge, we begin the adventure, a stimulation occurs and a more committed engagement with the world might ensue from this, a recognition of our need to renegotiate what and whom this engagement involves.

Patience leads not up, but down, it is for more engagement with a world that is significant-patient (and not for the sake of a reprieve from it). The way out of illusion is neither up nor beyond, but attention to the rippling of a wave, the light reflected on the cloud of a coke-tower. The depth of the world is nothing but its surface. Our problem is that we are not superficial enough.

Notes

1. *Ten Skies* for instance uses sound that Benning had recorded for other films.
2. The question of boredom has attracted manifold commentaries, but the two figures I'd like to isolate here are Heidegger on the one hand and Jameson on the other. Heidegger identifies different types of boredom, all revealing of the relations between the time of human existence and the significance of this existence. For Heidegger boredom is not simply that which drags us into a "silent fog" (1983: 80). The experience of what he calls "profound boredom" (1983: 134) is capable of triggering a renewed sense of the responsibility humans have over the significance of their existence. Jameson on the other hand has paid attention to boredom both in terms of aesthetic response and phenomenological problem, while also describing it as a theological concept, both at its origin and in its existentialist version (2007: 191). In his discussion of modernism and video art Jameson remarks how boredom can be a "precious symptom of our own existential, ideological, and cultural limits" (1991: 71). In his commentary on Derek Jarman's *Caravaggio* (1986) Jameson describes boredom, the mark of world-weariness, as "the price the viewer is asked to pay, as a kind of devotion to "art" as such, to the reappearance of a virtual religion of the image" (1998: 125).
3. Benning trained as a mathematician before converting to the visual arts, but mathematics as operational device, and thought process have never stopped feeding his filmmaking.
4. For more on this, see Grabar (1992), *Les Origines de l'esthétique medieval*.
5. For more on this, see Bakker (2012), *Landscape and Religion from Van Eyck to Rembrandt*.
6. Hilary Putnam has described a second naiveté, as involving "acquiescence in a plurality of conceptual resources, of different and not mutually reducible vocabularies (an acquiescence that is inevitable in practice, whatever our monistic fantasies) coupled with a return, not to dualism, but to 'the natural realism of the common man'" (Putnam 1994: 483).
7. For a survey of appreciation in the context of aesthetic theory see Allen Carlson's two volumes: *Aesthetic and the Environment: The Appreciation of Nature, Art and Architecture* and *Nature and Landscape: An Introduction to Environmental Aesthetics* (2000, 2012).
8. This is made possible largely by Benning's move to digital from *Ruhr* onwards.
9. For an interesting take on absence in photography see Buchloh (1990), "Thomas Struth's Archive."

10. The film *Milwaukee/Duisburg* (2011), makes this parallel very clear. Benning presents the work as follows:

> My father worked at the Falk Corporation in Milwaukee during WWII. He had a war industry's job building landing gear for B29 bombers. Those same bombers would later heavily bomb Duisburg. Duisburg was a highly concentrated industrial zone back then, as was Milwaukee. One could argue that perhaps Milwaukee was more representably German than Duisburg for its citizenry came from every region of Germany. Duisburg is located in Germany's Ruhr Valley. In any case Milwaukee was a very German town. In 1971 I made a short 16mm black and white film (Time and a Half) about a working class man. In that film there is a 14 second shot of him leaving the factory. In 2010 I copied that shot with my HD camera and slowed it down 133 times stretching the 14 seconds to 31 minutes. In 2009 I spent a week at HKL Steelworks in Duisburg. On November 4th I filmed trains collecting slag and pig iron from blast furnace #2, again with my HD camera. The shot is 31 minutes in real time. (2011)

This shot is also the standalone work called *Pig Iron* (2009).
11. This property of cinema is already identified by Aragon. See Aragon (2000).
12. Benning has produced replicas of Thoreau's cabin at Walden Pond and of Kaczynski's cabin in Lincoln, Montana. This project has resulted in exhibitions, books and, so far, three films: *Two Cabins* (2010), *Stemple Pass* (2012), and *Concord Woods* (2014). In *American Dreams: Lost and Found* (1984) Benning reproduces sections from the diary of Arthur Bremer, who was convicted for the attempted assassination of US Democratic presidential candidate George Wallace in 1972.

Works Cited

Alberti, Leon Battista (1991), *On the Art of Building in Ten Books*, transl. by Joseph Rykwert, Cambridge, MA: MIT Press.

Aragon, Louis (2000), "On Décor," in Paul Hammond (ed.), *The Shadow and Its Shadow: Surrealist Writings on the Cinema*, San Francisco: City Lights Books, pp. 50–54.

Bakker, Boudewijn (2012), *Landscape and Religion from Van Eyck to Rembrandt*, London: Ashgate Publishing.

Benning, James (2007), "Life in Film," *Frieze Magazine*, issue 111, November–December 2007, pp. 38–9, https://frieze.com/article/life-film-james-benning (accessed March 1, 2017).

Benning, James (2011), "Milwaukee/Duisburg," AV Festival. International Festival of Art, Technology, Music and Film: As Slow as Possible, Platform A, Middlesbrough. Available at www.avfestival.co.uk/documents/view/da1a60b1404cdd9f27447436dfce4402 (accessed March 1, 2017).

Benning, James (2012), *Nightfall* Q&A, Tyneside Cinema, Newcastle, March 3. Available at https://www.youtube.com/watch?v=1MqGt7OuOxE (accessed March 1, 2017).

Bloch, Ernst (1998), *Literary Essays*, transl. by Andrew Joron, Stanford, CA: Stanford University Press.

Buchloh, Benjamin (1990), "Thomas Struth's Archive," in *Thomas Struth Photographs*, The Renaissance Society at the University of Chicago, March 25–April 29, pp. 5–11.
Carlson, Allen (2000), *Aesthetic and the Environment: The Appreciation of Nature, Art and Architecture*, London: Routledge.
Carlson, Allen (2012), *Nature and Landscape: An Introduction to Environmental Aesthetics*, New York: Columbia University Press.
Cole, Thomas (1965), "Essay on American Scenery" (1835), in John McCourbrey (ed.), *American Art, 1700–1960*, Englewood Cliffs: Prentice Hall.
Dewey, John (1958), *Art as Experience*, New York: Capricorn Books.
Gibson, Walter (2000), *Pleasant Places: The Rustic Landscape from Bruegel to Ruisdael*, Berkeley and London: University of California Press.
Grabar, André (1992), *Les Origines de l'esthétique medieval*, Paris: Macula.
Heidegger, Martin (1983), *The Fundamental Concepts of Metaphysics: World, Finitude, Solitude*, transl. by William McNeil and Nicholas Walker, Bloomington: Indiana University Press.
Jameson, Fredric (1991), *Postmodernism: Or, the Cultural Logic of Late Capitalism*, London: Verso.
Jameson, Fredric (1998), *The Cultural Turn: Selected Writings on the Postmodern 1983–1998*, London: Verso.
Jameson, Fredric (2007), *Archaeologies of the Future: The Desire Called Utopia and Other Science Fictions*, London: Verso.
MacDonald, Scott (2007a), "James Benning's *13 Lakes* and *Ten Skies*, and the Culture of Distraction," in Barbara Pichler and Claudia Slanar (eds.), *James Benning*, Vienna: Filmmuseum Synema Publikationen, pp. 218–31.
MacDonald, S. (2007b), "Testing your Patience," *Artforum International*, 46(1): 429–37.
MacDonald, Scott (2009), *Adventures of Perception. Cinema as Exploration: Essays/Interviews*, Berkeley and London: University of California Press.
Mitchell, William J. T. (1994), "Imperial Landscape," in William J. T. Mitchell (ed.), *Landscape and Power*, Chicago: University of Chicago Press, pp. 5–34.
Novak, Barbara (1980), *Nature and Culture: American Landscape and Painting, 1825–1875*, Oxford: Oxford University Press.
Panofsky, Erwin (1971), *Early Netherlandish Painting: its origins and character*, New York: Harper & Row.
Panse, Silke (2013), "Land as Protagonist: An Interview with James Benning," in Annette Pick and Guinevere Narraway (eds.), *Screening Nature: Cinema Beyond the Human*, New York and Oxford: Berghahn Books, pp. 60–70.
Plotinus (1969), *The Enneads*, transl. by Stephen MacKenna, London: Faber & Faber, 1969.
Pugh, Simon (ed.) (1990), *Reading Landscape: Country—City—Capital*, Manchester: Manchester University Press.
Putnam, Hilary (1994), "Sense, Nonsense, and the Senses: An Inquiry into the Powers of the Human Mind," *Journal of Philosophy*, 91(9): 445–517.

Shaviro, Steven (2012), *Without Criteria: Kant, Whitehead, Deleuze, and Aesthetics*, Cambridge, MA: MIT Press.
Sitney, Adam P. (2003), "Landscape in the Cinema," in Salim Kemal and Ivan Gaskell (eds.), *Landscape, Natural Beauty and the Arts*, Cambridge: Cambridge University Press.
Stengers, Isabelle (2011), *Thinking with Whitehead: A Free and Wild Creation of Concepts*, transl. by Michael Chase, Cambridge, MA: Harvard University Press.
Whitehead, A. N. (1922), "Uniformity and Contingency: The Presidential Address," *Proceedings of the Aristotelian Society*, New Series, Vol. 23 (1922–3), 1–18.
Whitehead, Alfred N. (1967), *Science and the Modern World. Lowell Lectures 1925*, New York: Free Press.
Whitehead, Alfred N. (1979), *Process and Reality. An essay in cosmology*, New York: Macmillan.
Whitehead, Alfred N. (2007), *The Principle of Relativity*, New York: Cosimo Classics.
Whitehead, Alfred N. (2016), *The Concept of Nature: Tarner Lectures*, Cambridge: Cambridge University Press.

Filmography

Did you ever hear that cricket sound, 1971, 1 min
Time and a Half, 1972, 17 mins
Ode to Muzak, 1972, 3 mins
Art Hist. 101, 1972, 17 mins
Honeylane Road, 1973, 8 mins
57, 1973, 7 mins
Michigan Avenue (with Bette Gordon), 1973, 6 mins
Gleem, 1974, 2 mins
I-94 (with Bette Gordon), 1974, 3 mins
8 ½ × 11, 1974, 32 mins
The United States of America (with Bette Gordon), 1975, 27 mins
Saturday Night, 1975, 3 min
An Erotic Film, 1975, 11 min
9-1-75, 1975, 22 mins
3 minutes on the dangers of film recording, 1975, 3 mins
Chicago Loop, 1976, 9 mins
A to B, 1976, 2 mins
11 × 14, 1976, 80 mins
One Way Boogie Woogie, 1977, 60 mins
Four Oil Wells, 1978, continuous
Grand Opera. An Historical Romance, 1978, 90 mins
Oklahoma, 1979, continuous (also shown as a 4-screen installation)
Double Yodel, 1980, continuous
Last Dance, 1981, continuous
Him and Me, 1981, 88 mins
American Dreams (lost and found), 1984, 55 mins
Pascal's Lemma, 1985, continuous
O Panama (with Burt Barr), 1985, 27 mins

Landscape Suicide, 1986, 93 mins
Used Innocence, 1988, 94 mins
North on Evers, 1991, 87 mins
Deseret, 1995, 81 mins
Four Corners, 1997, 79 mins
UTOPIA, 1998, 91 mins
El Valley Centro, 1999, 90 mins
Los, 2000, 90 mins
SOGOBI, 2001, 90 mins
13 Lakes, 2004, 133 mins
TEN SKIES, 102 mins, 2004
One Way Boogie Woogie/ 27 Years Later, 1977/2004, 120 mins
casting a glance, 2007, 80 mins
RR, 2007, 112 mins
Fire and Rain, 2009, 1 min
Ruhr, 2009, 122 mins
Reforming the Past, 2010, 80 mins
Tulare Road, 2010, 18 mins (also shown as a 3-screen installation)
Faces 1973, 2010, 25 mins (also shown as a 2-screen installation with two objects)
PIG IRON, 2010, 31 mins (also shown as a 2-screen installation called *Milwaukee/Duisburg*)
John Krieg Exiting the Falk Corporation in 1971, 2010, 71 min (also shown as a 2-screen installation called *Milwaukee/Duisburg*)
Faces, 2010, 130 mins
Pascal's Lemma (document), 2010, 17 mins
Milwaukee 1971 Duisburg 2011, 2012, 31 mins
small roads, 2011, 104 mins
Two Cabins, 2011, 31 mins (also shown as a 2-screen installation)
One Way Boogie Woogie, 2011, 90 mins
Nightfall, 2011, 98 mins
YouTube Trilogy: 4 Songs, History, Asian Girls, 2011, 43 mins
Twenty Cigarettes, 2011, 98 mins (also shown as a single-channel installation)
After Warhol, 2011, 65 mins
One Way Boogie Woogie 2012, 2012, 90 mins (also shown as a 6-screen installation)
Stemple Pass, 2012, 123 mins
BNSF, 2012, 193 mins
postscript, 2012, 7 mins
the war, 2012, 56 mins
EASY RIDER, 2012, 96 mins

signs, 2013, 18 mins
natural history, 2013, 77 mins
Three Generations, 2013, 8 min
US 41, 2013, 56 mins
DATA ENTRY, 2013, 10 mins
HF, 2014, 11 mins
FAROCKI, 2014, 77 mins
Concord Woods, 2015, 122 mins
52 Films, 2015, 391 mins (also shown as a 52-computer laptop installation)
Levee Road, 2015, 37 mins (shown as a 2-screen installation)
Fresh Air, 2015, 45 mins
American Dreams, 2015, 85 mins
Ash 01, 2016, 20 mins (part of the installation *Untitled Fragments* 1)
Vallegrande, 1967, 2016, 2 mins (part of the installation *Untitled Fragments* 2)
In Memory of Benjamin Benally, 2 mins (part of the installation *Untitled Fragments* 2)
General Võ Nguyên Giáp, 2016, 2 mins (part of the installation *Untitled Fragments* 2)
thinking of red, 2016, 7 mins
Cuba, An Historical Romance, 2016, 3 mins
dancing in the street, 2016, 5 mins
Spring Equinox, 2016, 63 mins
Fall Equinox, 2016, 63 mins
Wavelength (2015), 2015, 10 min
Scorched Earth, 2016, 60 mins (part of the installation *Untitled Fragments 1*)
thinking of red, 2016, 7 mins
measuring change, 2016, 61 mins (also shown as a single-channel installation)
time after time, 2016, 44 mins
Red Cloud, 2016, 61 mins (part of the installation *Untitled Fragments 1*)
READERS, 2017, 108 mins
Retired, 2017, 3 mins
Graceland, 2017, 4 mins

Index

11 × 14 (Benning), 6, 15, 20, 23, 25
13 Lakes (Benning), 8, 9, 11, 12n, 21, 26, 27, 28, 32, 37n, 114, 123, 124, 129–41, 162–3, 165, 170, 173n
52 Films (Benning), 17, 19, 31–3, 34n
8 ½ × 11 (Benning), 6, 15
9-1-75 (Benning), 15

Aaron, Hank, 18, 19, 23
Adams, Ansel, 25
affect-image, 145–6, 151, 156
After Warhol (Benning), 29
Albers, Josef, 23
Alberti, Leon Battista, 166–7
American Dreams (lost and found) (Benning), 6, 12n, 16, 18–19, 20, 23, 25, 30, 32, 55, 63, 174
Andersen, Thom, 36n
Anderson, Bruce, 47–8
Anger, Kenneth, 20, 129, 139n
Anthropocene, 2, 99
Antonioni, Michelangelo, 32, 167
Arendt, Hannah, 101–2
Assemblage, 145, 150, 153, 156, 157
Auerbach, Erich, 140n
Ault, Julie, 31, 36n, 101

Back and Forth (Benning), 17
Baille, Bruce, 23
Barad, Karen, 98, 120–1, 123
Barbash, Ilisa, 37n
Barthes, Roland, 143, 157
Bateson, Gregory, 81, 86

Baudelaire, Charles, 140n
Beck, Martin, 36n
Bell, Rhonda, 36n, 56
Bembenek, Lawrence, 34n
Bennett, Jane, 98
Benning, Sadie, 22, 36n, 70n
Benson, Ezra Taft, 42, 52
Bick, Robert, 29
Bierstadt, Albert, 141n
Bitomski, Hartmut, 24
Black Hawk, 30
Blanchot, Maurice, 140–1n
Blightman, Juliette, 36n
Bloch, Robert, 20
BNSF (Benning), 3, 27, 114–16, 124, 162, 169
Bosch, Jerome, 131, 137, 139
Boudin, Eugène, 140n
Brakhage, Stan, 17, 18
Bremer, Arthur, 19, 55–6, 63, 170
Broughton, James, 17
Brown, John, 95–6, 111
Bruyn, Dirk de, 70n
Buchanan, James, 42, 46
Buñuel, Luis, 22
Burns, Anthony, 44

Cage, John, 12, 78
California Trilogy (Benning) *see El Valley Centro*; *Los*; *SOGOBI*
casting a glance (Benning), 7–8, 11, 12n, 21, 26, 114–19, 121, 123–5
Camus, Albert, 62

Index

Caniff, Milton, 132–3
Capra, Frank, 103
Cash, Johnny, 20
Cassavetes, John, 9, 11, 29, 144, 152–4
Castaing-Taylor, Lucien, 37n
Cavell, Stanley, 63, 102–4
Certeau, Michel de, 129, 131, 135, 140n
Ceylan, Nuri Bilge, 167
Chamberlain, John, 34n
Che Guevera, Ernesto, 48
Chicago Loop (Benning), 15
Church, Frederic, 165
close-up, 143–7, 149–50, 152–5, 157
Colbert, Claudette, 103
Cole, Thomas, 165, 167
Concord Woods (Benning), 7, 30, 94–111, 174
Conner, Bruce, 20, 23
Contemplation, 25–7, 86, 165–7, 169
Costas, Kirstin, 34n, 56–7, 60
Cumming, Alfred, 42

Dalí, Salvador, 22
Danner, Bob, 36n
Darger, Henry, 30
Davis, Mike, 49
defacement, 147, 157
Del Vikings, the, 20
Deleuze, Gilles, 7, 8, 75, 78–9, 87–8, 90–2, 120, 131–4, 140n, 145–6, 150–1, 154, 157
Demme, Jonathan, 6
Deren, Maya, 18
Deseret (Benning), 6, 12, 21, 24, 39–53, 123, 165, 168
devotio moderna, 166
Dindo, Richard, 31, 52
Disney, Walt, 16
Dreyer, Carl Thedor, 32
Duchamp, Marcel, 22
Dylan, Bob, 20

Easy Rider (Benning), 31
ecosophy, 65, 77, 83
Edison, Thomas, 32
Edwards, Blake, 29
Eisenhower, Dwight D., 20, 52
El Valley Centro (Benning), 7, 9, 12n, 21, 39, 123, 162, 168–9

Emerson, Ralph Waldo, 95–7, 99, 110
Erice, Víctor, 141n
Everly Brothers, 20
Evers, Medgar, 19

Faces 1973 (Benning), 8, 29, 143–5, 150, 152, 154, 156
facialization, 145, 147, 153–4, 156–7
Faroqhi, Anna, 36n
Finster, Howard, 22
Fisher, Eddie, 20
Fisher, Morgan, 23
Fitzgerald, F. Scott, 33
Flavin, Dan, 34n
Ford, John, 20, 21
Four Corners (Benning), 6–7, 12n, 21–2, 24, 25, 39, 75–81, 83, 90, 165, 168
Four Oil Wells (Benning), 34n
Frampton, Hollis, 6, 16, 17, 23, 28, 32–3, 76
Franco, Francisco, 141n
Fresh Air (Benning), 27
Friedrich, Su, 23
Fuller, Jake, 36n

Gable, Clark, 103
Gardner, Fred, 24, 47, 48, 51
Gehr, Ernie, 16
Gein, Ed, 28, 34n, 56, 60–2, 64, 67–8, 69, 70n, 136
Gianakos, Maia, 36n
Godard, Jean-Luc, 32
Gordon, Bette, 16, 17
Grand Opera (Benning), 16, 23, 28, 31, 34n
Griffith, D. W, 34–5n
Guattari, Félix, 6–7, 9–10, 12, 56, 59, 64–6, 67 69, 75, 77, 79, 81, 90–1, 145–6, 150, 154, 157

Haneke, Michael, 58–9, 62, 70n
Haraway, Donna, 98
Harman, Gregory, 106
Hawkins, William, 30
Hebdige, Dick, 31, 36n
Heidegger, Martin, 105–10, 158, 173
Him and Me (Benning), 16
Hitchcock, Alfred, 6, 20–1, 32, 60
Hodge, Joanna, 109

Holt, Nancy, 8, 123
Hooper, Tobe, 6
Hopper, Dennis, 11, 31
Hopper, Edward, 6, 165
Horwarth, Alex, 36n
Howard, Jesse, 30
Huillet, Danièle, 167
Hutton, Peter, 25, 36n

I-94 (Benning and Gordon), 15
Iimura, Take, 23
Immanence, 7, 79, 84, 91–2
Ivakhiv, Adrian, 9

Jackson, Michael, 59
James, David, 34n
James, Etta, 20
James, LeBron, 16
Jameson, Fredric, 173
Jarman, Derek, 173
Jenkins, R. Bruce, 32–3
Jefferson, Thomas, 24
John, Elton, 20
John Krieg Exiting the Falk Corporation in 1971 (Benning), 31
Johns, Jasper, 22, 76, 78, 80
Johnson, Sonia, 42
Jost, John, 36n
Judd, Donald, 34n

Kaczynski, Ted (Unabomber), 2, 3, 6, 7, 30, 52, 55, 56, 62–4, 66–7, 69, 70n, 94–111, 136, 138, 139, 170
Keaton, Buster, 35n
Keiller, Patrick, 140n
Keillor, Garrison, 136
Kelman, Ken, 17
Kennedy, John F., 19, 20, 50–1
Kennedy, Robert, 19
King, Martin Luther, 19, 36n
King, Rodney, 32
Knecht, John, 6, 34n, 36n
Kubelka, Peter, 17
Kushner, Rachel, 36n

Landow, George (Owen Land), 17, 23, 28
Landscape Suicide (Benning), 3, 6, 12n, 20, 28, 30, 34n, 55–71, 136, 165, 168

Lang, Fritz, 32
Last Dance (Benning), 34n
Last Poets, 77
Latour, Bruno, 97–8
Lee, Peggy, 20
Lemon, Steve, 36n
Lennon, John, 20, 29
Levee Road (Benning), 56
LeVecque, Les, 36n
Lin, Maya, 24
Linklater, Richard, 36n
Lockhart, Sharon, 6, 25, 26, 36n
Lorrain, Claude, 27
Los (Benning), 7, 12n, 21, 39, 75, 83, 85, 88–9, 163
Lyotard, Jean-François, 140n

MacDonald, Scott, 36n, 56, 129–30
McCall, Anthony, 23
McElwee, Ross, 32
MacInnis, Allan, 36n
Maciunas, George, 29
Macrobius, 139n
Mairs, Gary, 36n
Malcolm X, 19
Manson, Charles, 56
Manzini, Henry, 29
Marhöfer, Elke, 114, 121
Marx, Leo, 139n
Masokur, Sarinah, 36n
Massumi, Brian, 66
material-image, 117, 120–1
measuring change (Benning), 21, 114–15, 119
Mekas, Jonas, 17, 23
Meloy, Ellen, 53n
Mondrian, Piet, 21, 23, 165
Monet, Claude, 22, 76, 80
Moran, Thomas, 141n, 167
Murnau, F. W., 35n
Musikie, Zorana, 36n
Muybridge, Eadweard, 25

Natural History (Benning), 12n
Naumer, Helmuth, 141n
Nelson, Robert, 23
Nightfall (Benning), 3, 27, 36n, 162, 169
Nixon, Richard, 19, 55, 63

North on Evers (Benning), 6, 20, 21, 22, 23–4, 25, 28–9, 30, 31, 39, 56, 70n, 75–6, 78, 123

O'Brien, Michel, 36n
Ode to Muzac (Benning), 29
Oklahoma (Benning), 34n
One Way Boogie Woogie (Benning), 6, 11, 15, 17, 21, 23, 25, 26, 32, 123, 165
One Way Boogie Woogie/27 Years Later, 26, 165
Ono, Yoko, 29, 36n

Pabst, Georg Wilhelm, 32
Pakesch, Peter, 36n
Pascal, Blaise, 23
Pascal's Lemma (Benning), 17, 23
patience, 4, 9, 10, 160–3, 165, 168–73
Pierce, Franklin, 43–6
Plotinus, 165–6
Pollock, Jackson, 15
Porter, Edwin, 22
Presley, Elvis, 20
Protti, Bernadette, 28, 56–7, 61, 64, 68, 69
Proust, Marcel, 141n
Ptolemy, 136

Rainer, Yvonne, 6, 17, 23, 28
Ramírez, Martín, 30
Rancière, Jacques, 10
Ray, Johnny, 20
Reagan, Ronald, 51, 53n
Red Cloud (Benning), 27
Reforming the Past (Benning), 28–9
Rocha, Glauber, 167
Rolling Stones, 32
Rose, Peter, 23
Ross, Julian, 70n
Rothman, William, 102–4
Rowlands, Gena, 153
RR (Benning), 12n, 26, 32
Rugo, Daniele, 140n
Ruhr (Benning), 9, 12n, 15, 26, 160–1, 167, 169–70, 173n
Ruisdael, Jacob van, 134
Rusha, Ed, 21–2
Ruth, Babe (George Herman), 19
Ruzicka, Werner, 36n

Sampon, Sharon, 29
Sauvagnargues, Anne, 66
Scheeler, Charles, 22
Schipps, Jan, 52
Schmitt, Lee Anne, 36n
Schneeman, Carolee, 129, 139n
Serra, Richard, 161–2
Serrano, Andres, 33
Sharits, Paul, 23
Shiomi, Chieko, 29
Simondon, Gilbert, 56, 66–7
Sinatra, Frank, 20
Sitney, P. Adams, 16–17
Skoller, Jeffrey, 52
small roads (Benning) 20, 114, 123, 162
Smithson, Robert, 6, 8, 21, 62, 76, 86, 114–16, 119, 121–3, 125
Snow, Michael, 6, 16, 17, 23, 28, 33, 76
SOGOBI (Benning), 7, 9, 12n, 20, 21, 25, 39, 75, 83, 85–6, 89–90, 123, 162
Song, Yeasup, 24
Spray, Stephanie, 37n
Spring Equinox (Benning), 33
Stella, Frank, 23
Steinbrügge, Bettina, 36n
Stemple Pass (Benning), 6–7, 30, 32, 66–7, 70n, 94–111, 114, 136, 138–9, 141n, 174n
Stendhal (Henri Beyle), 138
Stengers, Isabelle, 6, 56, 64–7, 69, 71n
Stevens, George, 34n
Strand, Paul, 22
Stratman, Deborah, 36n
Straub, Jean-Marie, 167
structural film, 1, 2, 16–19, 22, 26–7, 144
Swan, Joanna, 36n

Tarkovsky, Andrei, 167
Ten Skies (Benning), 9, 21, 26, 27, 28, 32, 162, 165
text-and-image films, 17, 18–19, 39, 79, 83
Thoreau, Henri David, 1, 3, 6, 7, 30, 52, 56, 62–4, 94–111, 138, 170
Time and a Half (Benning), 31
time-image, 75, 80, 84, 87, 89
Tolliver, Moses, 22, 30, 76, 78, 80–1

transcendentalism, 94–111
Traylor, Bill, 30
Twenty Cigarettes, 6, 8, 29, 114, 143–5, 147–9, 158n
Two Cabins (Benning), 6–7, 30, 67, 94–111, 174n
Tyndall, Andrew, 23

United States of America, The (Benning and Gordon), 16, 20
Used Innocence (Benning), 34n, 56
UTOPIA (Benning), 21, 31, 33n, 39, 52, 83, 96, 165, 168

Valence, Richie, 20
Velez, Pacho, 37n
Vertov, Dziga, 35
Vigo, Jean, 32

Visconti, Luchino, 117, 119, 121
Vo, Danh, 36n
Vrvilo, Tanja, 34n, 36n

Wallace, George, 19, 55, 63
Walls, Laura Dassow, 97–8, 100
Warhol, Andy, 6, 11, 29, 146, 149
Weine, Robert, 35n
Whitehead, Alfred North, 9, 10, 131–2, 133, 160–1, 164, 168, 171–2
Wieland, Joyce, 23
Williams, Raymond, 56, 59–60, 65
Williams, Terry Tempest, 53n
Woodberry, Billy, 24
Worden, Bernice, 34n, 61

Yoakum, Joseph E., 30
Young, Brigham, 39, 43–7, 48, 51

EU representative:
Easy Access System Europe
Mustamäe tee 50, 10621 Tallinn, Estonia
Gpsr.requests@easproject.com

www.ingramcontent.com/pod-product-compliance
Lightning Source LLC
Chambersburg PA
CBHW070939240426
43667CB00036B/2382